OSCAR PETERSON

THE WILL TO SWING

GENE LEES

Prima Publishing & Communications
P.O. Box 1260 GL
Rocklin, CA 95677
(916) 624-5718

Prima Publishing & Communications
Rocklin, CA

Library of Congress Cataloging-in-Publication Data

Lees, Gene.
  Oscar Peterson: the will to swing / Gene Lees.
    p. cm.
  Reprint. Originally published: Toronto, Canada: L. & O. Dennys Publishers, c.1988.
  ISBN 1-55958-037-2
  1. Peterson, Oscar, 1925- . 2. Jazz musicians–Biography.
  I. Title.
ML417.P46L4 1990
786.2'165'092–dc20
[B]   89-48543
                                               CIP
                                             MN

90 91 92 93 RRD 10 9 8 7 6 5 4 3 2 1

Printed in the United States of America

CONTENTS

To Morley Callaghan,
for a kindness in a café many years ago
without which this book almost
certainly would not have been written

ACKNOWLEDGEMENTS

"Why do you have to research this book?" Ray Brown said. "You were *there* for most of it."

"Yes, Ray," I said. "But not for all of it. And memory fades. I'm cross-checking all of us."

And Ray sat still for yet another interview.

A list of the printed and broadcast sources I consulted will be found at the back of the book. For the most part, these sources are attributed in the text. Comments not thus acknowledged were made to me; the triplicated tapes and research material will be donated to Concordia University in Montreal; the Institute of Jazz Studies, at Rutgers University in Newark, New Jersey; and the National Archives of Canada in Ottawa.

I am indebted to journalist and broadcaster friends around the world for their generosity in seeking out information for me, particularly my brother, David Lees; Michael Hanlon, London bureau chief of the Toronto *Star*, who interviewed Roy McMurtry on my behalf; Mark Miller of the Toronto *Globe and Mail*; Lois Moody of the Ottawa *Citizen*; Michael Zwerin of the *International Herald Tribune* in Paris; Max Jones and Dave Howling of the *Melody Maker*; Max Harrison, critic, pianist, and contributor to many British publications; Peter Clayton of the British Broadcasting Corporation and the London *Sunday Telegraph*; Whitney Balliett of *The New Yorker*; Stuart Troup of New York *Newsday*; Naum Kazhdam of the New York *Times*; and Norbert Ruecker of *Jazz Index*. Broadcaster and record producer Ted O'Reilly of Toronto gave me the tape of 1944 CBC air checks.

I interviewed: Lou Braithwaite, Carol Britto, Ray Brown, Don

Cameron, Herb Ellis, Patti Ellis, Baldhard G. Falk, Maynard Ferguson, Percy Ferguson, Clare Fischer, Ambassador Robert A.D. Ford, John Foss, William Fraser, Hal Gaylor, Audrey Morris Genovese and Stuart Genovese, Dizzy Gillespie, Norman Granz, Jake Hanna, John Heard, Bonnie Herman, Eddie Higgins, Johnny Holmes, Oliver Jones, Suzanne Keeler, Roger Kellaway, Maurice Kessler, Mike Longo, Gerry Macdonald, Lois Mito (formerly Thigpen), Lyle (Spud) Murphy, Phil Nimmons, Oscar Peterson, Sandra King Peterson, André Previn, Bobby Scott, Evelyn Sealey, Eric Smith, Daisy Sweeney, Dr. Billy Taylor, Edmund Thigpen, Jiro (Butch) Watanabe, and Beverly Watkins. Daisy Sweeney, Oscar's sister, was unflaggingly generous with her time, her memories, and her insight.

I am indebted to Monty Alexander, Prof. Lorris Elliott of the Department of English of McGill University, Oliver Jones, and Cedric Phillips for background on the cultures of "the islands." John Gilmore was generous with his time and his files, and Oscar's friend (and mine) Eric Smith repeatedly read the manuscript and made valuable suggestions. Terri Hinte of Fantasy records was very helpful with the Pablo catalogue, as was Richard Seidel of Polygram in regard to the Verve, Limelight, and MPS material. Joan Brown Naylor of McGill turned up material and several important leads. Harald Bohne of the University of Toronto Press contributed with his comments. Richard Flohil of *Canadian Composer* was just there all the time, and so was his loft.

I thank my sister, Dr. Victoria Lees, of the Montreal Neurological Institute, for tracking down Wilfred Emerson Israel's 1928 master's thesis at McGill, and the McGill library staff for access to it; Dan Morgenstern and the staff of the Institute of Jazz Studies at Rutgers University for the use of their formidable assemblage of clippings; and Leonard Feather for material from his files. Thanks also to the staff of the John P. Robarts Library at the University of Toronto; Wayne Primeau of the Department of External Affairs in Ottawa; and Dave Dunn of the Hamilton *Spectator* library for clippings I did not expect to find.

Grants from the Canada Council and the Ontario Arts Council

ACKNOWLEDGEMENTS

paid in part for the research, and the publisher and I thank them for this vital assistance.

You'll often see in the acknowledgements of books some variant on the phrase "my appreciation to my patient and long-suffering editor." In the case of Malcolm Lester of Lester & Orpen Dennys, the phrase takes on special meaning for me. An undertaking I thought would take eighteen months took four years, and Malcolm never lost his cool. I thank him for that patience, and for suggesting the book in the first place.

Finally, and especially, I am indebted to the subject of this book himself. Oscar checked many parts of the manuscript for accuracy, clarifying details without interfering with my right to interpretation. This is not an authorized biography, but Oscar was patiently co-operative as I proceeded with the research. I thank him for that, for laughter long forgotten, and for so much music.

G.L.

It's strange, I need to know the human side
of all the great artists I like.

OSCAR PETERSON

INTRODUCTION

"Fan-tas-ti-co! Fan-tas-ti-co! Fan-tas-ti-co!" The crowd chanted the one word over and over, rhythmically, accelerando and molto crescendo, like a growing great wave that smashes at last on rocks, and a roar of renewed clapping rose in the air. Roger Kellaway and I were behind a huge canvas curtain, the backdrop of the stage, peering through peep holes, over the shoulders of the Danish bassist Niels-Henning Ørsted Pedersen and the English drummer Martin Drew, at the broad back of Oscar Peterson. He bowed low, his hands prayerfully pressed together before him after the Indian manner. Five thousand Italians applauded and cheered the end of his first concert in Milan in fifteen years. The spotlights made a halo of his hair, which was turning grey now. I had met him for the first time twenty-seven years before, when a barber in Hamilton, Ontario, refused to cut it.

This was the evening of April 8, 1984. The setting was a huge tent theatre somewhere on the edge of Milan, and the concert that preceded this moment had passed through every phase of Oscar Peterson's playing, from the bravura displays his detractors deplore, to the pensive lyricism that is one of the loveliest aspects of his work. To make that day in Milan only the more memorable to me, I had that afternoon introduced the bearded Roger Kellaway, then forty-four years old, widely admired by musicians and critics alike as one of the world's great jazz pianists, to Oscar, the childhood idol whom he had never before met, and who had in turn expressed his admiration for Kellaway to me. During an interview I had done with Oscar a year or two earlier, he'd said, "I love Roger

Kellaway." And I had copied that segment of the tape for Roger, who was thrilled by it.

While some critics have derogated the sheer technical brilliance of Oscar Peterson's playing, jazz pianists often name him as one of their favourites, and as an influence on their work. He was deeply admired by the late Bill Evans, himself one of the major influences on jazz piano, whose birthdate Oscar almost shared. Evans was born August 16, 1929, in Plainfield, New Jersey, Peterson on August 15, 1925, in Montreal, Quebec. Those who take astrology seriously will reflexively note that they were born in the sign of Leo, a characteristic of which is supposedly a great stubbornness. Evans was immovable when he had made up his mind to something. So is Peterson. Asked for his evaluation of Oscar, the Toronto trombonist Butch Watanabe, his friend for most of his life, said, "Well, first of all he's a Leo, and that makes him very stubborn. He is also very generous."

Milan became yet another on the list of cities in which I have spent time with Oscar. He could probably name them better than I. His memory is phenomenal. Once, when I was editor of *Down Beat* and interviewing him for an article I was writing, I asked him a question. Long afterwards, I put it to him again, curious to see whether I could elicit a different response. He grinned and said, "I answered that for you ten years ago in Chicago."

The Monterey Festival, sometime in the early 1960s. Fog coming in from the Pacific, the night air uncomfortably damp. Oscar had a serious influenza, a respiratory problem to which he was prone, probably as a consequence of childhood tuberculosis. He had a temperature of 104 that night and shone with perspiration. Other musicians and the festival staff thought he should not perform. Oscar went out on the stage and played with a power that belied his condition.

San Francisco and the Black Hawk, a famous jazz club that is now gone, once one of the regular stops on his endless tours. New York City and conversations at the Algonquin, where he usually stays. Newport, Rhode Island, where we both got caught in the jazz festival riot of 1960.

The Detroit Jazz Festival, in 1959. Afterwards he drove me from Detroit to Toronto. That time we were both going home. As we came out of the Detroit River tunnel in Windsor, a bagpipe band was marching down the street.

"Oscar," I said, "is the bagpipe a chromatic instrument?"

"Sure," he said. "They're in B-flat." That's when I realized he had absolute pitch. His family discovered it when he was five.

Los Angeles. Oscar's penchant for practical jokes is notorious. That night I decided to get *him*. It was in the Hong Kong bar of the Century Plaza Hotel, where I had gone with Lalo Schifrin, the film composer, and a prodigious pianist, to hear him.

"You really got me that night," Oscar said afterwards. "You know when you come off the bandstand that people are going to be coming at you. You're warm – at least I am – and you're perspiring, and still breathing hard, and the mind is still going. And people will come up to you and say, 'Oh, Mr. Peterson!' And if they come out with that line, 'You don't remember me, do you?' I immediately come back and say, 'No!' At such a time I might not recognize my brother or sister. A friend of mine once said, 'Oscar, if I were ever going to make an assault on you personally, do you know when I'd get you? When you come off stage. Because after a concert it's all lying open. And,' he said, 'all I'd have to do is go in there with a scalpel and do you up.'

"And I had to agree with him. You are vulnerable at that time."

He was playing splendidly that night at the Hong Kong. Lalo kept shaking his head and saying in his Argentine accent, "No! Impossible! Ridiculous! Stop!" And I got an idea. I had recently grown a beard and suspected that Oscar would not recognize me. I noticed at an adjacent table a man who was wearing thick glasses. I asked him if I might borrow them, explaining what I planned to do. The man lent me the glasses, saying he regretted that he would not be able to see what was to come. The practical joke is almost the Argentine national sport, and Lalo Schifrin is very good at it. He led me – I couldn't see – to the bandstand as Oscar was descending from it in a cloud of applause. I stood by, affecting a great dignity, as Lalo and Oscar exchanged greetings. Finally, Lalo said, "Oscar,

3

I would like you to meet Vladimir Gretchkov, the music critic of *Pravda*."

"How do you do, Mr. Peterson," I said in my best approximation of a Russian accent. "I am great admirer your music." There is nothing that renders an artist as uncomfortable as excessive and intemperate praise, and I overpraised him to the point where he was becoming visibly discomfitted. But he maintained his urbane politeness, saying, "That's very kind of you, Mr. Gretchkov, and I hope you're enjoying your trip to America." All the while I had never let go of his hand, never let him escape. And when the hook was really in, I took off the glasses and said in my own voice, "You jive mother!"

He was puzzled for a moment. Then he recognized me, went mock ferocious, and said, "Okay! That's it! I'll get you for this. Don't ever turn your back. I'll get you." Two or three years later, when I had almost forgotten the incident, he did.

I have chided Oscar that all great virtuoso pianists are a little strange. The monomaniacal devotion that goes into the physical and mental mastery of any musical instrument puts the practitioner, shall we say, out of the mainstream of human concerns. And this is only the more so in piano, which is not inherently an orchestral instrument, except when it is used as a solo voice *in front of* the orchestra. On a jazz date, there may be several trumpeters and saxophone players, but usually there is only one pianist. "Piano players are all a little nuts," I teased. "I wonder if it's because they get lonesome, shoved out there all by themselves."

"No!" he asserted, laughing. "They're *planning* on being out there alone!" Then he became serious. "It's because, I think, pianists have dreams of being the primary, all-encompassing soloist eventually in their careers. Pianists think of going out there by themselves, or with a trio."

"Maybe," I said, "that's why they choose the instrument in the first place."

"It goes beyond that," he said. "You choose the instrument, I think, as a matter of wonderment. It's a *lot* of instrument. You look down and see that whole keyboard with all its possibilities sitting in front of you. I'm sure it intimidates everyone at some point. It did me. I looked down and wondered what the hell to do with all those keys, and where they go, and how I'm going to make them work, and then the three pedals, with" – he laughed; pianists know what he means – "the mysterious middle one."

On the afternoon of the April day in Milan, Roger Kellaway and I were walking across the Piazza del Duomo, the beautiful paved square in front of the fantastic cathedral that was five hundred years in the building. It is still the largest cathedral in Europe, excepting the one in Seville and St. Peter's in Rome. It can hold twenty thousand people, and one could spend a lifetime studying the turrets and pinnacles and three thousand statues that adorn its façade. The weather was comparatively mild for April, and the pigeons rose in great flurries, to settle again on the pavement as the tourists threw corn and photographers took pictures for these pre-season visitors to send home. Roger had just completed an engagement in London and was vacationing nearby in Switzerland.

"What was the original attraction of Oscar's playing to you, as a pianist?" I asked.

"It was the whole trio," Roger said. "It was the will to swing. It wasn't just Oscar. It was Oscar, Ray, and Herb." He referred to Ray Brown, the great and pioneering bassist with whom Oscar was associated on and off from his early twenties, and Herb Ellis, one of the finest guitarists jazz has ever produced. With Oscar, they constituted the first famous Oscar Peterson Trio. (Barney Kessel played with Oscar for a year before Ellis joined the group.) "I was listening to the Stratford Shakespearean Festival album the other night," Kellaway continued, "and I got to reacquaint myself with an awesome pianist and trio. It certainly could have defeated me when I was young, because it was so brilliant. But it was the will to swing that I picked up from them, basically. I remember going into Storyville in Boston in the early 1950s to hear Oscar, with the intent of sitting in. And I never sat in. And that evening I *did* feel defeated."

"Oscar felt that way about Art Tatum."

5

"Understandably," Kellaway said. "I think Oscar comes as close as anybody could to Art Tatum. But I couldn't compare Art Tatum to anyone. Or Oscar either, for that matter. Oscar is his own person. The dexterity and the cleanliness of the sound are just impeccable, always. The will to swing. To get on the stand and pull it all together and have that kind of energy has always been to me the most astounding thing. One of the reasons I revere Oscar is that he plays the *piano*. He is a total musician. And in his relationship to the instrument, he plays what I call two-handed piano. All the things that differentiate the men from the boys. It's a mind-blower. He's absolutely complete as a pianist. It's a kind of tradition that I feel is my responsibility too, now. You know, the artist rarely has the opportunity to be acknowledged by one of his heroes, and that's already happened because of that tape you gave me, where he said, 'I love Roger Kellaway.' I still have it. That was a milestone in my life already. And now to meet him, at a hotel, and in Italy to boot. It feels like life on the road."

We passed along the great arcade that forms the south side of the piazza, past the elegant outdoor cafés and the excellent boutiques full of handsome shoes and Italian fashions, turned into a side street, and entered a small and beautifully appointed hotel.

At this point in his life, Oscar Peterson had received more awards and honorary degrees, including ten doctorates, than probably even he could remember, he had travelled to the Soviet Union as his country's representative on Canada's first cultural exchange program with the Russians (only to cancel part of the tour because of what he and his manager considered serious mistreatment by the Russians), and had been named companion of the Order of Canada, the nearest thing to a knighthood his country could give him. Excepting Glenn Gould, he was Canada's most famous musician. He was assuredly the first Canadian to have a major international impact in jazz. A virtuoso without peer, he was idolized by pianists around the world.

I called Oscar's room. He told us to come up. He was wearing a dressing gown as we entered. I introduced him to Roger. They shook hands as if they had known each other for years. Musically, they had.

I noticed that Oscar was walking a little heavily, as if in some pain.

"How's your knee?" I said.

"I've got a barometer in there," he said. "You know." Some years ago, Oscar had a torn cartilage removed from his knee.

"And the arthritis?"

"It comes and it goes," he said. He has had arthritis in his hands since he was very young; it runs in the family. No one has ever detected any sign of it in his playing, although at times he has been in great pain while performing. Another triumph of his will.

"Otherwise you're okay?"

"Three times and out. That's it," he said. He was referring to the breakup of his third marriage. I had heard about it on the grapevine. I did not pursue the subject.

"I hear your brother's pretty sick," I said. "I'm sorry."

"It's not good," Oscar said. His brother Chuck was in Royal Victoria Hospital in Montreal with emphysema, a heart condition, and kidney trouble.

"I was in Montreal last week," I said.

Oscar raised his eyebrows, asking a wordless question.

"Pretty sad," I said. "They've ruined it." The streets seemed dirty and crumbling, signs of the shrunken tax base caused by the flight of many businesses when René Lévesque's provincial government passed laws restricting and even prohibiting the use of English in many areas of daily life, in effect institutionalizing a linguistic racism.

"I refuse to speak French in Quebec now," Oscar said.

"I have the same feeling. And you know how I love the language."

"Roger," Oscar said, "there's a tune of yours I want to do. It's in one of your Cello Quartet albums, but I can't think of the title. It goes ..." And he sang the melody.

"That's the *Ballade*, in the second Cello Quartet album."

"I'd like to record that," he said.

"I'll get it to you," Roger said.

We chatted for a while about music and computers – Oscar always has the latest gadgets – and about friends and travelling. I had met him that morning when he arrived at Linate Airport. As he waited for his luggage to come off the carousel, I slipped up beside him, waiting for him to turn and see me, hoping for once to catch him completely by surprise. Throughout his life his friends have been retaliating for his practical jokes. When he saw me, he didn't turn a hair or raise an eyebrow. He said, "Hi," as if it were the most natural thing in the world for me to meet him at the airport of Milan. He is famous for this kind of control. I told him, in the car on the way from the airport, that Roger Kellaway was also in town and wanted to meet him. "Come on by the hotel this afternoon," he said.

And now it was time for him to start dressing for the evening's work. Roger and I took our leave, saying we'd see him at the concert.

Pianist Mike Longo, who studied with Oscar in the early 1960s, said of him, "I think his personality is like Liszt's." It is an interesting perspective. Lalo Schifrin once said, "In their own time, it was said that Liszt conquered the piano, Chopin seduced it. Oscar is our Liszt and Bill Evans is our Chopin." Almost all jazz criticism has viewed Oscar as the derivation of Art Tatum, although he himself acknowledges strong influences of Teddy Wilson, Nat (King) Cole, James P. Johnson, and almost everything in jazz piano that had gone before. Rarely is the influence of his sister mentioned, and never that of the Chicago pianist and singer Audrey Morris. Butch Watanabe said, "Art Tatum was the jazz influence on Oscar, but I don't think he was the pianistic influence."

Oscar studied in Montreal with a pianist of international repute named Paul de Marky, a Hungarian. De Marky studied in Budapest with Stefan Thomán. Thomán studied with Liszt.

CHAPTER I

MOUNT ROYAL'S SHADOW

Montreal for a long time held a racy reputation among Canadians, not without reason. When the rest of Canada, imitating the Americans, forbade the public serving of mixed drinks and therefore effectively barred night-clubs, French-speaking Quebec declined to comply, and night-clubs roared in Montreal while the consumption of beer and ale in adjacent Ontario went on in sullen and seedy "beer parlours." These beer parlours were segregated, with sections for men and others for women; a man could enter the latter only in the company of a woman. This was designed to prevent impromptu encounters and perfunctory indulgence in the sport for which men and women alike have shown an intemperate interest for some time.

Meanwhile, in Montreal, depravity flourished along old Dorchester Street in three-storey, stone-fronted whore-houses. Cartoonist Ed McNally caught this earlier Montreal in a mural drawn for the Montreal Men's Press Club, once housed in the high-rise Laurentien Hotel at Dorchester and Peel. The Laurentien was built in haste during World War Two close to the Canadian National (CNR) and Canadian Pacific (CPR) railway stations, both of which have a great deal to do with this story. When the press club moved to the basement of the older and more prestigious Mount Royal, the mural was photocopied and hung on the wall in the new location. It showed men chasing naked ladies over the rooftops and along the eaves of Dorchester Street. It captured an era.

The character of Montreal is, like that of all cities, the consequence of geography and history. The island it inhabits, which is 384 miles almost due north of New York City at the confluence of

9

the St. Lawrence and Ottawa rivers, was discovered by Jacques Cartier in 1535 on his second voyage to what we call North America. Huron Indians, who lived in a village they called Hochelaga, took him to the top of what he named Mont Réal – Mount Royal, as it is still known to those who speak English. Samuel de Champlain arrived in 1611, by which time the village of Hochelaga had apparently disappeared. Champlain laid out the site of a settlement.

The island extends north-northeast between the St. Lawrence River on the south and what the French-speaking residents of the city call Rivière des Prairies and the English-speaking call the Back River. It is ten miles wide at its maximum and thirty-two miles long, ending in the southwest at the village of Ste. Anne de Belleville and in the northeast at Bout de l'Ile – End of the Island. Montreal is bitterly cold in the winter – I once saw a German shepherd frozen to death on its feet in one of its suburbs. In the summer, since it is a river city and therefore very humid, it can be miserably warm, though the highest recorded temperature is 97°F.

The island comprises an almost horizontal stratum of limestone, which contributed to Montreal's distinctive architectural style, at least in the era before tall glass boxes. Those Dorchester Street bordellos were all fronted with this limestone, as indeed are churches, libraries, hospitals, museums, McGill University, the Montreal Neurological Institute, the waterworks, the house in which Oscar Peterson was born, and many of the city's distinctive four-plex and six-plex dwellings. Though conventional apartment houses were built, the city's French-speaking inhabitants and presumably landlords and builders showed a taste for private access to each residence; rows on rows of buildings have stairways curving or leading straight up to second- and even third-floor apartments. In the snow and ice of the city's bitter winters, these outdoor stairways are dangerous, but they reflect the French passion for separation, the intense individualism, and a long street of these buildings is curiously attractive. The patterned recurrence of these railed stairways sets up visual rhythms encountered nowhere else in the world. Even to the eye, the city of Montreal seems to swing.

Montreal is one of the great seaports of the world. Again, topography shaped its destiny. It is at the head of a thousand miles of wide water that slopes smoothly down to the Atlantic Ocean. Caravels and merchant ships had to halt here because of the Lachine Rapids, to the southwest of the city. (The first French explorers thought that they had reached China.) Above Lachine, one can travel by canoe or other vessel twelve hundred miles into the interior of North America. This was the route of the fur traders, and inevitably Montreal became the site of transfer of pelts from canoes to the sailing ships that bore them off to be worn by the ladies of Paris.

Excepting Louisiana and the little archipelago of St. Pierre et Miquelon (which is still French), all of France's North American lands were lost to the British in the Seven Years War. Montreal was peacefully surrendered to their forces in 1760, and the British moved with their customary political skill to reach a tacit accommodation with the Roman Catholic church: you support us as the legitimate and permanent government, and we will support you as the legitimate church.

Millions of years ago, this area of North America was geologically volatile. Lava erupted up through the limestone strata. Eons of erosion removed the softer limestone, leaving a volcano's core in the centre of modern Montreal. When Oscar Peterson was a boy, this graceful green mountain, Mount Royal, completely dominated the city, visible from almost anywhere. It rose like a great whale breaching in a sea of dwellings, its forehead toward the northeast, as if it were heading for Bout de l'Ile. On its dorsal slope rested the City of Westmount, then and now an English-speaking enclave. There the very rich Anglophones who dominated and exploited the French lived out their lives in lofty indifference to the suffering of their subservients, who could look up at them from their limestone houses on the city's floor. The dominance of Mount Royal, which is 769 feet high, has been diminished by the downtown clustering of skyscrapers, but its crest is still the best place to view the city. On a clear day you can see into the Green Mountains of Vermont in the south. In autumn, the colours seem to come first to

Mount Royal, spilling slowly and gloriously down into the city itself. The Dorchester Street whore-houses are gone, replaced by tall buildings or parking lots, and the street itself has been widened into a main thoroughfare – and renamed Boulevard René-Lévesque.

Slavery existed in Central America among the various Indian groups before Columbus arrived. The introduction into America of the chattel slavery of Africans, purchased from other Africans, was the work of the Spaniards after they tried to use the native Caribbean Indians who, as the Canadian historian A.R.M. Lower put it, "as an alternative to slavery, died." The descendants of Africans were already working in Jamaica when England took it from the Spaniards in 1665, and Britain in 1833 became the first European nation to condemn and prohibit slavery.

The English were not, however, guiltless of cruelty, and there were uprisings in the islands. In Jamaica, many slaves escaped into the hills to mount guerrilla warfare against their masters. They made occasional treaties with their enemies, but the struggle continued, and after a particularly bothersome rebellion in 1760, the English burned its leader at the stake and hung some of the others in irons to starve and be eaten by birds. Jamaican blacks arrived in Halifax as early as 1791; their population swelled in 1796 when the English moved five hundred of the more rebellious element there.

You will look in vain through the indexes of standard Canadian history textbooks for the word "slavery," which is the reason Canadians believe it never existed in their country. It did. The last slave sold in Canada, one Emmanuel Allen (whose first name, let us note, is Oscar Peterson's middle name), aged thirty-three, drew a price of £36 in a Montreal auction on August 25, 1797, six years after the settlement of those rebellious five hundred in Halifax. Slavery was abolished in Upper Canada (modern Ontario) by act of Parliament on May 31, 1793, and in Lower Canada (now Quebec) in 1834 on the British order prohibiting it throughout the Empire.

But slavery was never a pinion of the economy, as it was in the United States, and the black population of Canada was small. In

1804, there were 142 slaves in Montreal. One of the sources of Canada's black population was the "Underground Railway," by which escaped American slaves made their way north to freedom. Its terminus was in the area around Windsor, Ontario, directly across the river from Detroit. Its importance has been somewhat exaggerated, however: many of those who arrived by this route were less than enchanted by the new country and went back.

The big influx of blacks into Montreal was the consequence of the railways. Oscar Peterson's very life was shaped by the railways. By the end of the nineteenth century, four railways serviced Montreal, the Canadian Pacific (CPR) and Canadian National (CNR), the New York Central, and the Delaware and Hudson; the latter two ran by contractual arrangement over the rails of the two Canadian lines, connecting Montreal to New York. The Pullman Company had made it a policy to hire only blacks to wait on its white sleeping-car customers, and when sleeping-car service was extended into Montreal, Pullman sent up blacks to do the same work in Canada. In 1897, an estimated three hundred blacks, mostly American – as opposed to West Indian – were living in Montreal, most of them working for the railways. During World War One, more American blacks were recruited from New York City, Philadelphia, Chicago, Washington, DC, and the South.

At the same time, a substantial immigration from the West Indies began, and more blacks moved to Montreal from Halifax. Both of Oscar Peterson's parents followed this route. In 1928, when Oscar was three, and already able to read and write, 90 per cent of the black men of Montreal worked for the railways, in sleeping and parlour and observation cars, as cooks, and as red-caps. They looked on this work as their own and bitterly resented and resisted attempts to open it up to European immigrants. For that matter, they resented the hiring of American blacks. On May 19 of that year, this letter appeared in the Montreal *Star*:

> I read in a recent issue of the *Star* a statement by the CPR concerning the number of so-called trained and experienced porters brought to the city from the United States. Now I should like to ask

13

the CPR how it is that they have a colored instructor to [show the newcomers] how to make down beds and treat passengers. There are plenty of capable coloured West Indians who are better qualified than the men who have been brought in from the United States, and we appeal to the public to support us. We help to support the government of this country and pay taxes, so that it is only just to us to put an end to this unfair practice.

West Indian from Jamaica

One of the friends of Oscar's youth, Lou Braithwaite, said, "If you were black in this city when I grew up, you could be a dancer or a pimp – or you could work for the railways. I swore I'd never work for the railways, and I ended up spending my life doing it." Braithwaite, a Barbadian by ancestry, worked as a redcap at Windsor Station, the CPR's Montreal terminus.

As the black population in the vicinity of the two main railway stations increased, old limestone mansions began to be converted into apartments and boarding-houses and rented to these families. The CPR owned a lot of this land. Most of the city's black residents lived in a strip between the two railway lines, the CNR on the south and CPR on the north, Windsor Street on the east and Glen Road on the west. There were small pockets of black population elsewhere in the city, including, in the east, a group of French-speaking immigrants from Guadeloupe and Martinique. But the group that lived between the railway lines was the largest and most coherent; the area was known as the St. Antoine district. There was a similar but smaller such colony in the nearby community of Verdun, which is walking distance away.

Anticipating the summer rush, a CPR agent would visit New York, Philadelphia, Washington, DC, and Chicago, as well as black universities in the South, to recruit summer labour. These temporary workers boarded in the St. Antoine district and went home in the autumn – along with bookies and stable boys and walkers who came for the racing season, then followed the horses south when the weather grew cool.

Sometime shortly before or during World War One, a young

boy named Daniel Peterson joined the merchant marine and left his native island of Tortola, one of the British Virgin Islands, which lie to the east of Cuba and the Dominican Republic. In time he became an able seaman, sailing to South America, Canada, the United States, and England. "I always wanted to play the piano," he said years later. "But we didn't have pianos aboard ship and I was never ashore much. I solved my problem by buying me a collapsible organ. All folded up, it looked just like a suitcase. Wherever I went, my suitcase went with me." Aboard ship he taught himself music, studying theory from books he purchased when he was ashore. By the time he became a bos'n, he was a modestly accomplished organist.

In 1917 he landed in Halifax and made his way inland to Montreal, where after two years he went to work for the CPR as a sleeping-car porter. He married a shy young domestic named Kathleen Olivia John, also from the Caribbean, from St. Kitts, one of the Leeward Islands.

Kathleen John was of an educated family. Her father, Ishmael John, was a school superintendent who died when she was very young. The family was apparently highly musical, and an uncle, Vance John, was a pianist who was about to begin medical studies at McGill University when he was killed in an automobile accident. Kathleen John had two brothers, who became pharmacists, and three sisters. It was the family's plan that the two brothers, on completing their educations, would help send the sisters to school, but one of the young men married a fellow student and disrupted the plan.

In 1985, Oscar Peterson's elder sister, Daisy Peterson Sweeney, then sixty-five, an esteemed teacher of the piano, recalled that opportunities for the girls were scarce in St. Kitts. "There was," she said, "a company called Pittford and Black that had a steamship line to Halifax. The owners were in the West Indies at the time, and they said to my grandmother, 'Why don't you let the girls come to Canada and they can work for us and they'll have an opportunity?' Mum was always amazed by the fact that my grandmother wouldn't let them out of the yard even, and if any noisy people came down, she'd close the shutters, because you're not in that class. It ended, however, that this opportunity came along and she let her two daughters come to Canada. My aunt was a cook and my mother was a housekeeper. They were paid the grand old sum of five dollars a month. And Mum used to send some home. I think the woman she worked for was a bank manager's wife. After they were there for a while and realized there was more money to be made in Montreal, they came up to Montreal.

"She worked until she got married, the same kind of work. You weren't allowed to do anything else. I worked as a domestic for years. I even went to the children's hospital once when they advertised for chambermaids. The woman said, 'The only thing I have for you is to clean toilets.' That didn't bother me, because somebody has to clean toilets. I said, 'When can I start?' She said she'd call me, but of course she never did."

The man Kathleen John married is remembered by everyone as an extremely quiet and very powerful man.

"My father could sit all day and play solitaire," Daisy Sweeney said in her soft accent, a musical mixture of Caribbean inflections and Canadian vowels. "Play solitaire and smoke a cigar. On the other hand, he'd read to us. I remember a book of poetry he read to us. Different books. There used to be a Sunday newspaper called the *Standard*. He would read that to us and ask us to explain it to him. This was his involvement with education. He didn't have much himself, but he had a hunger for it, always. When my brother Fred was seven and I was six, the teacher gave us a sheet of paper and said we could all draw anything we liked. Fred and I decided to do long division and have a race doing it. The teacher came around to see what we had done. The other children had drawn stick figures and trees or whatever you draw in grade one. And Fred and I had done long division. We could all read and write fluently by age three. Well, the teacher took us into the office. And Fred and I were saying, 'I didn't know we made any mistakes.' We were scared. And the teachers looked at what we had done and they put Fred up to grade two, but they left me where I was because I was too young.

"When we were ten my father gave us this book a little more than an inch thick about psychology. We didn't know what psychology was." She chuckled quietly. "It is still doubtful what it is. We were not only supposed to read, we were supposed to memorize it, because some man on the train had told him you could look a man in the eye and know who he is, and you wouldn't be fooled. My mother objected to this, and after a while the book disappeared. I guess he realized it was too advanced for us."

It is one of the few things, apparently, about which he ever relented. Like J.S. Bach, he taught music to his wife and all his children. All of them practised diligently under the wilful eye of this deeply determined man; all of them learned to play piano – and other instruments besides.

Trombonist Butch Watanabe said, "I was a little afraid of Mr. Peterson."

"A little?" said Lou Braithwaite, when the remark was quoted to him. "A *lot*. I'd be out playing with my friend Richard Parris, who is now a very fine saxophonist. In that black neighbourhood, if you were running along and passed any adult, regardless of whether you knew them, you had to stop and bid them good day, and then you continued on. I remember running with Richard and other friends on St. James Street past the Peterson door. Mr. Peterson would be sitting there. You didn't want to stop every time you went by. But you did. He had that overwhelming quality about him, and you stopped, every time. And he never said a word to you."

CHAPTER 2

BETWEEN THE TRACKS

In 1949, the year Oscar Peterson made his Jazz at the Philharmonic concert début in Carnegie Hall, Canada had about 18,000
blacks in an overall population of about 13 million. According to
the Canadian census of 1951, the majority, 45.2 per cent, lived in
Nova Scotia, 38.4 per cent were in Ontario, and only 3.1 per cent in
Quebec. There were approximately as many black Americans
south of the border as there were white Canadians north of it – 13
million in a population of about 135 million. One American in 10
was describable as black, but only one Canadian in about 722.

So Oscar Peterson was part of a minority within a minority, an
English-speaking black in a white city whose primary language was
French.

In 1928, when Oscar was three, Wilfred Emerson Israel submit-
ted for his master's degree in sociology at McGill a treatise titled
"The Montreal Negro Community." He estimated the black population of the city at between 1,200 and 3,000. Israel left us a fascinating portrait of the St. Antoine community at that time – of
small boys playing softball, football, and lacrosse in back alleys
hung with wet wash, sometimes flecked with soot from the two railways; of vegetable pedlars and ice men; of loafers and gamblers
and bookies and con men, all drawn by the racing season each
summer and resented by the permanent residents.

"The bookie transacts his business," Israel's typed manuscript
says, "on a strictly cash basis. Each office is equipped with a battery
of telephones by means of which he receives reports of the local
results as well as those taking place in other parts of the world. By

means of the bookie, who takes advantage of modern communications and the mobility of city life, the opportunity of this expression of the self is extended to all classes, colors, creeds and nationalities."

Israel took careful note of the three different elements in St. Antoine's black community – West Indian, American, and Canadian, meaning those whose families had been in Canada for some generations.

"In the West Indian family," he said, "the husband occupies the dominant and superior position. He is the bread-winner of the home. Largely under British influence and tradition, his conception of the position of his wife is one of the home-maker. To him, her place is in the home. To her, he delegates the task of attending to his bodily needs and comforts. His life outside the home is largely a personal one and the wife knows little of her husband's outside interests. Matters of rent, light, gas, telephone and accounts other than groceries are all part of his duties. With the father insisting that he be the support of the home, he has to develop habits of thrift, and this is soon copied by his energetic wife. The allowance system to her is a constant challenge to be able to show a balanced accounting or a surplus in her expenditures. It is the claim of this group that every West Indian Negro carries some form of insurance."

Some West Indians, however, claim that the male dominance was more apparent than real. Since, during the days of slavery in the islands, men worked in the fields from early sunup until sundown, women held control of the family, and the father was seen as a sort of absent tyrant who inflicted punishment for misdeeds when he came home after work. Behind the façade, these people say, West Indian society was essentially matriarchal.

Israel says:

"It has been shown that the West Indian group are rural people. They have to accommodate themselves to this organism which has been called the city. It is only in the most serious cases of economic depression that the traditional roles are reversed and the wife attempts the shouldering of the economic burden of the family.

The home education of the children is one of restrictions, rather than allowing the freedom of city expressions. The West Indian parents cling tenaciously to the patterns of child development to which they were subjected. As a child matures with his wider contacts, he tends toward the development of city ways. Seeing life through the adult vision in terms of the child, is for this group a difficult task. Thus often it has been found that the conflict occurs between the parent who is clinging to the past and the child, who is leaning towards the behaviour of the city. As the English or Anglican Church is the established body in those islands, the religious education tends toward keeping the child away from the established Negro church in this city. Thus there are Negroes and their children to be found attending the different Anglican churches in this city."

The Peterson family at first attended St. Jude's Anglican Church but felt the chill of prejudice there and moved to Union United Church, with a large black congregation, an important centre in the social life of that surrounded community. The United Church of Canada, formed the year Oscar was born, became the country's largest Protestant denomination, linking the Methodist and Congregational churches and two-thirds of Canada's Presbyterians.

Israel contrasted the life of St. Antoine's West Indian families to that of its American blacks. "The husband" in these American families "no longer dominates the wife and rules as a monarch. The city experience has filled her with that spirit of independence, and he is accepting this. Like the modern woman, she knows that marriage is not the escape from the world of reality. There is economic opportunity in the city, and marriage to her is a matter of choice. In the American cities, her economic life is expanding, and the husband has to put her on an equal footing, or she refuses his proposal. She knows her husband's outside business interests and experiences and shares his success and his failures. A tolerant attitude toward the child and his taking on the city pattern in his behavior is characteristic of this group. The children enjoy the freedom of action necessary for their development, and make wide contacts. This American father is more of the companion than merely the stern but just father. He makes pals of them and enters fully into their confidence."

Israel apparently knew the West Indian community, but he seems naïve about the black American experience, overlooking important differences in the two histories. For one thing, the British in the islands – despite an occasional execution – do not seem to have mistreated slaves to the extent the mainland Americans did. American blacks were forbidden to learn to read and write. The British educated many West Indian blacks, and even sent a few of them to school in England, to make them more effective managers of their sugar plantations. The Americans mixed together Africans of different linguistic groups, so that they could not communicate and plot rebellion. The British did not do this – which may be one reason they had so many rebellions and mutinies in the islands.

American slave-holders commonly showed no respect for family ties among blacks, selling them off separately, taking husbands from wives, children from parents. This weakened these links, and even the very tradition of family. The British allowed the blacks to live as families. American slaves were not allowed to own land. The British let them have individual family farm plots, which encouraged independence and the development of managerial skills.

While Britain passed its Abolition Act in 1833, and provided for payment of compensation to those forced by law to free their slaves, it took the Civil War to end slavery officially in the United States, and even afterwards various laws were put in place to keep black Americans in a state of submission and de facto bondage.

Finally, and this is one of the most significant differences of all, the blacks very early became the majority of the population in the islands. "Where I come from," as one West Indian put it, "I am not part of a minority." And, Lou Braithwaite said of islanders, "They are more British than the British."

Oscar was born in a limestone house on Delisle Street, the fourth of the family's five children. The house, which in 1988 was still there, was at one time the parsonage of the Union United Church.

Fred was the first-born, followed by Daisy, Charles, Oscar, and May. The exposure to music began before any of them could remember. Oscar has said, "There's a good way and a bad way to expose children to music. If they're exposed in the wrong way, it can turn them against it. Fortunately we were introduced to it in a good way, and we all learned to play."

Oscar began playing trumpet as well as piano when he was five years old. At the age of seven, he contracted tuberculosis and was confined for thirteen months in Children's Memorial Hospital. When he left the hospital, he was pronounced cured, but his lungs had been weakened and his father decided he should give up trumpet to concentrate on piano. Both his brothers, Chuck and Fred, played piano. Oscar says that Fred was the best pianist in the family, but he died in 1934 at fifteen of tuberculosis, when Oscar was nine.

In 1944, the public relations department of the CPR put out a press release on its musical porter and his family. It is a curious document to read, utterly of its time and place, and reflecting the forgotten PR man's unease with the subject.

"Eighty-eight keys, ten nimble fingers and a sense of rhythm born years ago on the Mississippi levees," it begins, though neither Oscar nor any of his ancestors had ever been anywhere near a Mississippi levee. "These together paint a word picture of Montreal's Oscar Peterson, who at 19 bids fair to emulate the pianistic success of Duke Ellington and the late 'Fats' Waller.

"One of the four living musical Petersons, the sepia brood of Daniel Peterson, a Canadian Pacific sleeping car porter, Oscar is a rare individual who ran an amateur contest into what promises to be a stellar career at the piano keyboard.

"Built like a piano himself, genial, mahogany-stained Oscar is close to six feet tall" – he was already six-foot-two – "and measures about four octaves wide at the shoulders. His broad smile displays a set of ivories fit to make the ivories on any piano keyboard turn yellow with envy, and it reflects too, the immense personal pleasure and satisfaction he derives from his 'work' ...

"With five pianists under one roof, the Petersons, a mutual

admiration society, don't worry much about where their next music is coming from, and it's a rare day when one of the family at least is not at the piano, respectfully noting the classics or beating out the latest 'jive'. One of their favourite tricks is four hands at the piano, and they frequently engage in what one of them terms 'musicales' in the family living room."

As a study in unconscious racism, the document is classic. But it does fill in some details about the family and gives us a glimpse of the tragic Chuck: "While Charles, 23, got his early musical start at the piano, he later went into brass, specializing in trumpet, which he calls 'my baby.' He also played with local dance bands before he donned the King's uniform four and a half years ago.

"Three years he spent attached to an artillery unit, and then he transferred to the Montreal Garrison Band playing tuba under the direction of Sgt. Major W.G. Black. His 'oomp-oomp-oomp' is heard regularly in Montreal railway stations, where the music of the garrison band greets returning overseas veterans."

One of his bandmates was clarinetist Lou Braithwaite. They were discharged from the army together at the end of World War Two. The CPR press release is incorrect in suggesting that the trumpet was Chuck's instrument of choice. His true love was the piano, but you don't play piano in army bands. And all the Peterson children played brass instruments as well. But Chuck had every intention of being a pianist when he came out of the army. Unable immediately to get work as a musician, Chuck Peterson went to work in an aluminum plant. He reached into a drop press to pull out something that had stuck. The press came down and crushed off his left arm below the elbow.

"I remember when it happened," Lou Braithwaite said. "We had a band, just a group of us, and we were cursing Chuck that night because he wasn't there and he had all the music. He was working on the stamp machine. When we went to the hospital to see him, the marks he had made on the wall with the other hand, from the pain, were black."

Oscar said, "I was with Johnny Holmes' orchestra when it happened. We had been working out of town, and I was coming home from Ottawa by train, and one of the porters said, 'What are you doing on board?' I said, 'Just going back home,' and he said, 'It's a drag what happened to your brother,' and I said, 'What are you talking about?' And he said, 'He lost his arm this morning.' That's how I heard about it."

Years later, a group of musicians were sitting around a hotel room during a Jazz at the Philharmonic tour. Someone asked Oscar how his brother was doing. Oscar said that he was doing studio and other work on trumpet in Montreal and was just fine. Somehow it came out that he had lost his hand in an industrial accident. And someone asked how it happened. Oscar told how Chuck put his hand into the machine...

"Stupid motherfucker," one of the musicians, not noted for tact, interjected.

Oscar grabbed him by the lapels of his suit, picked him up bodily, slammed him against a wall, and said, "You say one more word about my brother and I'll kill you."

Oscar liked the piano, he would say later, so much that he could not be kept away from it. "I practised from nine a.m. to noon," he told me in 1959, "took an hour off for lunch, practised from one to six in the afternoon, then went to dinner, and went back to the piano about seven-thirty. I'd keep practising until my mother would come in and drag me away from it so the family could get some sleep." But his own statements at other times suggest that he resisted the ordeal the way most children do.

In 1982, Oscar said during an interview for a Canadian Broadcasting Corporation documentary on his life, "The interesting thing about my dad is that he became a musician because of being a sailor. From what I understand he was a bos'n on a ship and he bought himself [that] little organ, I never did find out exactly what kind, and taught himself to play. And when he decided to settle in Canada – he sailed to Canada – and met my Mum, he taught my Mum how to play. And then he decided as the children came along that we should all have a workable knowledge of music. And I think it was wonderful. He worked a marvellous system, actually. He taught the older children, and then he expected them to pass on what they had learned step by step by step. Daisy did a lot of teaching in the house, and she helped me tremendously.

"Daisy is a great tutor. Daisy has great patience. She understands human weaknesses, and she can relate to someone having difficulties. And Daisy is a great pianist." Oliver Jones, ten years younger than Oscar and a neighbour during their youth, who emerged as a strong jazz pianist in the mid-1980s, was also trained by Daisy. He described her thus: "I always found her very, very easy. Her attitude was always very pleasant. But stern. If you didn't practise, she let you know it." Interestingly, and perhaps significantly, he has a technique similar in clarity, rapidity, and balance to Oscar's.

In 1946, when he was twenty, Oscar told an interviewer, "I owe a good deal to my mother. In the write-ups about me my father always gets the credit for teaching me to play, but my mother should get some credit too. When I wanted to swing music, she backed me up and said she thought there might be some future in it." Daisy in turn said of him, "He had the range and the depth that I've never seen as yet in pupils."

Daisy Peterson, later Daisy Sweeney, born May 7, 1920, remembers growing up in Montreal during the Depression and World War Two as "pleasurable, though sometimes painful." The family, she said, was rich not in material things but in culture and thrived in an environment that was socially stimulating, because "everyone knew everyone and felt responsible for each other." It is a memory of the Depression shared by whites and blacks alike. Lillie Fraser Peterson, Oscar's first wife, told an interviewer in later years that her family had been poor, but not as poor as the Petersons. She said that Oscar had never forgotten his burning embarrassment over his patched pants on his first day in high school.

Oscar would later celebrate nearby Place St. Henri in his *Canadiana Suite,* evoking its mood with a vigorous stride piano. The style recalls an era, but also "I used it because Place St. Henri was a bustling and busy area," he said.

Wilfred Israel's master's thesis tells us a great deal about the life of Oscar's father. "The post of porter is one that can be filled only by those in the prime of life. In some rare cases young men at 19 have been employed. On the trans-Canada trip, the travel is five nights and four days when Vancouver is reached. Here the porter has two nights and three days to rest at the quarters provided him by the [railway]. Then follows the return trip to Montreal followed by a rest of four days and three nights. While travelling he is permitted on this run to retire from one a.m. to five a.m. after which time he is on duty until the following day at one o'clock again. On the shorter runs he retires at 11:30 p.m., arises again at 3:30 a.m., followed by working until the night is again come. These men experience great difficulty in getting rest, for with a full car of passengers, [they] must attend their needs at all hours.

"The heat of the prairies is often excessive in the summer. Many complain of the dampness during the rainy season in crossing the prairies. Thus most of these men endeavour to locate themselves on the shorter runs whenever possible.

"Salaries are kept at the same level on the two roads. The first six months he draws $82.50, followed by an increase of $2.50 per month for a full year. This is increased to $87.50, which rate is maintained until three continuous years of service have been completed. Following the completion of three consecutive years of satisfactory service, the maximum of $95 is granted. Tips are always obtained on the different trips. These vary with the men, length of the trip, and the patrons. A round trip has been known to net the porter amounts varying from $15 to $35."

Israel says that the rest of the black population of the St. Antoine district – the 10 per cent that didn't work for the railway – earned from $9 to $21 a week. Daisy says that in the depths of the Depression, the family had a comparatively decent income, though it was hardly rich.

In 1949, when Oscar made that famous first Carnegie Hall appearance, the CNR employed 585 porters, of whom 340 were Canadian-born; 96 had immigrated from the United States, 118 from different parts of the British West Indies, and 31 from other parts of the British Commonwealth. The figures for the CPR were doubtless much the same. In an article titled "Three Thousand Nights on Wheels" published that year in *Maclean's* magazine, the writer McKenzie Porter gave us a vivid portrait of the life of a black railway porter in Canada. He wrote of a man named William Ruffin, but most of what he had to say about Ruffin applied equally to Daniel Peterson.

A railway porter's salary by then had risen to $187 a month, and he could expect to pick up about $50 more in tips. His uniform was provided by the railway, and his food on the train was free. He could eat anything he wanted within reason from the dining car menu – and the food on Canadian railways at that time was excellent. Porters, however, were inclined to eat lightly. They were on guard against stomach ulcers caused by nervous indigestion, in turn caused by the constant motion.

When the run was from either Toronto, where Ruffin lived, or Montreal to Vancouver, some three thousand miles away on the west coast, he would work on a sixteen-day cycle, reaching Vancouver on the fourth day. On the sixth day he would leave Vancouver, arriving back home on the tenth day. Then he would have seven days off. In twenty years, that amounted to three thousand nights and days spent over the click of the wheels.

"His routine is never the same," Porter wrote. "Some people sleep late, others rise early. Occasionally men will sit up all night yarning in the club car and go to bed just when others are shaving. He is kept on the hop. Yet to look at him, you would think from his bland smiling composure that he is your personal servant, wishing you would find him something to do.

"Generally he begins his day by cleaning the shoes of his stateroom passengers. Around six some of these are calling for coffee. Often he has a couple of mothers who give him baby formulas to prepare. He knows every infant food on the market and how to adjust quantities to every age. Between six and seven a.m. he dusts the club car, polishes the woodwork, and tidies up the magazines. While passengers are breakfasting in the diner he transforms their compartments from bedrooms to sitting rooms.

"Soon after breakfast he is making morning coffee in his own kitchen, which separates the compartments from the club car and is so narrow there is room only for standing. He also serves soft drinks from a refrigerator....

"During the afternoon, when passengers are given to dozing, he has his account books to make up. At night it is coffee and soft drinks and bed-making again."

Passengers expected porters to know the schedule exactly. Every once in a while one of them would ask, "Are we on time?" And the porter would look out the window at the coastal landscape of New Brunswick, the villages of Quebec, the bleak moon-like beauty of northern Ontario, or the great seas of wheat interrupted only by lonely grain elevators, or jutting peaks of the Canadian Rockies, or the frantic plunging waters of the Fraser River gorge, and he would glance at his pocket watch and say, "Two minutes behind, sir," or "Twelve minutes ahead." Daniel Peterson knew the contours of the land, the headlands and houses and valleys and crossings and bridges and church steeples of five thousand miles of CPR line.

The pieces that make up Oscar's *Canadiana Suite*, recorded first in 1964, proceed across Canada from east to west, which is the way the country thinks, in the precise sequence of the railway journey from the Atlantic to the Pacific: *Ballad to the East, Laurentides Waltz* (les Laurentides is the French name for the Laurentian Mountains of Quebec, and anyone born and raised in Quebec, like Oscar, tends to think of them that way), *Place St. Henri, Hogtown Blues* (Canadians traditionally dislike Toronto and have since time out of mind called it Hogtown), *Blues of the Prairies, March Past,* which refers to the Calgary Stampede parade, and *Land of the Misty Giants* (the Rocky Mountains). Those pieces are like views from a train window; or perhaps memories of a father's descriptions of the land when he would come home from his journeys and supervise his son's piano lessons.

McKenzie Porter wrote that a porter often is "guardian to a child traveling alone and nearly always finds some elderly woman glad to help him with the responsibility. He tries to get the shy type of passengers into conversation by drawing them into sharing coffee tables. Sometimes he sees passengers begin the journey in a flurry of warm comradeship and end it bitter enemies.

"He keeps his eye on the men who spend the entire journey in an alcoholic miasma, and on the parties which build up between men who have whisky in their compartments and women who are bored. If mixed parties keep quiet and do not offend the rest of the passengers they are left alone. If they become noisy he tips off the conductor.

"He must do his utmost to remember what his passengers forget. He is always picking up after people. If many articles were lost he would fall under suspicion. So to protect his job [he] goes to great lengths in running things down."

Sometimes a porter would have to play midwife, and infants would come into the world in his compartment. Usually, however, he would be able to find a doctor among the passengers when a woman came to her time.

Tips ran to about fifty cents per passenger in each twenty-four hours, and to get them, porters made a ritual of politeness. "No porter can afford to be surly," William Ruffin said. The railways, he said, treated porters well but would not let them rise to any higher position. Why, Ruffin wondered, if they could make the white man's bed, couldn't they also take his tickets? There was only one way they could be promoted – to become instructors of porters. And the chances of that were one in a hundred.

Ruffin, who was born in Chicago, had become a Canadian citizen. He said, "I know that if I had an altercation with a white man that ended in court I would get a just hearing. In some parts of the United States I would be judged guilty before the proceedings opened." He noted that a black man had recently been acquitted of murdering an English war bride. "Cases like that," Ruffin said, "make me proud to be a Canadian."

None the less, Ruffin and his wife once were refused service in a hotel beverage room, and he was denied admission to the old Palace Pier ballroom on the Toronto lakefront when Duke Ellington was appearing there.

Ruffin lived in Toronto, about 350 miles west-southwest of Montreal. Ruffin worked for the CPR, Daniel Peterson for the CNR. But they must have known each other. Ruffin worked for a year for the CPR and they both made runs to Vancouver. Given the small community of black Canadians and the even smaller community of black Canadian railway porters, it is almost impossible that they were not acquainted.

Daniel Peterson once told Oscar about nursing a family – a husband and wife and their young children – all the way across the country, seeing that the children ate and went to bed on schedule and the like. When they reached Vancouver, the husband proffered the reward. A dime. But maybe it was all they had.

Oliver Jones said, "I don't think I ever saw Mr. Peterson smile." After those trips, he was probably smiled out. One begins to see why he was determined that his children would not live a life like his own, why he would force on them the one educational gift he had to offer – music. And first he taught Daisy. He started her, and then she went on to more academic teachers.

Young Daisy Peterson earned $4.50 a week as a domestic, $3 of which she paid out for her piano lessons. She continued to study under adverse conditions until she earned an associate degree in music from McGill University in 1947. She and Oscar and all the family suffered severely from the effects of racism.

"Once," she said, "when they had uprisings in the States, some people would say, 'You're lucky you don't have to go through this.' I'd say, 'How do you know?' They have no clue, they might see me living here, or see someone working in a store, see some tokenism, they'd say, 'Oh you're lucky.' And it's not so. As we grew up and were called 'nigger,' we didn't like it. Then the other kid is called carrot top. Or something else. Your friend could easily be a white friend, and it might be fine until you went to the parents' home. But basically children are free, they'll call all kinds of names. When you hit sixteen or seventeen, you began to realize there was a difference.

"To be fair, can you name me a race that isn't racist? Racism exists among black people with black people. I was discriminated against because I was darker than other girls. If we had plays, you had to look white. How does it make a child feel? If I go into your home, I don't expect to be able to walk all over and have the feeling that I have in my home. But when I *am* home, if I feel the same discrimination, where do I go to? Because this is the end of the line. When I changed from the Anglican church and became a member of the United church, which was a black church, and discrimination was really rampant, I couldn't believe it.

"I remember that even Oliver Jones was discriminated against. Oliver is very dark, like me. I was one of his Sunday school teachers. And I had to fight with one of the leaders because of her wanting to put him in the back. Now this didn't happen in a white church. There was a white church, an Anglican church in Montreal; whenever any blacks came in, they were shunted to the back in one corner. If that happens there, you say, 'Well, I'm going home.' Home being a black church. If you go to a black church and you're rejected, where else do you go?"

Oscar said, "Daisy was the best example of it. She was the best piano teacher around, and never got the job at the Negro Community Centre. She won't tell you that. But I can say it, and I want somebody to dispute me. For years they kept appointing people to teach piano there, and I imagine there was some payment for it, minuscule or whatever it was. But not Daisy."

When Oscar was ten, he and another boy were the only blacks in his class. Someone threw a ruler. The teacher said, "I'll bet one of the niggers did it." Oscar stood up and screamed, "You apologize for that!" All his indignation got him was a trip to the principal's office.

CHAPTER 3

SWINGING IN ST. ANTOINE

Oscar's father worked mostly the Toronto–Montreal run on the CPR and during World War Two made occasional trips to Halifax on troop trains. Oscar has described the discipline he imposed: "My dad would leave and he would give us each a task, pianistically. You had to know this, you had to know that, and when I come back from Vancouver or St. John's, have it together. There were no ifs, ands and buts. Have it together. It was that simple.

"He would come back and then he would call each of us in turn into the room where the piano was, and he would say, 'Okay, fine, may I have the scale? What did you have?' 'I had the G scale.' And he'd go through the scales, the arpeggios, all the things we were supposed to have learned. And when he found one of us, usually me, I guess, had been playing games and wasn't practising, he'd sit there with a little strap, and if he knew for a fact ... I think my Mum used to cue him; he'd come in off the railway, and my mother would say, 'You know, for whatever it's worth, he may have signed the book, but I don't think Oscar spent a half an hour on the piano while you were gone.'

"But usually that was the routine, he'd go through this work book, from point one to the end, and say, 'Well, what have you done and what haven't you done?' And if you did well, he'd say, 'Fine, now here's what I want you to do next week.' I think this was all designed to give us a sense of responsibility, of having goals to reach, having certain debts we had to honour musically, and we had a time limitation to do them in.

"I think at nine I was playing the usual things that kids play, *The Minute Waltz*, and some things I wouldn't even *attempt* to play now.

33

And I would hear my older brother, Fred, fooling around with things like *Oh Dem Golden Slippers* and *Tiger Rag* and I'd say, 'What *is* that?' And finally I found out that it was jazz, and it kind of intrigued me."

According to Lillie Fraser Peterson, Oscar's first wife, the discipline was more severe than Oscar describes. "His father used to beat them with a belt," she told an interviewer for *Maclean's* magazine years later. "His sister Daisy used to get it worse than Oscar. She told me about a time when their father assigned them both a very complicated concerto to learn. They knew they would have to play it without a mistake before he got back. Well, Daisy practised for three, four hours every day, just terrified. Oscar didn't touch the piano, lolled around and read comic books. The day before their dad was due home, he went over to the piano and played the whole thing through perfectly."

Oscar's mother was friendly with William Thomas, a bandmaster she had known since her Halifax days. He had now taken up residence in Montreal and formed a community band. "Fred and Chuck had been in a boys' band, and then joined this band, playing trumpet," Daisy recalled. "As they came up to our house to rehearse one night – on Plymouth Grove, which is no longer there – they needed some piano music. So I was asked to play it. I was about twelve years old. Oscar would have been seven. And so I used to play the piano and finally they got me a trombone, because I was interested in that too. It was a mishmash of instruments, as they had in the good old days. We had tuba, we had a fine clarinetist in a Mr. Bowman from the States, and a violinist, Mr. Spooner. A Mr. Evelyn also played violin. It was all classical and band music. Oscar and I were the only children in the band. Naturally, for him, it would be boring to play his part over and over. So of course he heard the clarinet going to town, and he'd play along with it. The bandmaster would say, 'Stick to your part!'"

Oscar studied for a short time with pianist Lou Hooper. Born May 18, 1894, in North Buxton, Ontario, near Windsor and the upper end of the Underground Railway, one of eleven children, Hooper was of mixed Irish, African, and Amerindian blood – his mother was full Cree.

The family moved across the Detroit River to Ypsilanti, Michigan, when he was three. He sang solos in church and at twelve played piano and trombone in the Hooper Brothers' Orchestra. He studied piano at the Detroit Conservatory, working the while in dance and theatre orchestras. The band played regularly at the Koppin Theater, working with such acts as Ma Rainey, Ethel Waters, and Sammy Davis Sr. Graduated with a bachelor's degree, Hooper moved to New York in 1921 and continued studying through 1923 and '24 at Columbia University, meanwhile teaching at the Martin-Smith Music School, a subsidiary of the Damrosch Institute, which later became the Juilliard School of Music.

Hooper almost immediately became a figure in Harlem jazz, playing with banjoist Elmer Snowden and clarinetist Bob Fuller. They recorded as the Three Jolly Miners, the Three Hot Eskimos, the Three Monkey Chasers, the Rocky Mountain Trio, the Three Blues Chasers, the Bob Fuller Trio, and the Choo Choo Jazzers, for Columbia, Vocalion, Okeh, and other companies. Researchers have turned up a great number of Hooper recordings from his Harlem days. He earned $7.50 a side, and no royalties.

When he was seventy-five, Hooper was interviewed by the Montreal *Gazette*. He said of the Harlem part of his life, "Oh man, those times were something else. I knew Fats Waller and Willie 'the Lion' Smith and the Duke. I remember one night at a place called the Hoofer's Club there was the Lion, Fats, Luckey Roberts, and the great James P. Johnson, all playing against one another. And then Fats got up and made that famous statement, 'Ladies and gentlemen, here is an artist.' James P. took a bow and the session broke up.

"I played at the Lafayette Theater in Harlem, too. I was in the pit when Bessie Smith played there, and I was there the night that Louis Armstrong came to New York. He made his debut with the Fletcher Henderson band, playing the *Whatcha Callem Blues*. The people received him almost boisterously, but he didn't like New York and went back to Chicago shortly after that."

Throughout the 1920s, Hooper accompanied on recordings trumpeters Johnny Dunn and Louis Metcalf, as well as Ethel Waters, Ma Rainey, and Mamie Smith. He accompanied Paul

Robeson in 1926, then toured with Lew Leslie's *Blackbirds of 1928*, a revue that has been called the first major black musical. One member of the company was dancer Bill (Bojangles) Robinson. The show closed in 1929 at His Majesty's Theatre in Montreal. Hooper went back to Detroit for a time, then in 1932 returned to Canada permanently.

In Toronto, Hooper joined Myron (Mynie) Sutton's near-legendary Canadian Ambassadors, an all-black dance band that played throughout Quebec and Ontario. He formed and led a male choir, the Hooper Southern Singers, in concerts and on radio, worked in dance and jazz bands, accompanied Billie Holiday in a 1939 Montreal appearance, and taught piano. He spent part of World War Two overseas in the Royal Canadian Artillery as a pianist and entertainer, then returned, almost forgotten, to work in Laurentian resort hotels. In 1962, he was rediscovered and began to be recorded. He joined the faculty of the University of Prince Edward Island in Charlottetown in 1975 and died in Charlotte-town in 1977.

In an unpublished autobiography – the manuscript of which is now in the National Archives of Canada in Ottawa – the pianist recalled getting a phone call from Daniel Peterson, asking if he would take his son Oscar as a student. "I was not fully aware of his playing ability," Hooper wrote in his curiously courtly style, "nor the theoretical knowledge he already possessed. Suffice to say, I was in for a delightful surprise when I arrived at the Peterson home for the first lesson."

Hooper describes Oscar as a plump boy, "looking very neat in an overly snug dark suit, buttoned up to the top and with knee-pants." He continues: "My first pleasant experience came, when I was presented to him, in his polite manner and the pleasantly modulated voice in which he replied. As I came to know the parents and other members of the family at that time, I discovered this kind of courteous dignity to be a strong characteristic of all of them.

"When, on that first day, I asked Oscar to play for me, I was indeed astonished, not only at what I was hearing but at the intelligent interpretation; the easy and adequate technique while playing entirely from memory. This from a boy of eleven was, to say the least, unusual. Then followed a short period of basics – scales, arpeggi, keys, chords, minor versus major. He knew them all, as well as possessing nature's gift of perfect pitch, which I observed and tested fully....

"Following a few lessons with young Oscar and realizing his outstanding potential, I advised Mr. Peterson that, in view of Oscar's present ability, I had decided to select only such musical pieces as would challenge to the utmost his musicianship, leaving him to deal with them in his own way. As I observed the results through biweekly visits to his home, I was satisfied that this practice was proving satisfactory: it freed Oscar to forge his own illustrious way.

"Eventually we parted, I to leave Canada for six years of military service. When I returned to civilian life in 1945, I soon began to hear the name of Oscar Peterson, always in words of highest praise, and during a visit to his home, hearing him play I quickly understood and agreed. His playing that day was to me an experience in controlled power, facility, and gentleness. I heard Oscar from time to time following this meeting, and learned he was doing some studying with Paul de Marky."

Daisy was already a student of de Marky's.

Pianist Paul Alexander de Marky was born in Gyula, Hungary, May 25, 1897. He emigrated to Canada in 1921, continuing to perform throughout Europe, the United States, and Canada while teaching from 1929 to 1937 at the McGill Conservatory. Oscar studied with him throughout his years at Montreal High School.

Oscar said, "Paul de Marky came into my life at a very important time. I was fourteen. I went to this man. He totally awed me with his beautiful sound on the instrument, his beautiful touch, and his command of the instrument, and I was so inspired by him I can remember unbeknownst to him going early to my lessons because I found he would practise, and I'd sit and listen to him. He'd be sitting there playing and playing, with this beautiful sound that he'd get out of the instrument.

"After the lesson, he'd say, 'What are you doing now, in your field, in the jazz field, what are you working on?' And I'd be teaching myself different tunes. I remember playing *The Man I Love* for him. He'd say, 'I don't hear the melody singing. The melody is choppy. Make it sing.'"

In 1982, de Marky, then eighty-five, recalled those lessons. "I taught him," de Marky said, "technique, speedy fingers, because that's what you need in modern jazz. Tatum had the speediest fingers. I gave Oscar Chopin studies. And then mostly, as I found that he was so good at melodic ballad style, I gave him the idea of big chords, like Debussy has them. Big rich soft chords. And his ballad playing is remarkable, when he plays those old-timers like *Laura* and *Tenderly*. If you have a natural talent for your fingers and harmony, they can't go wrong if they wanted to."

"I had a certain amount of confidence," Oscar said, "but Paul de Marky really sort of made a believer out of me, from a musical and artistic standpoint. It's one thing to know you can play, to know you can skate up and down the rink, but as to how well you look doing it, how much finesse you have, how much confidence, how much interest you can create in your audience, I guess that all has to do with it. He made me believe that I did have something to offer the music world."

Hooper is Peterson's link to the Harlem of the 1920s, de Marky the link to the nineteenth-century tradition of bravura piano playing.

Oscar once told his friend André Previn: "My first bruising with Art Tatum came at a very tender age, in my teens. I thought I was pretty heavy at school, you know – I'd play in all the lunch hours with all the chicks around the auditorium. And my dad was watching all this quietly, and he got the feeling that I was getting a little too egotistical about it. And one day he came home and said, 'Listen, there's something I want you to hear. It's a record.' And he put it on, I'll never forget – it was Art Tatum's *Tiger Rag*. And, truthfully, I gave up the piano for two solid months; and I had crying fits at night."

38

"My dad was the type that always made sure you kept your feet on the ground," Daisy said. "He always made you think you could do better. I remember Oscar saying once that he was annoyed with my father because every time he thought he'd get praise from him, he'd say, 'Oh yes, I heard someone that did far better.' That was very discouraging for a while."

Oscar somehow survived this constant pressure from the father. But it destroyed Daisy as a public performer.

"Really, outside my dad was a lot of fun," she said. "He kept to himself. If my father was downstairs, we were upstairs, and if he came upstairs we went downstairs. We weren't pals, that's for sure. He might say, 'Did you do your practice?' or did you do something else. But when we were at the table at suppertime, he didn't tell jokes so much as he acted them. For instance, my mother might set the table, he might unset it. She'd be looking for the salt and pepper, and she'd say, 'Well I'm sure I put it there.' He'd say, 'Well if you don't know where you put it, you must be crazy.'" (It is a style of humour we will see later in Oscar.)

"My father was firm and very stern," Daisy said. "He never took us any place. Mum was a home person. She'd send us out and say, 'Now you know I'm with you, and I'm thinking of you, and you do your best.'

"One thing he did that was unpleasant that I always remembered, although he wasn't aware of it. He felt pretty proud of us, and he'd give a little added push. I had to play a solo that day and he said, 'Now remember, no mistakes.' Well, in the first place, no one makes mistakes because they want to. He said, 'If you make a mistake when you start, people will lose interest.' And if you made one at the end, no matter how well you had played at the beginning it would undo everything. Now up until then Fred and I had enjoyed going playing. Well, I made a mistake at the beginning, middle, and end. And I always remembered it. And from that time on, if I had to play, I was just a bag of nerves. I never enjoyed playing in public again."

Everyone who knew her then remembers Daisy Peterson as a pianist of stunning virtuosity. Johnny Holmes recalled phoning

39

Oscar at the house one day. As they talked, Holmes heard someone playing Chopin in the background. "Who's that?" Johnny said.

"Daisy."

"I've never heard *The Minute Waltz* played that fast," Johnny said. "She's going to get through it in about thirty-five seconds."

"Yeah, but Johnny," Oscar said, "she's playing it with her left hand."

In his last high-school years, Oscar played, along with trumpeter Maynard Ferguson, in a band called the Montreal High School Victory Serenaders, led by Ferguson's year-older brother, Percy, now a professor of psychology at Adirondack State College in Glens Falls, New York. Oscar's father disapproved of his playing jazz, but his mother supported him. Maynard's father, also named Percy, was a respected teacher, principal of Aberdeen School, one of the English-speaking elementary schools within Montreal's unique bilingual school system, since abolished. He allowed the band to rehearse in the school's kindergarten, and Oscar's mother was able to point out that he was in a respectable place under respectable auspices. Mike, as Percy Ferguson is still called by Maynard and friends, remembers Oscar as "serious and responsible, particularly for someone that age. He was honest and punctual, never the one who was late. And he was very big. I still have pictures of us somewhere, rehearsing at the school."

As the high school's star trumpet player, Maynard was impressed into playing the bugle at the raising and the lowering of the flag, even in bitter winter cold. He says Oscar would stand inside a glass door, in the warmth, pointing at him and laughing helplessly. He says that Oscar and he were very close in those days, and that he has never lost the feeling. Oscar was already becoming a celebrity, Maynard says.

Montreal High, the city's major English-language high school and a very good one, on University Avenue just above Sherbrooke Street and thus a stone's throw from McGill University, had at that time about twenty-five hundred students. One of Oscar's schoolmates was Hal Gaylor, who later became a well-known bassist, working with Chico Hamilton, Benny Goodman, and Tony Bennett. Hal remembers going to Oscar's home to listen to records. Oscar drew his attention to the bassist on one record. He said, "That was Ray Brown. Some day I'm going to have a trio, and he's going to be my bass player."

Another schoolmate was Don Cameron, the drummer with the Victory Serenaders. He remembers Oscar sitting during recesses at a baby grand piano in the foyer of the school, surrounded by crowds of excited fellow students as he played boogie-woogie at tempos none of them had imagined possible.

In the autumn of 1942, recalled Cameron – who kept a diary during that period and is very precise about dates, places, and times – the Victory Serenaders played an engagement at a place called the CPR Club. "Oscar never wanted to leave the piano," Cameron said. "In the breaks, he'd go right on playing. I remember him playing Harry James' *Trumpet Blues and Cantabile*, the whole arrangement, note for note."

One evening when Oscar was fourteen, Daisy asked him to go for a walk with her. She knew that Ken Soble, who conducted a nationwide amateur contest on the Canadian Broadcasting Corporation (CBC), was holding Montreal auditions. She took Oscar to the CBC studio. She had to push Oscar, who was then extremely shy, onto the stool and make him play. Soble immediately scheduled him for the program and put him on the air. Oscar went through the semi-finals of the competition and won, then went on to Toronto to win the finals and a cash prize of $250. This led to a weekly broadcast on Montreal radio station CKAC, called *Fifteen Minutes' Piano Rambling*. He performed during the war years on CBM, the CBC's English-language outlet in Montreal, and nationally on *The Happy Gang*, a CBC network radio program whose alumni include Robert Farnon.

Oscar fell under the influence of a pianist named Harold (Steep) Wade, who played with the house band at Rockhead's Paradise, one of several clubs in the black neighbourhood. Across the street from Rockhead's was the Café St. Michel, another St. Antoine Street jazz club.

41

"Steep was like a godfather to me, musically," Oscar says. "First of all, Rockhead's wasn't exactly in the safest part of town. I used to go there every night just to hear the guys play. They used to sneak me in because I was under age at the time. Steep used to call me 'kid'. On different nights when he used to go for a walk or listen to someone else's music, he'd say, 'Okay, kid, go on and play the show for me. I'll be back.' That's where I really served my jazz apprenticeship – in that environment."

The St. Antoine district had a thriving night life, clubs where jazz bands appeared, and white audiences. In his 1928 thesis, Wilfred Israel wrote: "Two Negro buffet parlors are being operated on St. Antoine Street at Number 1256 over a tavern, and the other at Number 1323 over a Chinese laundry. Both premises have been former private residences. At Number 1256 the partitions between some rooms have been removed, giving greater floor space for dancing. For a period this location was known as the Owl Club. Membership and admission today is on the basis of being known to the management. These two houses are the Negro cabarets of Montreal. The cabarets or nightclubs are the night life of this group. During the day, only the casual visitor is to be seen seeking admission. After 11 o'clock at night, the patrons are to be observed drifting in the direction from their homes and from the auxiliary social centres in the sporting district. The jazz band of piano, violin and two saxophones grinds out the sensuous blue harmonies with a syncopation that sets the body in ready motion with sympathetic vibrations. With sounds of Broadway's favourites floating through the windows lowered from the top, the patrons come in increasing numbers. By midnight, these places are filled to their capacity. From then till daylight, the dominance of the saxophone is challenged by the laughter of both male and female voices. Nearby residents have, they claim, learned the words of *Follow the Swallow Back Home* and *Whispering* while struggling unsuccessfully to drop off in their blissful slumbers. Another claimed learning the piano version of *Girl of My Dreams*.

"The lady patrons of these cabarets are largely whites. These girls of the teen-age and early twenties, some of them, are never seen in this district except at night, come from all sections of the St. Antoine district. Above the hill has its representatives also. Here the young are engaged in the promiscuity phenomenon as outlined by Burgess. Coming from different sections of the city, they enjoy the freedom and abandonment of their new contacts. There is an emotional excitement to these girls from the fact of being in strange surroundings. The eating and drinking with the dark soft-skinned male supply that thrill and emotional release of unsatisfied wishes which she has sought so long. Live, eat, drink and be merry, for tomorrow I may die, has become her philosophy for this brief but fascinating period. The patriotic *God Save the King* at five o'clock in the morning brings the night's festivities to a happy conclusion. With the breakup of these parties, the revelers are observed slowly wending their respective paths homeward. Often a young girl will show facial signs of the glorious night that has been hers. Some walk after the pattern of the drunkard in their tired march home to rest for the frolic of tomorrow. The charming white girl introduced into this group does so as a compensation for her loss of status amongst her own white groupings. It represents her attempt to remake her social world. Some of them have grown up in this immediate locality, known as the sporting district. Here they have contact from early days with these men. They have never had any other attachments nor have they lived in white groupings. They are the victims of the social and economic environment and from which they have not nor ever can escape. Maintaining their status in such a world of casual groupings forces them to exercise their physical charms to the utmost. They adopt a bravo blase attitude towards all. Two of these girls were seeking one of their male friends in a tavern on St. Antoine Street shortly after 10 o'clock. One peeked through the sliding doors, calling to her beau, 'Come on there, shake your big fat lazy [ass] out of the street there.' On another occasion a white resident of the district was loitering on his particular corner when one of these girls accosted him with 'Say, what the [fuck] are you looking at, eh?'"

Israel replaced the profanity with blanks, but they're easily filled in.

Oscar finally dropped out of Montreal High School. He says, "The strongest memory of my dad is the day that I came home and told him I wanted to leave high school. And that was the day he told me I could leave, not to be another piano player, but to be the *best*. He didn't see the same obstacles that I saw. I'd say, 'Gee, y'know, this can't be done.' And he'd say, 'Why not? It got there. If it got there, you can remove it. Or if it isn't there, you can put it there.' It was that simple to him. And I think he instilled a great determination in me. Because he was a determined man."

But the move was not made without doubts. "After I made the decision to go into music," Oscar said, "I remember thinking about it and saying, 'How do you manage to put this all together, how do you string this together to make it financially and environmentally feasible?' I'd say, 'It's okay to play, but what do I do? Do I play a concert this week? You have to be good to play a concert. How do I get to that stage? How do I make money until I get to that stage? Do I play in an orchestra? And if I got into an orchestra, does it mean that I'm going to be stuck there for the rest of my life? Or do I do some studio work? And does it mean I'm going to be stationed there the rest of my life? And how do I get to make recordings, and what if the recordings don't work?' I can remember sitting up one night thinking that there really was no way for me to make a decent living being a jazz artist."

We catch an odd and vivid glimpse of Oscar at the age of twenty in an article published in the October 15, 1945, issue of *Maclean's*. The article describes him sitting in the window of a Montreal music store, playing a piano, the traffic stopped still by the crowds, policemen trying to clear the people away. "Swing!" said a soldier just back from the war. "Oh boy, is that swing!"

CHAPTER 4

DOMINION NETWORK

Oscar was a member of the Johnny Holmes Orchestra from 1942 through 1947. The personnel also included Maynard and Percy Ferguson, Nick Ayoub, and Al Baculis. Oscar has repeatedly said that the experience in the band helped him grow as a ballad player at a time when he was caught up in boogie-woogie. (Indeed, he had become known as the Brown Bomber of Boogie-Woogie.)

Holmes said, "The amazing thing is that when he came into our band at seventeen, he had a technique I think every bit equivalent to what he has now. But he was a diamond in the rough."

"Up to this time," Oscar said, "I'd been playing anything I wanted to play any way at all. I went up and sat in with the band, and I enjoyed it. And I suddenly thought that this is another facet of music that I hadn't really been exposed to – a big dance orchestra. And I wanted to get some experience in that way."

An article in the January 12, 1946, issue of the old Canadian *Liberty* – quite separate from the American magazine of the same name – said, "Despite his comfortable income, Peterson continues to live on Montreal's shabby St. James Street West, down by the railway tracks and the canal. Canadians know St. James Street as the workshop of high finance, but not many persons who live outside of Montreal know that it is also a narrow, straggling, dirty street of factories and tenements. That's Oscar's street, although his home is well furnished ..." Daisy Peterson did not share the writer's opinion of the district. "It was a beautiful area," she said. Much of its charm went, however, when a modern freeway was slashed through it.

The *Liberty* article goes on, "Peterson is the only coloured man in the Holmes band, and despite a bit of pressure caused by racial prejudice, Johnny Holmes took Oscar with him and the band to a summer assignment in the Laurentian Mountains, at Ste Adele, last year." Later it says, "Montreal, like its sister cities everywhere, is not consistent about racial prejudice. Johnny Holmes' band, with Oscar at the piano, has played in the homes of rich young debutantes at coming-out parties, and Victoria Hall, the band's regular stand, is in one of Montreal's better areas. The bobby-soxers and others plague the black boy for his autograph and they crowd around the bandstand five deep on Saturday night to listen in ecstasy as Oscar 'sends' them.... In the band, Oscar enjoys high popularity, and Holmes gets very bitter about the prejudice shown on occasions to his number one attraction. 'You couldn't meet a finer guy anywhere,' he says."

The *Liberty* piece describes Oscar: "big and broad and a shade darker than most Negroes. When Oscar smiles, his huge face is suddenly alight with white and his shy eyes smile too, so that strangers get a feeling of personal warmth and eager friendliness. There isn't anything peculiar about this, because he is a genuine person who has not been spoiled."

One of his friends in the Holmes band was Gerry Macdonald, a saxophonist who later became a recording engineer and founded the Choice record label. Gerry recalled going to Oscar's house to pick him up for a job on a bitter winter night when the streets were covered in ice. Gerry had a motorcycle with a sidecar. Somehow Oscar managed to crowd his large body into the sidecar. Gerry, who was slim and slight of build, gave the motorcycle the gas, and it spun around the axis of Oscar's weight in the sidecar, ending up on the sidewalk. Finally Gerry managed to get the motorcycle rolling, and they drove off to the job, the handlebars turned sharply to the left to compensate for Oscar's weight, trailing laughter behind them in the night.

Macdonald recalls too a tour of Ontario made by the band. Oscar's absolute pitch was already well known to musicians. As the band bus moved down a dark highway, the musicians began to drop off to sleep. But Oscar was bothered by the hum of the engine. Finally he walked up to the driver and said, "Would you mind speeding up or slowing down? I can't sleep in B-natural." Oscar says he remembers the motorcyle ride, but he doesn't remember such an incident on a bus. "I tried to hide the thing about pitch," he said.

Johnny Holmes said that at one point he had to audition several girls who wanted to sing with the band. One of them was tone deaf. With Oscar as accompanist, she made her way through a song, constantly changing tonality. Holmes recalled, "Oscar would follow her wherever she went, whatever key she wandered into. And he never cracked a smile. It was positively surreal."

Oscar too remembered the incident years later. "I just kept looking down at the keys," he said. "If I'd looked up, and if I'd seen Johnny, I would have laughed. It would have been all over."

William and Beatrice Fraser lived in Verdun, walking distance from Oscar's home in the St. Antoine district. William Fraser was, like the heads of so many households in the district, a railway porter. He worked for the Canadian Pacific. Both his sons would become porters as well. Friends recall that all the Frasers were involved in the church. They were a quiet family, everyone remembers, Lillie, the eldest child, even more so than her sister Joan, and she was shy. She had two brothers, George and Bill.

Oscar had been noticing her for some time at church. "She was a sweet girl," he said. "I just fell in love with her, that soft, warm, straight-ahead person. I walked over to her one day after Sunday school. It was the bobby-socks era, and I still remember what she was wearing, a tan suit with a little beige blouse, and she had on brown loafers and little ankle socks. She had gorgeous long hair. I don't know why I said it. I said, 'You're the one I want to be the mother of my children.' It was the first time I really ever said anything to her. I saw her at the social clubs in the black church. Occasionally I would play part of a concert there.

"One night she and some of the other girls were in a play. I held her up backstage and told her how much I liked her. My buddy Hilton Braithwaite, who I went to high school with, took me down to her house and introduced me formally to her parents."

We can date that introduction exactly: March 17, 1943. Lil

recalled it in an interview printed in *Tan Romances* ten years later.

The September 1953 issue of the magazine carried an article titled "How He Proposed" over the byline "By Mrs. Oscar Peterson." Its language should be treated with caution, since it was doubtless dictated to a writer, who would then have organized the material. However, Lillie Fraser Peterson almost certainly approved the text prior to its publication, and the information can be considered reliable.

"To say that I was thrilled at having this famous fellow in my home would be putting it mildly," she said. "I liked the way he said involved things in such simple language. Although he was only a boy, he looked and thought like a man. Certainly, his wonderful music was enough to turn any girl's head.

"We later went to a dance and I got an opportunity to see and understand more about him. I found that he was just a plain fellow who loves beautiful things and expresses this love in his music. There was nothing mean or small in his makeup and no chance at all for him to ever become big-headed over whatever the future held for him.

"We began seeing one another frequently. I met his mother and father and his sisters and he met my parents.

"On Oscar's birthday, that August 15, I was at home preparing to go away on vacation, when the doorbell rang. It was Oscar. He had some presents for me as he usually did on these visits. But this time I sensed something special.

"'Look, Lillie,' he said, 'there's something we've got to do before we get too far down the line. I feel I'm going to get some good breaks pretty soon and I don't know anyone I'd rather share it with than you. I figure I can earn enough to support you and, without beating around the bush, you know I love you. So, let's you and me get married.'

"When he produced the ring and put it on my finger, I was really thrilled. After Oscar had left the house, I ran around the neighborhood showing it to all my friends."

Thirteen months later, in September 1944, Lillie Fraser and Oscar Emmanuel Peterson were married at Union United Church by the Reverend Charles Este, with Oscar's brother Chuck as best

man and Joan Fraser, Lil's sister, as maid of honour. Lil said later
that Oscar's mother and her own thought they were too young to be
taking the step. Oscar was nineteen, Lil seventeen.

Two of Oscar's friends were the musician brothers George and
Hugh Sealey, both of them now dead. George Sealey's widow,
Evelyn, remembers a happy young couple:

"I met them at George and Hughie's rehearsals. Oscar loved to
tease. He loved to play jokes. That man could tease you to tears.
And then when he saw that it was too much for you to take, he'd
stop and hug you. You could get into a conversation with Oscar that
would last three, four hours, going from one subject to another. A
very interesting young man, even at that age.

"When I married George, Oscar was at my wedding. And when
he married Lil, we went to visit one another back and forth. And we
would all go out together. The best time I can remember is a picnic
we went on on Mount Royal. About ten of us, couples. This is
when I really got to know Oscar and Lil. None of us had any children then. I can remember Hugh talking to him like a Dutch uncle.
Hugh was about eight years older than Oscar, and he'd been working a lot longer.

"Lil had the most direct look. She always kept her hair long.

"How that Oscar Peterson could tease. He used to come to our
house for rehearsals. I belonged to a women's club. I had to bake a
cake that night to take to the club. And when I came to get the cake,
I'll never forget the look on those men's faces. There were about
five of them, George, Allan Wellman, Oscar Peterson, a bass
player, looking like the cat that ate the canary. They'd eaten the
cake. Gone. Fini. I had to go across the street to the grocery store
and buy a package of cookies. The following month it was my turn
again. Then I got wise and made two cakes and put one in a tin and
left the other one out. And they ate that one again, but I still had
one.

"Another thing he did. I was in the hospital, having my son
Hugh. Oscar is his godfather. And in came Oscar and my husband.
They had flowers and God knows what. And I saw all the nurses
scurrying. One of them was so red in the face. I said to George,
'What's the matter with that nurse? She looks like she's going to

cry.' George said, 'OP did it again.' It was a little before visiting hours. Oscar said, 'We've come to see Evelyn Sealey.' She said, 'Well you'll have to wait for visiting hours.' He said, 'No, we can't wait.' And she wanted to know who they were, and Oscar said, 'He's the husband and I'm the father.'"

Lillie Fraser bore Oscar Peterson five children. They came a year apart, Lyn, born in 1948, Sharon, 1949, Gay, 1950, Oscar Jr., 1951, and Norman, 1952 – one a year for five years.

She was a big woman, despite her shyness. And she was from Nova Scotia. Ray Brown came to know her during this period. "And every time I went to Montreal, she was pregnant," he said. "So I called her Big Scotia."

Fifteen months after Oscar and Lil were married, just before Christmas of 1945, Oscar was on his way home from shopping in downtown Montreal, his arms full of packages. He saw a taxi pull over to the curb. As its passenger was paying the driver, Oscar moved forward to enter the still-open rear door. A woman rushed up and said that *she* wanted that taxi. Before Oscar could even reply, the previous passenger turned on him, called him a "dirty nigger" and hit him in the face. Oscar fell to the street and the woman got into the cab, which pulled away. A policeman who witnessed the incident turned his back. Oscar, by then weighing 246 pounds, most of it muscle, rose in silence and hit the man who had hit him, sending him sprawling. The man picked himself up and, calling for the cop, took another punch at Oscar. When Oscar hit him this time, he had the sense to stay down. The policeman now told Oscar he was under arrest.

"You turned your back when he hit me," Oscar said, bending to pick up his packages. The policeman said they could finish the argument at the station. "If you want to take me to the station," Oscar said, "you'll have to use that gun." And he walked off, leaving his assailant and the cop to stare after him.

Daisy recalled an incident when Oscar was working with his first trio at the Alberta Lounge. A white patron at a front table kept making requests, something jazz musicians usually do not appreciate. But to keep the man happy, Oscar played the tunes he wanted.

At the end of the set, the man, who turned out to be an American with a Southern accent, said, "You are one of the most brilliant musicians I have ever heard. But as a nigger, I hate your guts."

"There was a great deal of subtle intimidation, if there be such an animal," Oscar said in the spring of 1986. "They'd refuse you by saying 'I'm sorry' in front, but it was still a refusal. The famous Ritz Carlton, where I stay now when I'm in Montreal – never mind getting a room there, they didn't even want me playing there."

Once the Johnny Holmes band was booked to play a dance there for the IODE – Imperial Order Daughters of the Empire, a group comparable in composition and character to the Daughters of the American Revolution and populated by ladies of high social status. The dance, an annual affair called the Blue Orchid Ball, was to be held on a Friday night at the Ritz Carlton, then and now the city's most prestigious hotel. Two days before it, on Wednesday, Holmes got a call from the hotel manager, a Monsieur Cantin.

"Mr. Holmes," he said, "you've got a nigger in your band."

"We've got a *coloured* boy," Holmes said, that being the accepted polite term at the time.

"Well I don't want him in the hotel," M. Cantin said.

Holmes said, "Now do you mind if we notify anyone who wants to use the band that we can't play the Ritz because you don't allow coloured people?"

"I don't care what you do," the manager said.

"Okay," Holmes said. "I'm going to put a notice in the *Star*, the *Herald*, and the *Gazette*" – the three English-language Montreal dailies of the period; only the *Gazette* remains – "that our band can never play the Ritz because you don't allow coloured people."

"Is this blackmail?" Cantin demanded.

"You call it anything you damn please," Holmes said, and hung up on him.

Shortly thereafter Holmes got a phone call from a woman named Maude Cleugh. Mrs. Cleugh was the grand regent of the IODE. She was also Johnny's wife's aunt. She said, "Johnny, why are you giving Mr. Cantin at the hotel trouble?"

Johnny told her what had happened. She said, "You'll get a call in about twenty minutes."

And Cantin called Holmes to say, "Okay, you can bring that nigger in."

At the dance on the Friday, Holmes featured Oscar on every third number while the hotel's manager skulked angrily in the balcony.

"What I went through as a student," Oscar told Len Lyons, "was probably what everyone else grooming themselves for the classical field goes through – Czerny, Hanon, Dohnányi. All of these things just serve to broaden digital control. It was something I wanted to get behind me as quickly as possible.

"Probably I started feeling comfortable around the age of sixteen or seventeen. That's when I started feeling that I could transmit to the keyboard most of what I conjured up mentally. Prior to that, it was a scuffle. I'd be thinking something and then run into a snag on executing it. That used to bug me.

"I'd start out in the morning with scales, exercises, and whatever classical pieces I was working on. After a break I'd come back and do voicings; I'd challenge the voicings I'd been using and try to move them around in tempo without losing the harmonic content."

The Merchant Navy Show
July 11, 1944
Canadian Broadcasting Corporation
Announcer: Rusty Davis

Big-band theme music: *Mr. Five by Five*

Davis: (voice-over, then orchestra fades down and out behind): Oscar Peterson! Friends, tonight we'd like you to meet a coloured boy whose amazing fingers have been cutting a rhythmic blazing path to success over the airwaves for the past three years now. Three years back, Oscar, then fifteen, won a nationwide new-talent contest, and today, still going to school, he manages to make his presence felt on as many occasions as his homework will allow, filling engagements over the radio networks. A combination of Art

Tatum, Teddy Wilson, and counterpart of the composite picture of America's great coloured pianists, young Oscar Peterson, six foot three, two hundred and twenty pounds of terrific musical sense and piano technique, has accepted *The Merchant Navy Show*'s invitation tonight, and we're mighty happy he could make it. You will be too when you listen to … Oscar Peterson! (Formal cue-card applause) Oh, and now, hang on to your seats, folks, here's Oscar Peterson, and his version of *Chinatown.*

Piano with bass and drums. [The tune is not *Chinatown* but *China Boy,* and the style is largely that of Teddy Wilson.]

Davis: Oscar, that was terrific! Tell me, boy, how many hands you got?

Oscar: Just two, Mr. Davis, just two. But I like to make 'em work hard.

Davis: You're not kidding. Tell me, Oscar, you're still going to school, aren't you?

Oscar (very wooden, obviously uncomfortable with the stereotype): That's right. My folks would tan my hide if I missed a day.

Davis: Your dad would have his hands full there!

Oscar: That's what you say. My pop ain't no pygmy either.

Davis: Ha-ha. Well, Oscar, how did you manage to learn all you know about hitting those keys? Boy, you sure play 'em solid.

Oscar: Well, it's this way, Mr. Davis. I do a lot of extra-curricular study.

Davis: Extra-curricular study?

Oscar: Yes, I've been studying very hard on the three Bs.

Davis: The three Bs?

Oscar: Yes, barrelhouse, beat-me-daddy-eight-to-the-bar, and boogie-woogie.

Davis: Ah, boogie-woogie! Tell us something about that, Oscar.

Oscar: Mister, that's something you just don't tell about, you demonstrate.

Davis: You say words that make sense. Ladies and gentlemen, Oscar Peterson at the piano again, and it's ... *Boogie-Woogie Cocktail*! (Spontaneous moans of enthusiasm from the audience)

Piano with bass and drums: *Boogie-Woogie Cocktail*

(Hot applause, whistles, shouts)

"No, it wasn't a matter of countermelodies. It was a matter of comping as if I were playing for a soloist, comping without having the voicings break down. I didn't want to sound like I just came up with a chord to get myself out of a situation or to get myself to the next chord. Voicing is putting something down for your right hand to play off of. See, you really play off of your left hand. Most players think of themselves as playing off of the right hand because there's so much activity there. What's really happening is that the right hand is determined, although that's probably too strong a word, by the left-hand formation. The left hand can add tonal validity too, by augmenting with clusters what the right hand is playing. But it's the left hand that starts the line off and determines its basic movement."

The Merchant Navy Show
August 15, 1944
Canadian Broadcasting Corporation
Announcer: Rusty Davis

Big-band theme music: *Mr. Five by Five*

Davis: Oscar Peterson! Yeah, man. He's nineteen years of age today. Friends, a lot of you who are familiar with our six-foot-two eighteen-year-old, now nineteen-year-old coloured boy, well, he's definitely taken Canada by storm as the greatest thing in barrelhouse, boogie-woogie, and beat-me-daddy-eight-to-the-bar, since

Mr. Steinway started making those pianos. Heard regularly on *The Saturday Night Little Review,* young Oscar also did more than a fair job of making himself solid with *Merchant Navy Show* fans on one of the first editions of this year's series of programs. I know you'll be glad to welcome back ... Oscar Peterson! (Applause to cue card) Now we'll seat him at the piano, and very quietly, he'll begin Hoagy Carmichael's *Stardust.*

Piano with bass and drums: *Stardust*

Davis: Well Oscar, tonight I was going to ask you up to the microphone for a special interview, but I know it's your birthday, so how about just being nervous in a boogie manner and bring us *One O'Clock Jump?*

Piano with bass and drums: *One O'Clock Jump*

"After the movement of the voicings, I'd go to the right-hand lines alone. I'd try to play the melody with real feeling, as if I were playing a horn, pedalling and controlling the touch so it wouldn't sound staccato. Then I'd duplicate the right-hand linear playing in the left hand. I figured I'd develop a lot of control that way. Sometimes I'd play fours with myself. That comes in handy after you finish a right-hand line and you want to move down to a different pedal tone. You're not relegated to simply hitting it. You can move down or up, tying things together, walking."

940 on the Dial
November 22, 1945
Canadian Broadcasting Corporation
Interviewers: unknown

Ted: Well, Oscar, could you give us a lowdown on some of that jive talk?

Oscar: Well, you mean you want me to beat my gums, and some of that rug-cutting and [inaudible].

Ginny: Well, Oscar, there seems to be quite an argument as to what kind of music you play. Is it jazz, hot jazz, or swing?

Oscar: Well, I think it's definitely swing. I don't go actually for the term jazz, or jazz music itself.

Ginny: I know I'll sound very ignorant in such matters, but what's the difference?

Oscar: Well there isn't actually any verbal difference, it's in the music itself. Jazz is, to my opinion, it's not organized, like swing is organized. Swing is more or less along the … well, made-up line. It's impromptu, like jazz in places, but then it's much more organized in other places.

Ted: Well, when we talk about musicians ad libbing, Oscar, in playing, is that ad libbing included in jazz?

Oscar: Well, it's included in both of them, Ted. Jazz can be every man for himself, and then, at times, there's ad lib. And it's the same with swing. Swing is organized, and then there's times when there's solos, what you call ad lib, at the same time.

Ted: It still sounds awfully complicated to me. Where does boogie-woogie come in?

Oscar: Well, boogie's more or less a happy medium between the two, because there was jazz, originally, from what I can understand, there's jazz, then boogie-woogie, and now today the fine swing that many of the bands and solo artists are putting out on records and so forth.

Ted: In other words, it's developed from one to the other to the swing of today.

Oscar: That's right. And boogie is actually the medium between the two.

Ginny: Your own syncopated swing, I understand it's made up of what you call a walking boogie, or bass, with the left hand, is that right?

Oscar: That's right. It's playing the left hand, the chords in syncopated octaves, and making up a pattern on the melody in the right hand, at the same time, completely independent of the left hand. At first to learn it is quite difficult, but once you master it, it's easy from there in.

Ted: Well it's very effective, and I know when you put them both together you get this own particular style of your playing.

Oscar: That's right, Ted, I try to keep my playing more or less individual to the rest of the other pianists around....

Ginny (slight tone of amazement): Didn't you study with Paul de Marky?

Oscar: Yes I did, Ginny, I studied a number of years more or less off and on. Mr. de Marky was very kind to me in that he never forced me to be an actual pupil of his. I looked to him more or less as an adviser, and he really approved of swing and he helped me along with it, and criticized in any way he could, at the same time helping my technique with the classical exercises and so forth.

Ginny: That's very interesting, because we always think of Mr. de Marky as a ... classic uh ... well, he ... his concerts are always given over to classical music. Incidentally, he's accepted an invitation to drop in next week – Wednesday of next week, isn't it, Ted?

Ted: That's what you said, Ginny. Well I've heard some of your recordings, Oscar. Have you made any recently?

Oscar: Yes, I made two more recordings, one of which'll be out in the next few weeks, it's *C Jam Blues* and *If I Could Be with You One Hour Tonight*....

Ginny: Do you spend much time practising, Oscar?

Oscar: Well no, Ginny, I don't get very much time to practise. If I do I usually cram it into about three or four hours at it, and then other times I go without. It's kind of tough keeping up on the popular songs. The only way I can do that is by buying the records. I find it a lot easier to just listen to someone else's ideas on them and

57

formulate my own opinions on what the other person has done. And as a result I usually have a tremendous record bill and so forth.

Ted: Well are you playing with any name bands?

Oscar: Yes, I'm playing with Johnny Holmes' orchestra. He's also my manager, and he, I can say, is more or less even more responsible for my technique today than anyone else, because when I hit the band, Johnny broke me down into the category I am now. I was unable to play slow ballads at the time, knowing nothing but fast numbers and boogie-woogie. He took me under his wing and coached me and criticized in every way that would help me....

Ginny: Would you like to tell us what are your favourite *American* name bands?

Oscar: Well, I like Les Brown, for the reason that he's a sweet band and at the same time he's a good swing band. And I also like Tommy Dorsey's orchestra.

Ted: Well haven't you had a number of interesting offers to play with name bands in the States?

Oscar: Yes, I had an offer from Jimmie Lunce ... uh from Count Basie first of all, he asked me if I ever got to New York to look him up. And I had an offer from Jimmie Lunceford. At the time his band was here his pianist was being drafted, and he asked me to fill the spot. But at that time my draft status was unsettled too. And there were a couple of fellows in the jam sessions that we were holding in town here, that came up from the States, such as Mezz Mezzrow and Frankie Newton, that asked me to go away with them, but for my opinion, music is opening up in Canada and there's a much greater future on its way for all the young musicians in Canada and I'd like to stick and be here when it does. It's well on its way, and I feel that too much Canadian talent is wandering down into the States as a result.

Ginny: Well that's very lucky for us, and here in Montreal we're particularly happy to say that you're one of our own products. We hope for you continuation with the success that you've had, and thanks so much for coming in.

Oscar: Thank you, Ginny, and thank you, Ted.

"Each hand is constructed differently, and you'll never make them play the same way. My theory is to have the phrase under your hand with whatever it takes to do that. If you find yourself reaching awkwardly, you know that for your hands there's bad fingering there somewhere. At this point, the fingerings just fall under the hand for me. Each finds its own. If you think of the whole phrase you want to play, you shouldn't have to think about fingering at all. It should be that well integrated from your mind through your heart and soul to your hands."

"It's very difficult for me to rehash some of this," Oscar said forty years later. We were sitting on a sofa near a window, in his living-room in Mississauga, not far from Toronto. Spring was coming up in his garden. "My mother was a very peaceful woman. So was my father, a peaceable man. We were taught, in a biblical way, not to attack fellow human beings. So my initial approach to any kind of racism was subdued.

"I sensed that people, including Johnny Holmes, got put into situations that were a little too big even for them. I can't say they didn't handle it – Johnny handled it as best he could. But his bringing a band into the Ritz Carlton with a Negro in it didn't change anything in the hotel the next day. They made an *exception*. I didn't want to be the *exception*.

"This is something that has always been hard for me to sidestep. People say, 'You've got to take the opportunity, you've got to go in there and break that.' Many of the times I went in there and broke things, whether in Montreal or Toronto or wherever, I had the feeling it was only temporary, and mainly because it was me. And that used to bug me more than anything else.

"The kind of prejudice that I experienced at home here in Canada was certainly not as violent as I saw it in the United States. But that didn't make me feel any better as a human being.

"And it didn't give me any more self-credibility."

CHAPTER 5

THE ALBERTA LOUNGE

It was only a year prior to that 1946 *Liberty* article that Oscar told his mother he wanted to record. There was virtually no recording industry in Canada at the time. None the less, she urged him to call one of the record companies and simply say that he wanted to record. With trepidation, Oscar telephoned Hugh Joseph, who was in charge of RCA Victor recordings in Canada.

"It has worked out well," Joseph said after Peterson's first boogie records exploded across Canada. "I had the boy in mind for some time because his popularity was growing and the young crowd in Montreal were talking about Holmes' band and the boy at the piano. I guess we would have got after him if he hadn't approached us. He is under contract to us now and we are happy about it." Peterson's first four records had sold in the thousands, to the company's happy surprise.

Oscar began an association with RCA Victor Canada that was to last four years. The first side he recorded was *I Got Rhythm*. It was followed by about two dozen sides, including one called *Oscar's Boogie* and Ellington's *Rockin' in Rhythm*, which for a long time he used as a theme. "They weren't too representative of my playing at the time," he said years later. Listened to now, they are very poor Peterson. He had not yet assimilated the various elements of his work. But they were played at ferocious speed and demonstrated what a prodigious technician he was.

In 1946, Oscar played a concert for the patients of a tuberculosis hospital in Kingston, Ontario. "Various organizations would come to me, as they do now," he said long afterwards, "and say, 'We have a group of people who are shut-ins. Would you consider playing?'

As long as there's a piano available, it's the easiest thing in the world to go and do a half-hour for them. Maybe because I was a shut-in at Children's Memorial Hospital, I know that feeling. I know how much we doted on anything that came to us. At that time, TB really cooped you up. It was not like going in for an appendectomy. I think that always made me sympathetic to it, I related it to my own stint in the hospital." And, of course, to the loss of his brother Fred.

Aside from his work with the Johnny Holmes band, Holmes often booked Oscar and a rhythm section throughout Quebec and Ontario. Oscar would sell out theatres in northern Ontario mining towns because of his constant exposure on such radio programs as *Light Up and Listen* and *The Happy Gang,* a major CBC network show at the time.

On one of these trips, he and the group came close to losing their lives. They were on a tour of Timmins, North Bay, Sudbury, and Kirkland Lake. "We were in a bad motor accident," Oscar said. "The car turned over four times. Johnny was in the car with us. But we made it." Holmes was hospitalized, Oscar was unhurt.

By late 1947, Oscar was leading a Montreal trio at the Alberta Lounge, a room seating about a hundred people, across Peel Street and around the corner from Windsor Station, the Canadian Pacific terminal out of which his father worked. The group's personnel included Clarence Jones, drums, and Ozzie Roberts, bass. Guitarist Bernard Johnson later replaced Jones. Radio station CJAD decided to do "remote" broadcasts of the trio for fifteen minutes every Wednesday night. Assigned to be the announcer of the show was Oscar's old schoolmate Don Cameron, who had given up playing drums – after a final engagement with Oscar in a quartet at Queen's University in Kingston, Ontario, on October 31, 1947 – for a career in broadcasting. Cameron, with his usual precision, recalled that the first broadcast was aired the evening of December 9, 1947.

During an intermission at the Alberta, Oscar was approached by a young man from Toronto who requested a tune. They chatted for a while. The young man, who would always remember Oscar's graciousness at this meeting, was named Eric Smith. Smith, who was then twenty-six, was a veteran of the Royal Canadian Air Force. He had flown at least seventeen missions as a navigator in Lancasters over Germany, taking part in raids on Heligoland and Berchtesgaden, Kiel and Hamburg and Cologne – a city he would, many years later, visit with Oscar. Former Flying Officer Eric Smith, born in Toronto, son of a Jamaican father of African descent and an English Jewish mother, would become one of the closest friends of Oscar's life.

It was at the Alberta that Oscar also met Norman Granz. A legend has grown up that Granz, on his way to Montreal's Dorval Airport in a taxi, heard one of Oscar's broadcasts from the Alberta, was astounded, ordered the driver to go to the Alberta Lounge instead, heard Peterson, and swept him off to sudden fame with Jazz at the Philharmonic at Carnegie Hall.

Granz has said, "The cabby had some music playing, and I assumed that it was a disc that some disc jockey was playing, and I asked him if he knew the station. I'd like to call them and find out who the pianist was with the trio. And he said, 'No, that's not a record, it's coming live from a club called the Alberta Lounge.' He said, 'It's Oscar Peterson.' And I said, 'Well, forget the airport, turn around and let's go to the club.'"

Oscar's version is this: "I couldn't believe he was sitting in the lounge. And he sat and talked to me, and he said, 'Why do you make those terrible boogie-woogie records? That's not you, you don't play like that.' I said, 'Well, that's what I was asked to do at the time.' He said, 'Well, I'd like you to take a shot at the American jazz market, I think you could bring something to it, I think it would be a tremendous innovation, the fact first of all of the way you play, and secondly the fact that you're not an American.' He said, 'I think it would be great.' And when I finally agreed to do it, he decided it should be in Carnegie Hall. I was thinking of a smaller city. But he decided the proper place would be Carnegie Hall. He said, 'Take your best shot, you'll know in one shot. You won't have to dilly-dally. If you make it, you'll know it. If you don't make it, you'll know that too.' "

There are some serious problems with the story, no matter that Granz and Peterson are the authorities for it. Oscar already had a considerable reputation among American musicians, including some with whom Granz worked, and he had had a good deal of American press. Besides Jimmie Lunceford and Count Basie, Coleman Hawkins, Woody Herman, and Ella Fitzgerald were aware of him and in the habit of dropping by the Alberta when they were in Montreal. Hawkins said he had been profoundly impressed by him as far back as 1945. Oscar had even received a long review in *Metronome*, at that time *Down Beat*'s competitor. In 1947, Jim Butler wrote in the magazine, "His better [RCA Victor] sides, *Blue Moon*, *One Hour with You*, *China Boy*, and *Louise*, show a good amount of clean harmonic ideas. His slow and medium-tempoed recordings show off his ideas, which incidentally are closely similar to those of Nat Cole, to the best advantage. On up tempo numbers many fluffs are apparent. With further experience, however, these faults should be corrected."

Butler even gives us, in this near-forgotten review, an insight into Peterson's relationship with Johnny Holmes. "Early last August," Butler said, "this writer had the chance of hearing Johnny Holmes' fine, jumping band which still features Oscar. At this point it might do to mention that Oscar and Johnny have built up a very fine friendship. Holmes, who was Oscar's manager for a time, would give his right arm for his idolized pianist. Oscar's loyalty to Holmes is quite obvious. With the popularity he has gained through the country, especially in his recent personal appearances, Oscar could easily have a permanent job as a single attraction in any number of local night spots. Instead, Oscar prefers to remain with the Holmes band, insisting that he gets more kicks by following the latter policy.

"On [a] par with his personal loyalties is his desire to remain in Canada instead of accepting some of the big offers he has received from American band leaders, such as Jimmie Lunceford. Realizing that competition below the Canadian border is also much stiffer, Oscar is wise in sticking to Canada for the present where he has virtually free rein in his line.

"If Oscar Peterson continues to improve as steadily as he has done in the past year there is no reason why he can't be in the same class as Teddy Wilson, Erroll Garner and, yes, even Art Tatum."

Butler's piece, which long precedes Mike Levin's much more famous and quoted review in *Down Beat*, makes clear that it is all but impossible that Granz had not heard of him until he was taking a cab to Montreal Airport. Even the *Metronome* piece was not the first exposure Peterson had had in the United States. In 1944, a full three years before it, *Down Beat* had headlined: "Count Basie raves about young Canadian pianist!"

And there is that *Liberty* magazine article of January 12, 1946, which described him as "the most commercially successful pianist of his age in Canada – and perhaps the most commercially success-ful anywhere" and said that both Basie and Lunceford had made special trips up from New York to hear him. Oscar had already turned down a bid from Hollywood, and an American tour was in the planning stage. It was to follow a three-month tour of Canada. The *Liberty* article, written by Harold Dingman, said that Oscar was constantly jamming with New York musicians during their vis-its to Montreal. "On two occasions recently," Dingman wrote, "he set huge crowds wild in His Majesty's Theatre with Frank[ie] Newton and Wilbur de Paris when they came up on tour."

According to Lou Hooper and Gerry Macdonald, Dizzy Gil-lespie also discovered Oscar at this time. Hooper was there when it happened. His manuscript relates: "One night when name bands were being booked into the former nightspot called Chez Maurice, the Dizzy Gillespie band was the current attraction. My son and I were there, as we both dug Dizzy's playing. Oscar had finished his appearance at the Alberta Lounge, and had come into the hall while the band was playing a set. His name was immediately spread by the real cats via the grapevine through the hall, on its way to the bandstand. Evidently Dizzy had not heard Oscar play, and he invited him to join the band for a set. The look of sheer disbelief on

Diz's face when Oscar took his spot in the number with a display of solid dance-band piano which, even in its great rhythm, did sound here and there as though four or even six hands might have been combined in the performance, was something to see."

"I was with Oscar that night," Macdonald recalled. "I remember it vividly. I already knew Dizzy, at least to speak to. Oscar and I came in and walked through the crowd up to the bandstand. The piano was at the front left of the stage. Very soon, when Dizzy's band had just finished a number, the crowd began clapping rhythmically and calling, 'We want Oscar, we want Oscar!' Dizzy looked around as if to say, 'Who the hell is Oscar?' It got so loud that finally Dizzy beckoned him to come up on the stage. Oscar sat at the piano. They decided to play *What Is This Thing Called Love?* Oscar took about sixteen bars of introduction, and Dizzy's eyes were like saucers with disbelief. They got into the tune and then Oscar took a long solo. The guys in Dizzy's band just wigged out. The audience was screaming and yelling.

"After the gig I had to go home, but Oscar told me a day or two later what happened. He went somewhere with Dizzy and he played for him until eight o'clock in the morning."

Oscar of course remembers well his first encounter with John Birks Gillespie, one of the founders of the bebop movement and one of the most important figures in the evolution of jazz, the master trumpeter who with saxophonist Charlie Parker vastly enriched, if not revolutionized, jazz in the 1940s. Dizzy has all his life been an antic humorist, which bears on Oscar's memory of their meeting.

Chuckling, Oscar said, "Dizzy was as Dizzy is. He was very off-handed about everything. He came down to the lounge." (This was probably the night after the sitting-in session described by Hooper and Macdonald.) "I came off after the set. I said, 'Hello, Mr. Gillespie.' He said, 'You know something funny? You're crazy.' And he kept laughing. 'You're crazy.' The next day he came to my house for dinner, and my Mum was very taken with him. That evening we went out to a club on Mountain Street, with Arabian decor. It had a fountain. Dizzy said, 'Come on, I want you to play for me.' I said,

'Dizzy, I don't play in here.' He said, 'I want you to play for me.' And he walked straight through the fountain, right through the water, clothes and everything! It was around twelve-thirty at night, after we had been out listening to some other people. He sat down near the piano, and said, 'Play something, play anything at all.' And I played for him.

"I remember Coleman Hawkins first heard me at the Café St. Michel. He said to me, 'I'd like to take you back to New York and have a whole bunch of cats hear you.' Roy Eldridge was something similar. Duke Ellington started calling me the maharajah of the piano. "

We can fix the time of the meeting with Dizzy within a few weeks. Leonard Feather, in his book *From Satchmo to Miles*, mentions getting a phone call from Montreal from a wildly enthusiastic Gillespie. Dizzy told him, "Leonard, there's a pianist up here who's too much. You've never heard anything like it!" It was towards the end of 1948. So Leonard Feather too knew of Oscar that far back.

According to Hooper, Dizzy wanted Oscar to join his band there and then. In later years Dizzy and Oscar would record together innumerable times. Gillespie has said that Oscar is, aside from being one of his favourite pianists to listen to, one of his favourites to play *with*.

Finally, there is a self-evident contradiction in Oscar's version of the first meeting with Granz: he says that Granz denigrated the boogie-woogie style of the records as not typical of Peterson's way of playing, which indicates that Granz knew the records before hearing that radio broadcast.

Oscar remembers vividly that he first noted the Granz brown-and-white saddle shoes. Then his glance travelled upwards. "I saw the eyebrows," he said. "And I thought, 'My God, Norman Granz!'"

And it wasn't their first meeting.

"He doesn't know it," Oscar said, "but he met me one night prior to this. A year before. Downstairs at the Café St. Michel. I was coming in, it was after a Jazz at the Philharmonic concert and I

67

had gone somewhere for a bite to eat or something, and I came down to the St. Michel and heard all this music. I knew what was going on, the guys were upstairs playing, right?

"I walked in, and I heard the doorman saying, 'Well I'm sorry, sir, you're going to have to pay. I don't care who you are, you're going to have to pay.' And I recognized Norman. He said, 'No, I'm not paying to get in here. You've got all my guys, they're sitting in upstairs, I'm not going to pay.'

"So I said to the doorman, whoever it was, 'If the worst comes to the worst, I'll pay for it. Don't charge him.'

"Norman said, 'How would you like it if I go up there and pull all those guys off the stand?'

"I told the doorman, 'Don't be silly.' I finally prevailed. I went over and I meant to apologize to Norman and he brushed me off, he didn't want to hear it. I forget what he said, I wish I could remember it. He was very scathing.

"I said, 'Mr. Granz, I'm Oscar Peterson, and I'm sorry about this.' I didn't say my name that he should know it. I was just saying hello to him. I said, 'I'm a fan,' and so and so. And he didn't want to hear it, and he blew me off, blew me away. I could totally understand him being upset. He didn't want to hear it. None of that.

"I said, 'Would you like to go up with me?' I can remember he had his hands in his pockets. He went upstairs. I quick went to the guy at the door and gave him the sign, 'Don't mess with him.' The guy gave him a nice table. Norman didn't want to sit there, he said, 'I want to sit back here,' and he sat at the back. I stayed for whatever time, then he just got up and left, I remember that.

"This was a year before the Alberta. But he didn't know who I was, and I didn't play that night."

Granz indeed took Oscar to New York in September 1949 and planted him in the Carnegie Hall audience, planning to introduce him as a visitor from Canada. Granz was in the practice of introducing a surprise guest whenever his company played Carnegie. One year it had been Lionel Hampton, another year Billie Holiday. This night it was to be Oscar Peterson.

Another myth has it that Buddy Rich refused to play with Oscar that night. This is not so. Bassist Ray Brown remembers what happened.

Granz asked him and Rich to accompany his new discovery. They agreed readily. "I knew who Oscar was," Ray said. "I had heard him and met him up in Montreal. We used to take the train back from Montreal to New York, and he played around the corner at the Alberta Lounge. All you had to do was take your stuff to the station, then go over and listen to him before your train left. We stopped off and heard him a couple of times, when we were up there playing concerts.

"Buddy had a drum solo to play. And you know Buddy. When he plays his solos, he plays until he's exhausted. He just plays until he's two inches from being dead. His solo usually came before the intermission, because they almost had to take him off in a laundry bag. Buddy played a solo that night at Carnegie Hall and came off completely wiped out. Norman said, 'Okay, I'm going to bring Oscar on.' Buddy said, 'Norman, I don't think I can go back out there.' Norman said, 'What am I going to do?' Oscar said, 'Ray Brown and I'll do it.'

"So that's how it happened. Out of these things, something good always happens. We went out and played, and tore it up anyway. We played *Tenderly*, and later on we went into the studio and made a record of it, and it was a hit record. But that's how the duo started, because Buddy was too wiped out to play." A week after Ray described these events, in April 1987, Buddy Rich died. Ray had talked to him on the phone only days earlier.

In the October 21, 1949, issue of *Down Beat*, Mike Levin, the magazine's New York editor, reported, "A Montreal citizen, Oscar Peterson, stopped the Norman Granz Jazz at the Philharmonic concert dead cold in its tracks here last month. Balancing a large and bulky body at the piano much in the fashion of Earl Hines, Peterson displayed a flashy right hand, a load of bop and [George] Shearing ideas, as well as a good sense of harmonic development. And in addition, he scared some of the local modern minions by playing bop ideas in his *left* hand, which is distinctly not the common practice. Further than this, Peterson impressed musicians

69

here by not only having good ideas and making them, but giving them a rhythmic punch and drive which has been all too lacking in too many of the younger pianists. Whereas some of the bop stars conceive good ideas but sweat to make them, Peterson rips them off with an excess of power which leaves no doubt about his technical excess [sic] in reserve."

Recalling that period of his life, Oscar said, "When I went to the United States, I'd go into the studio to do radio shows or television shows, and I'd look over and there wouldn't be any blacks in the orchestra, and I knew really that it was a clique thing, everyone had their pets, and they did what they did. This is why black musicians had to go the way of the jazz route. We had no other route to go. And I decided that if the only way I was going to make it happen was to frighten the hell out of everybody pianistically, then that's the way I was going to make it. If that's what it took to get the attention, then I was going to do my best to do it that way."

Long afterwards, Oscar was asked whether, had the classical concert stage been open to black players at that time, he would have gone in that direction rather than into jazz. He thought for a moment and said, "No. I'd still have taken the direction I did. Because of the creativity of jazz."

CHAPTER 6

NORMAN'S CONQUESTS

The relationship with Norman Granz would prove to be the most important and lasting of Oscar Peterson's life. Oscar would have three marriages and a succession of trios, but from then on only one manager, Granz. He would even name one of his sons Norman. The vast majority of Oscar Peterson's enormous output of recordings would be produced by Granz and, usually, issued on record labels owned by Granz. From the time they first met, Oscar Peterson has never made an important career decision without consulting Norman Granz. With the possible exception of the long association of Louis Armstrong with Joe Glaser, there has never been an instance in jazz of so long a relationship between an artist and manager, and certainly not one involving so close a personal friendship.

In 1955, noting that jazz had achieved in a short time a notable degree of acceptance as an art form, with a jazz course instituted at North Texas State University, the appearance of Oscar Peterson at the Stratford Shakespearean Festival in Canada, performances by Dizzy Gillespie in Yugoslavia and by Louis Armstrong in Africa's Gold Coast (later Ghana), Leonard Feather wrote in *Esquire* magazine:

"That jazz, which a decade ago was hardly ever heard in a concert hall, far less recognized by the U.S. government, could have reached this summit of prestige and propaganda value was astonishing to some, incomprehensible to others. To many observers, however, it may have seemed like nothing more or less than a logical outgrowth of the efforts on the part of one man to launch jazz as an international commodity. The man in question is Norman

Granz, an irascible, slangy, expensively-casually-dressed, impulsive, epicurean, much-hated and much-loved man who, at 38, is not only the world's foremost jazz impresario, but also can claim to have made more money exclusively from jazz than anyone else in its relatively short and turbulent history.

"Granz, who has often stated that his objectives are, in the order of their importance, to make money, to combat racial prejudice and to present good jazz, is an enigma whose many-sided character is known only to a few friends, mostly musicians who have worked for him over an extended period."

He has been described as a tight man with a dollar and bearer of grudges. His relations with the press have sometimes been abrasive. Ted Williams, the great jazz photographer who was then on staff at *Ebony*, recalls that once in Chicago, angry for some reason at press photographers, Granz imposed the ingenious punishment of covering the spotlights with red gels, knowing that black-and-white film will not register red light. So the cameramen were effectively barred from photographing the concert. Many people, however, cite examples of Granz's generosity, particularly to musicians whose work he values.

Oscar once said, "Norman is shy. People mistake this for arrogance."

Granz is tall – six feet – and good-looking. His hair had thinned by his thirties. His eyebrows, which have repeatedly been described as Mephistophelean, curl up at their outer ends. Leonard Feather, in his *Esquire* portrait, noted his expression of "aloof disdain" and the succession of "pouting blondes" in Granz's life.

Granz was born in Los Angeles August 6, 1918, which makes him, like Oscar, a Leo. His family at the time lived near the Central Avenue area. They moved down the coast to Long Beach, where his father owned a department store, and later to the Boyle Heights district of central Los Angeles, a lower-middle-class area, where the family knew straitened circumstances after his father lost the store in the Depression.

Granz reminisced about Long Beach to Feather, saying it was "predominantly a Midwestern community in its thinking. We were one of about half a dozen Jewish families in the whole city. I remember there used to be a gag about all the retired businessmen from Iowa settling in Long Beach. And I think I remember the Ku Klux Klan used to parade there in their nightshirts. But I don't recall that it had any influence on me at all at the time. I suppose that the reason I can mix so easily with minority members arose from my playing with the kids on Central Avenue, when it was a heterogeneous district with all minorities represented." Granz says of the later part of his youth, "Mickey Cohen and I came from the same area in Boyle Heights. Mickey Cohen became a gangster; I didn't. Nobody forced him to become what he became."

Granz was graduated from Roosevelt High in Boyle Heights in 1935. He went to work in a brokerage office to earn the money to study at UCLA. "There was never enough money for a car," he told Feather, "so I spent the better part of my life in buses and streetcars. During daylight-saving time, with a three-hour time difference (between Los Angeles and New York) and Wall Street opening at ten, I'd have to be at work at six a.m. to get the board clean for a seven a.m. opening. In those days the clerks worked with chalk and chamois; we had no automatic boards. And during that time I played basketball at UCLA and stayed up at nights studying." Granz picked up invaluable financial insights during his days in that brokerage house.

Granz joined the United States Army Air Corps some months prior to Pearl Harbor. "The war was already on in Europe," he told me in 1987. "And I felt we would be drawn into it. They were putting out notices on the campus that if you enlisted, you could choose your branch of service. So I enlisted. It was obvious in the days after Pearl Harbor that I wasn't going to become a pilot. They gave you a choice. You could become a bombardier or get out of the Air Corps and wait for your draft call.

"So I took my discharge. I went to New York and discovered 52nd Street."

At the time, 52nd Street was like some kind of incredible fermentation vat for jazz. It was possible for Granz to walk from one club to another to see one great jazz player after another – many of whom he would later produce on records.

"Then I came back to Los Angeles," he continued, "and began

to book my jam sessions at the Trouville Club. I got drafted about May, and I got Basie and Nat Cole to play for the draftees. Then I got shipped to Texas. I applied for officer's training. They did an IQ test on you and another for mechanical aptitude. I proved to be not very mechanical, but I apparently got a good score on the IQ and it looked like I was going to go to officer's training. The army was very segregated in those days, and I had begun to mix with a lot of the black GIs. My reputation for that had already begun with the night-clubs. And I found out I wasn't going to officer's training.

"As a company clerk, I had access to a lot of literature. I came across a regulation that said if you had applied for officer's training and been rejected, you could apply for a discharge on the grounds that if you weren't good enough to be an officer you weren't good enough for the army, which I thought was extremely strange reasoning. But I applied for it and got my discharge in 1943 and started my things in Los Angeles." He was twenty-four years old. Granz had been a big-band fan until he heard the famous Coleman Hawkins record of *Body and Soul* in 1939. This remarkable recording was one of the harbingers of the bebop revolution that would arrive within five years. In any case, it was Granz's introduction to small-group jazz at its most creative.

But his reason for becoming an impresario, he has repeatedly said, was less a love of music than a sense of social outrage. Though black jazz musicians were playing all over Los Angeles, they were doing so largely before white audiences – many places would not let blacks enter as customers. This condition existed in Chicago, Kansas City, and most American cities. In Los Angeles, the discrimination was as fully institutionalized as it was in the American South: it was the firm and simple policy of night-clubs not to admit black patrons. And, as we have noted, the same policy often applied in Canadian clubs and dance halls.

Granz had been presenting occasional jam sessions at the Trouville Club, in the Beverly-Fairfax area of Los Angeles. He was particularly disturbed by the tears of Billie Holiday after its management refused to let some of her black friends come in to hear her.

Finally, Granz went to Billy Berg, a well-known night-club operator, with a proposal. Granz was aware that a new union ruling required that regularly employed musicians be given one night a week off. "Give me Sunday nights when the club is dark and the house band is off," he told Berg, "and I'll give you a jam session and a crowd of paying customers." Berg expressed interest.

Granz attached three conditions to the deal. First, rather than use drop-in musicians playing for pleasure, he wanted the players to be employed and paid, which would allow him to advertise them in advance; second, tables were to be placed on the dance floor, which would make it impossible to do anything but listen; third, the club would be opened to black as well as white patrons, and not only on Sunday night but all week. Berg agreed.

"I think the cats got $6 each," Granz recalled. "And those were good days for getting musicians in Los Angeles. Duke Ellington's band was around town; Jimmie Lunceford's men were available; Nat Cole, who had the trio at the 331 Club, was my house pianist; Lester Young and his brother Lee were regulars."

Drummer Lee Young described Granz at that time as "a real Joe College type, with the brown-and-white shoes, the open collar, the sweater and the general Sloppy Joe style; he was just a guy that was always around, and at first we wondered what he did for a living. He was a lone wolf. We'd drink malteds together – neither of us ever drank liquor – and before long I'd be going over to his side of town and he'd be visiting mine, and we'd be playing tennis."

The late Nat Cole knew Granz as far back as 1941. "He'd bring a whole bunch of records over and we'd listen to them together and have dinner," Cole told Leonard Feather. Cole's stature as a singer has completely overshadowed his importance as a pianist. Cole was to have an enormous influence on Oscar Peterson, and on Bill Evans as well, which fact alone defines him as one of the substantial formative forces in jazz history. He had not begun to sing when Granz first knew him. Cole said: "He had that sloppy Harvard look, and even in those days he wouldn't knuckle down to anybody. A lot of people disliked him, but I understood his attitude; he just knew what he wanted and exactly how he was going to get it. I remember when the booking agents used to call him a capitalistic radical, which of course wasn't right."

Sunday became Billy Berg's most lucrative night of the week, a

75

success that was not unnoticed by other club owners. Other clubs had different dark nights, and Granz set up a circuit of them for his musicians, putting himself in an advantageous situation with owners, for whom he made money, and with musicians, whom he was able to offer four or five nights of work a week.

In early 1944, Granz initiated a series of jazz concerts at a place called Music Town in South Los Angeles. He presented, along with his regulars, musicians from visiting bands, including the tenor saxophonist Illinois Jacquet, at that time known chiefly for his work with Lionel Hampton and Cab Calloway.

At this time, twenty-one young Chicanos had been arrested after what the press called the "Zoot Suit Riots," charged with murder, convicted, and imprisoned in San Quentin. The case became a *cause célèbre* in southern California, and a defence fund was established. Granz remembered: "There were so many kids accused that it smacked of a prejudice case. Orson Welles and Rita Hayworth and a lot of other Hollywood people were involved in the thing, which was called the Sleepy Lagoon Defense Committee. I didn't even remember where Sleepy Lagoon was, and I didn't know what the hell was going on with the case, but it did seem to be a prejudice case, and this was a chance to try out one of my ideas, which was to put on a jazz concert at the Philharmonic."

The concert was held at Philharmonic Auditorium on a Sunday afternoon in July. The cast of musicians included Nat Cole, who was on the verge of enormous commercial success; Les Paul, then known as a jazz guitarist, who would later sell his highly commercial overdubbed guitar-and-vocal records in the millions; pianist Meade Lux Lewis, one of the great boogie-woogie masters; and saxophonist Jacquet, whose screaming high notes, according to *Down Beat,* sent the audience of young people wild. The concert raised $500 for the Sleepy Lagoon Defense Fund.

For the rest of that year Granz presented Jazz at the Philharmonic as a monthly event. The following year, as World War Two approached its end, he took his company of players on a tour of the West Coast, which got as far as Victoria, British Columbia – and heard Oscar for the first time, on a juke-box. "But it broke me," Granz said. "I had to hock everything I owned to get the musicians back." It should be noted that other impresarios in similar conditions have been known to leave their artists stranded. It is also notable that Granz by now had something to hock.

His reverses were temporary. He was about to become a significant factor in the record industry.

Granz had tried to sell various companies on releasing material recorded in his Jazz at the Philharmonic (JATP) concerts. Experienced record men thought the idea was ridiculous – you didn't put out "live" recordings of concerts complete with applause and other audience noises.

Granz went to New York carrying a stack of his JATP recordings. This was before the general use of electromagnetic tape in the record industry, and the music was on bulky twelve-inch acetate discs. He opened the Yellow Pages of the telephone directory at record companies, the first one of which, in the alphabetical sequence, happened to be Asch Records, owned by the late Moses Asch. Granz telephoned him and made an appointment. He was trying to sell records from another session he had supervised, this one by singer Ella Logan. Asch had no interest in this material but, as Granz was about to leave his office, asked about the other batch of records he was carrying under his arm. Granz unwrapped and played *How High the Moon* from one of his JATP concerts. "Asch flipped," Granz recalled to Feather. "He put the records out as Volume One of *Jazz at the Philharmonic,* and it was incredibly popular. I imagine it sold about 150,000 albums, but I never got an accounting, because Asch eventually not only lost the rights, he lost his whole company."

The record, which featured a long solo by Illinois Jacquet and the drumming of Gene Krupa – billed as "Chicago Flash" because he was under contract to another label, though most young jazz fans knew who it was – had an enormous impact. This was the first jazz-concert recording ever issued. (The recording of the famous Benny Goodman 1938 concert at Carnegie Hall was not released until 1950.) And *How High the Moon* became for a time a sort of national anthem of jazz.

The period saw the sundown of the big bands and rising interest in small-group jazz played by veterans of those bands. Granz was the right man at the right place at the right time to take advantage of the situation. One of the main causes of the decline of the big bands was the spreading business failure of the ballrooms and dance pavilions that operated on the outskirts of cities all over North America, which in turn was caused by the conspiracy of automotive, tire, and road-building interests to buy up and dismantle the superb interurban trolley systems that, among other things, carried young audiences to those locations. Jazz had to take to the night-clubs in small-group formats: there was nowhere else for it to go, excepting concert halls. And it was Granz who opened their stage doors for jazz musicians. He was the first producer to present small-group jazz with the emphasis on improvisation, as opposed to the orchestrated big-band form of it, in a touring company. After the success of *How High the Moon*, Granz's players began criss-crossing the continent.

In 1947, when he was twenty-nine, Granz met a tall blonde girl named Loretta Snyder Sullivan, who was passing out leaflets at a JATP concert in Saginaw, Michigan. Granz proposed to her the next night. They were married almost a year later, and in 1949, in Detroit, she became the mother of his daughter. They were divorced in 1952. Loretta later complained that he never took his mind off his business.

"Moreover," she told Feather, "I was ill-advised enough to tell him I disliked some of his records."

From the very beginning, Granz was criticized for appealing to the lowest level of jazz-audience taste, with emphasis on the high-note tenor of Illinois Jacquet and, later, drum battles between Gene Krupa and Buddy Rich.

"The critics used to review the audience as harshly as the musicians," Granz told writer John McDonough in an interview published in *Down Beat* in 1979. "They criticized them for cheering too loud, whistling too much and so on. And they accused the musicians and myself of soliciting this kind of behavior from the crowds. I used to answer reviews like that, because they ignored so many other aspects of the presentation. They said Illinois Jacquet and Flip Phillips played differently in the jam sessions than they did with [Lionel] Hampton or Woody Herman. That was nonsense. Critics would ignore a set by Lennie Tristano, hardly a panderer to public tastes; a set by Ella Fitzgerald, who did mostly ballads; or a set by Oscar Peterson or the Modern Jazz Quartet."

Granz would sometimes stride angrily onstage and tell an audience the concert would not continue until they became quiet. The jazz fans of Paris are notoriously unruly, and Granz had one of his most memorable confrontations with a crowd there, at the Théâtre des Champs Elysées.

Clarinetist Buddy de Franco was performing with the Oscar Peterson Trio. "The French felt that no white man could play jazz anyway," Granz said as he recalled the incident. "Buddy got into a solo on *Just One of Those Things*" – Granz always remembers what tune was being played at the time of any given incident – "and just couldn't get out of it. That happens to people sometimes. It was a very fast tempo, and Buddy just kept going. The trio started to exchange glances. The audience began to get restless, then they started whistling and throwing coins. I don't know how they stopped it, I think Oscar just went *clunk* on the piano and ended it. Buddy came off stage just shaking, he was very hurt. And I got mad.

"I got out a chair and went out onstage and sat down. First of all, I told them I wasn't going to speak French to them. And then I said, 'Okay, and I'll tell you something else. You paid me a certain amount of money for two hours of music. I already have your money in my pocket, and I am not going to give it back. This concert ends at five o'clock. Whether you want to listen to this yelling or to music is up to you.' And gradually they began to shush each other up, which is the way it had to be done, and the concert went on.

"I had a number of friends at that concert. One of them was the screenplay writer Harry Kurnitz. He said to me afterwards, 'I've never seen anything like it. That's the first time anybody ever got the best of a French audience.'"

In 1955, Granz said, "I don't like to talk about exciting an audience, because it always implies *in*citing. Jazz has always been, to me, fundamentally the blues and all the happy and sad emotions it arouses. I dig the blues as a basic human emotion, and my concerts are primarily emotional music. I've never yet put on a concert that didn't have to please *me*, musically, first of all. I could put on as cerebral a concert as you like, but I'd rather go the emotional route. And do you know, the public's taste reflects mine – the biggest flop I've ever had in my life was the tour I put on with some of the cerebral musicians like Dave Brubeck and Gerry Mulligan."

That statement takes on a certain irony when read today: not long thereafter the Dave Brubeck Quartet became so hugely successful that it made the cover of *Time* and fell under criticism for "being commercial." And Gerry Mulligan would become comparably popular; Granz would himself record Mulligan.

In earlier times, jazz was kept firmly segregated: white players never appeared onstage with black players, except in after-hours clubs where they could go to jam. The first integrated orchestra was organized in 1937 in Scheveningen, Holland, by Benny Carter, who used white European and black American and Caribbean jazz players. Within a few years, Benny Goodman was featuring Lionel Hampton, Teddy Wilson, and Charlie Christian with his band, Artie Shaw hired Hot Lips Page, and Tommy Dorsey hired Sy Oliver – all examples of black players joining white bands. Finally, Count Basie hired Buddy Rich, an early example of a white player in a black band, and Dizzy Gillespie from his early days as a leader manifested indifference to colour in his hiring practices.

Granz perceived that integrating the performers was not enough: audiences had to be integrated as well. And he used the economic power that JATP gave him to do it. Promoters seeking to book his concerts were presented with contracts forbidding discrimination at the door. JATP played the first concert for an integrated audience in the history of Charleston, South Carolina. Granz cancelled a New Orleans concert when he learned that while blacks were being sold tickets, they would be segregated from the white audience. He put his artists up at the best hotels, often hotels that had previously been barred to blacks, and moved them from one engagement to another by airline, rather than the long dreary bus rides that are among the many ordeals of the jazz life, and on at least one known occasion he chartered a plane to get his company out of a southern city after a concert rather than let it spend a night under Jim Crow conditions.

In 1947, Granz set up the first of what would prove to be a series of record companies, Clef Records, which was distributed by Mercury Records, a Chicago company. He commissioned the brilliant graphic artist David Stone Martin to design the album covers of the new label. Martin turned in a memorable series of pen-and-brush drawings in his distinctive spidery line style, which had a curiously improvisatory quality that suited it well to the subject matter and made him as famous among jazz fans as the musicians he portrayed. Martin's vivid drawing of a trumpet player in the throes of creation, seen from a low left angle, became the logo of Clef Records. And Granz too became as famous as any of his artists.

This, then, was the formidable figure, a tall, good-looking, very famous self-made millionaire at thirty-one, who came to hear Oscar Peterson at the Alberta Lounge, and took him off to Carnegie Hall in September 1949.

In the aftermath of the Carnegie concert, Granz, already Peterson's manager, had many offers for the pianist's services. He passed them up, urging Oscar to return for the time being to Canada.

He said, "I think you've done it now, but let's just cool it. Let's do this properly. I want to find out first what direction you *want* to go in. Then we'll sit down and talk sensibly about the things I think you should be thinking about doing. There's plenty of time. You've done it now, you've garnered the attention."

And Oscar went home to Canada – with a partner. Ray Brown.

CHAPTER 7

MAKING TIME

Prohibition lingered on in Ontario well after the Americans had rescinded it. Even into the late 1940s, while it was possible to get a beer or an ale in one of its dreary beer parlours and liquor by the bottle only in government-owned stores, public sale of mixed drinks – cocktails – was proscribed. There were no bars. At last this remnant of Prohibition was abolished, and restaurants and hotels rushed to establish cocktail lounges. One of these, in Hamilton, was the Hunting Room of the Fischer Hotel, an attractive little bar in a basement. Oscar Peterson and Ray Brown were booked to play the room in the first week of May 1951.

A problem for the travelling black musician, Oscar said years later, recalling the events of those few days, was finding in a white community a barber who could give him a decent haircut.

"In the South of the United States," Ray Brown said, "you couldn't go into a white barber shop. And you weren't *comfortable* in a white barber shop in New York City. In Montreal, you could find a black barber. But not in Hamilton. There was very little black population. So I walked into a barber shop, picked up a newspaper and sat there, and got into the first available chair. The guy said, 'How do you want it?' I told him, and he cut my hair. That night Oscar said, 'Hey, you got a haircut.' I said, 'Yeah, and the guy didn't do too bad.' And I told him the shop. So he had to feel comfortable about walking in there, since my hair'd already been cut."

The next day, Friday, May 4, Oscar and Ray played golf. When they returned, Oscar went to the recommended barber shop at 75 King Street West. Its proprietor was Glenn McQuaid, who was not there at the time. One of the barbers in his employ told Oscar that the shop was closed. Oscar went away, returned, and was again told the shop was closed. But another man walked past him and was immediately seated for a haircut.

Oscar returned to the Fischer Hotel and called the police, requesting that an officer accompany him to the barber shop as a witness. The police said it was unnecessary (in any case, this was a civil, not criminal, matter), that he need only tell the barber shop's personnel that if they again refused him, he would take up the matter with the crown attorney's office. Oscar again returned to the shop, asked one of the staff why he was being refused a haircut, and was told, "That's my orders." He went back to the Fischer Hotel and described the events to Lloyd Fischer, its owner. Fischer called the crown's office.

All of this is reported in the Hamilton *Spectator* of May 5, 1951, for which paper I was then a young reporter. For years I believed that I wrote that and the subsequent stories on the incident, but when I examined them later they appeared to me to be collaborations between me and whoever covered city hall – probably Bruce Murdoch – at that time, assembled by the rewrite desk from material furnished by both of us. In one of the paragraphs that I seem to have written, there is an inaccuracy about Oscar's brother Chuck, which tends to prove the unreliability of journalism as a source of history.

"Interviewed last night," the story reads, "Mr. Peterson said that he had encountered discrimination at Chatham several years ago.

"Proud of his Canadian heritage, it had been his boast on United States tours that Jim Crow did not live in Canada – it was a great country.

"'He used to laugh at discrimination and say that you never got it in Canada,' Mr. Brown interjected." So Ray was apparently present during this first conversation I ever had with Oscar Peterson. Now, of course, one can imagine how mercilessly he must have razzed Oscar in private over the incident. One can picture him, with the eyebrows raised, saying, "Oh yeah, man? You don't have this kind of thing here, right?" And now we know that Oscar –

and Daisy and the whole family – had suffered deeply from discrimination in Montreal.

"Mr. Peterson said it was still a great country," the story continues. "He was proud of his brother who had lost an arm while serving in the Canadian Army in the last war." Either I misunderstood what Oscar told me or the rewrite desk botched what I told them.

"'But when something like this happens to you, it almost makes you feel that you are not a man,' the jazz pianist said. 'It hurt to watch that man walk past me and get served.

"'I have three little girls. And it sort of makes me wonder what kind of world it will be when they grow up,' Mr. Peterson added ruefully."

The incident stirred a furor, making headlines across Canada. It would not have in the United States, where such acts of discrimination were unnoticed commonplaces, an as-yet undisputed part of the social fabric.

On Monday, May 7, McQuaid told the *Spectator*'s reporter, probably me, "I cut the hair of Mr. Peterson's companion only a few days previous to the present incident, and I would have cut Mr. Peterson's on Friday if I had been present.

"But I am the only man in the shop qualified to cut a negro's hair. I learned the art 31 years ago. You would break perhaps five combs if you didn't know how to do it. I have cut negroes' hair in the past in my shop and I will continue to do so in the future. That is not discrimination.

"This chap came in my shop when I was absent and he was told that the shop was closed. Instead of, in a democratic way and like a gentleman going elsewhere, he went to the police. When he returned another man got in the chair."

Hamilton's mayor, Lloyd D. Jackson, said to the newspaper, "I hate to see the stinking thing called racial intolerance raising its head in the city. I am ashamed to think it would happen here. I never dreamed any one would refuse to cut the hair of a negro."

The city already had an anti-discrimination clause in its licensing bylaw, and one of the city controllers said he intended to have it tested and to strengthen it if it should prove weak. On Tuesday, May 8, twelve members of the Hamilton Club of the National Federation of Labour Youth began picketing McQuaid's shop. On Thursday, various local labour leaders denounced the picketing as Communist-inspired. Now it was McQuaid's turn to go to the police. He said the pickets were obstructing pedestrian traffic and he wanted them removed. On May 19 the city's Trades and Labour Council said it would "press for an anti-discrimination bylaw with some teeth in it." A delegate of the city's barbers to the city council meeting denounced Ray and Oscar for patronizing a non-union barber shop, saying that had they gone to a union barber shop they would not have encountered discrimination. On May 29, by which time Oscar and Ray were long gone from town, the city was discussing turning the licensing of barber shops over to the Police Commission. And on June 5, the newspaper reported that the incident was closed. Henceforth business licences would be issued with a printed warning against any kind of discrimination. This was five years before Martin Luther King led the bus boycott in Montgomery, Alabama.

Glenn McQuaid wrote a letter to the city's Board of Control saying that the refusal to cut Mr. Peterson's hair was a "greatly regretted error that would not be repeated." The board ruled that "Mr. McQuaid did not merit punishment as he was absent when the incident took place."

And finally, the paper reported, "Mayor Jackson said that he had been told by the pianist that he would prefer to have the matter dropped."

Years later Oscar was able to chuckle over the incident. "After Ray had been there, and then took me to the shop, the poor guy probably panicked," he said. "He probably thought, 'Now I'm going to get all of *them*!'"

Toronto stockbroker Maurice Kessler, one of his friends, has said, "Oscar has an enormous capacity for forgiveness."

In the meantime, Oscar's international reputation was growing. Even *Time* magazine had begun to take notice of him.

In the magazine's morgue in New York, in files marked "For Use Only On Company Projects," are three memoranda about Peterson by *Time* researchers, two written in 1951, one in 1953.

The first is dated August 4, 1951, exactly three months after the May 4 barber-shop incident in Hamilton. Written in élite type on an old non-electric typewriter and pencil-corrected, the memo, from one Peg Rorison to John Mecklin, is slugged "Re: OSCAR PETERSON, Negro Canadian Pianist. This is a verbatim transcript, grammatical and stylistic anomalies included:

Norman Granz is credited with "discovering" Peterson, and is the owner and manager of *Jazz at the Philharmonic,* a jazz concert group that tours the U.S. in the Fall, and for which Oscar Peterson is now the starred pianist. Peterson records for Granz under the name of the *Jazz* group for Mercury labels.

I called Granz Aug. 3 (at MU 7-8450, 522 Fifth Av.) who was delighted with our plans for a story, but feels doubtful that Peterson will make a New York engagement now. He is scheduled for a night-club engagement in Cleveland Aug. 6 until the 27th; will be off then until the 30th, and on Labor Day, will appear in Providence. On September 14, he'll begin his tour with *Jazz at the Philharmonic* which will open at the Bushnell Memorial Auditorium & the following night stomp at Carnegie Hall. As this will be the beginning of a 52 or 3 city tour from Sept. – December, Granz considers it the best time to peg a story. Of course Granz will be particularly pleased with our story then, as owner of the *Jazz* group, and he also plans to release a Peterson album then, coinciding with the beginning of the tour.

The story on Peterson's delays is that last year, when he was touring with *Jazz* etc., their engagements were frequently extended as were his night-club engagements afterward, and since he was on a 3-month visitor's visa & he had played here from Sept. – March, he had to have an extension. Because Immigration officials don't like continued visa extensions, they suggested that he apply for a permanent working residence visa, which he promptly tried to get. It was supposed to come through on August 1st, but was delayed.

I asked Granz how he came to be interested in Peterson. He said he was the organizer of *Jazz* etc., a collection of all-star soloists (Ella Fitzgerald, singer; Coleman Hawkins, Lester Young, Buddy Rich or Gene Krupa, drums; Roy Eldredge [sic], trumpet), and he heard of Peterson first in '45 and was moderately interested. He heard of him again in '46 when he played in Montreal, heard more about him in '47, and finally in '48 he heard some of his records, RCA labels & not distributed in U.S. In '49, he flew up & heard him in Montreal, liked him so well he brought him back to the U.S. with him. The following week *Jazz* gave its opening at Carnegie Hall, Peterson gave an impromptu performance and played so well that it was recorded. (Ck. is album selling now or is it the one to be released in the Fall?) However, Peterson didn't tour with the group because neither they nor he thought he was quite ready. In 1950, he was taken in as a permanent member of the group, and toured with them Sept. – Dec. in 52 (ck.) cities. After this he scored a triumph by winning "Downbeat's" pianist popularity poll (he has since risen to 4th place in "Metronome's" 1951 Year Book, just out), and worked in nightclubs until March when he returned to Canada. He is 24 [Rorison got this wrong], has three children, all girls. Has classical piano background.

What kind of music does he play? Not boogie-woogie, no one does in Canada, it's not a style that would develop further. [What Rorison meant by that is hard to imagine.] He's been likened to Art Tatum, Teddy Wilson, Al Garner [sic], George Shearing. "The Tatum idea is closest," but Granz thinks "he's really more reminiscent of King (Nat) Cole [sic] in his earlier days when he played mostly piano, with an emphasis on swinging. Like most jazz players, he's influenced by Earl Hines, once removed through King Cole. Actually, he's developed his own style and will probably have a school of his own. Every time I call Canada & ask to speak to Oscar Peterson, the operators ask where he's playing now. In fact, in 1949, *when I flew up to Montreal to hear Peterson* [emphasis added] but didn't know where he was playing, I got into a cab and someone was playing piano over the radio. I asked the cabbie who it was & he said, 'Oscar Peterson. He's playing at the Alberta Lounge, I'll take you there.' I didn't know much about jazz in Canada, think it's mostly visiting American musicians. In fact, it's interesting that Peterson could develop in such an insulated clime. Though Buffalo is only 80 miles from Toronto, the 'new' records there are a year or two years old in the States. And Peterson is a modern player with his own style. The same isn't true of Europeans – they listen to our records & copy them. Peterson proves that a good jazz musician can develop without (jazz) training. He's got a prodigious technique which with him is a point in his favor though often it gets in the way of classical pianists when they try to play jazz."

Granz expects to be here about a week and will be delighted to answer any further questions.

The memo indicates that Granz at the time was unfamiliar with Canada and the jazz players who were developing there. Canadians interested in jazz were acutely aware of American developments and acquired the Dizzy Gillespie–Charlie Parker Savoy and Dial recordings as soon as they came out, as well as Granz's own JATP recordings. There was a scarcity of some records in Canada during the war years, but it ended in 1945, and before that the more determined fans smuggled them across the border from the United States, the early Nat Coles on Capitol among them. Canadian jazz lovers heard the same jazz disc jockeys the Americans did, went to Buffalo and Detroit jazz clubs, and heard visiting American jazz artists and big bands who came through regularly. By 1947, my high school friend Kenny Wheeler – later an internationally acclaimed and often avant-garde jazz trumpet player and composer – had drawn my attention to Miles Davis. There was a thriving jazz movement in Montreal even then, and Paul Bley, who would become known as one of the prickliest of the jazz avant-garde, was the pianist who replaced Peterson at the Alberta Lounge when Granz took him to New York in 1949. Four years later, Bley was with Sonny Rollins in New York; and the year before, 1948, I started writing for *Down Beat*. That Granz should have had only slight knowledge of Canada is not surprising – most Americans did and, for that matter, still do.

Regardless of that, Granz's perception of Peterson's playing is astute, particularly in that he minimizes the debt to Tatum and accurately measures the influence of Nat Cole. You hear it even now in the way Oscar plays those rolling eighth-note triplets, redolent finally of the remarkable piano fantasies of Earl Hines.

There is an addendum to the Rorison memo: "Peterson got O.K. from govt., but there's law in Can. that citizens must have police records from 'all the provinces', & Peterson got all in except Ottawa's. Holding Birdland for an additional week."

There was no such law in Canada, and in any case Canadian law was not relevant to American immigration regulations. It was the American authorities who demanded that an applicant for a visa supply a clean record from the Canadian police. Rorison thought, apparently, that Ottawa was a province.

About five weeks later, another *Time* researcher, Bonnie Howells, filed the second memo, this one to Jim Pitt. It reads:

Re: Dinner interview with Canadian jazz pianist Oscar Peterson at Hyde Park Restaurant, 998 Madison Ave., Sept. 13.

Big (250 lbs., 6 ft. 1½ in. tall), young (26) and as cheerful and hearty as the music he plays, Negro pianist Oscar Peterson is unique in jazz annals, for he hails from neither New Orleans, Kansas City, Chicago nor Harlem. Peterson is a Canadian boy, Montreal to be specific, but the fact that he was born a long way from the main stream of jazz has in no way impeded his rocket rise to fame.

Interviewed Sept. 13 at dinner (at the swank Hyde Park Restaurant 998 Madison Ave.), Oscar had two things on his mind, his food (he had just finished two appearances on disc jockey programs in Newark and Woodside, Long Island, needed fortification for three more to follow that evening), and his upcoming 46 city tour with *Jazz at the Philharmonic.* An affable, intelligent conversationalist, Peterson talks and dresses – custom tailored grey tropical worsted suit, French silk tie, heavy gold cuff links – with the confident, but not ostentatious air of a man who not only has arrived but expects to stay around quite a while. He exudes the same kind of healthy enthusiasm toward his music that he does toward his eating and he eats in a big way, topping off large portions of Vichyssoise, creamed chicken livers, a baked potato, salad and four hot rolls with a huge slab of apple pie a la mode washed down with milk. His milk drinking and his keen eyesight – he is a careful and interested observer of everything going on around him – are two characteristics he does not have in common with his idol and inspiration, blind, beer-drinking Art Tatum, with whom he is often compared.

Like most musicians, Peterson doesn't care to be compared with anyone, though Tatum is number one piano man in his book and has always been his greatest inspiration. "Unless a man is an out-and-out copyist, you can't put him in a category and I've never admired anyone enough to copy him." As for Tatum, "even if you copy him note for note, that spark of originality that is Tatum's genius, just won't be there." Peterson confessed – and his reviews affirm – that he has also been compared to George Shearing and Nat "King" Cole. "But we're all different," he emphasizes.

One Canadian music critic, Mike Nevard, says that in Peterson's playing "there are touches of Erroll Garner – though a Garner with perhaps more subtlety – distinct flavorings of Shearing – but Shearing with a beat – and … ineradicable traces of Tatum."

Peterson says the reason he is often compared to other pianists is because his playing is not confined to one style (most critics give him credit for this), but that he "plays like I feel. This means mastering the piano, not letting it master you. It also means that you have to make use of everything that has been done before in music, adapting it to your own creative ideas."

Whether or not Peterson actually makes use of everything that has been done before in music is a moot question, but he does have a thorough musical background and was trained originally to be a classical pianist. "A classical background is essential to a good jazz pianist," Peterson says, "and you can spot one who hasn't had that training after eight bars or so."

For the rest of the memo, Howells runs over Oscar's early background, gets some of it wrong, quotes him as saying he was playing Schubert and Scarlatti when he was six, and notes that his hands would reach an octave and a fifth and that he practised four or five hours a day, warming up with Czerny and playing Debussy "for his harmonies" and Chopin "for his conceptions." There's one interesting comment. Oscar said his father was still his severest critic: "He's never come out and said he's liked anything I've done. Sometimes, after hearing me play he'll say, 'You're not gonna go up and get your pay for that!'" And, again, Granz is quoted as saying that he'd been hearing Peterson's records from 1945 to 1948 and was only "moderately impressed." The memo says that Oscar by now was making $1,500 to $2,000 a week. And it quotes Granz as saying, "Oscar's youth, tremendous energy and ever growing popularity should keep him up there in the big money for another quarter of a century."

These memoranda did not apparently convince *Time*'s editors that Oscar was worth a story. Two years later, on December 16, 1953, a correspondent – identified on his copy only as Allen – filed from the magazine's Los Angeles bureau to an editor named Art White in New York a report that apparently turned the trick.

Oscar Peterson settled his massive frame on the piano bench, like a hippopotamus squatting on a river bank. As his six-foot-two-inch, two-hundred fifty-three pounds slouched solidly before the piano, Oscar's inspired fingers rambled over the keys, proving to his audience the skill, technique, and harmonics that Peterson near peerless [sic], have won for him the Downbeat best piano player award for the fourth, repeat fourth consecutive year (announced Tuesday).

This week, at the pseudo-swank, dark-lit Tiffany Club, Los Angeles jazz joint, (Shearing, Holiday, etc.) Peterson treated his listeners to the songs that make him great. With the single spot beaming on his fat, happy, sweat-drenched face, Oscar broke into a fast, technically exacting "Southwinds," in which he exhibited one of his finest attributes: near-perfect technical ability.

His long, spatulate fingers frisked about the keys with great speed, and yet, he never played a muffled note: every one clean and sharp. His trills sung; his progressions moved fast, with fine harmony. But hearing Oscar is not the whole treat. While he played, he constantly mouthed tones, like a muffled scat singer. As he puffed like a strained stevedore over a particularly tough passage, his lips moved in whispering accompaniment. This habit of following his playing with his mouth stems back to the time when Oscar was a trumpeter, thought he would [sic], until TB forced him to quit.

From the rocking "Southwinds," Peterson moved smoothly into "The Surrey with the Fringe on Top" which started off like a jet and got faster. Peterson has a standard song treatment; he opens with the melody, plays it for a few bars, then takes off on his own, improvising, harmonizing, working in various strains that seem to fit the music. He listens to his wingmen (Herb Ellis playing excellent guitar, Ray Brown, one of the best basses). His face beams whenever they give him a good riff [whatever that means]. Then Oscar picks up the song, plays his clean, imaginative piano, rippling over the keys, then diminished chords, then back to the original melody, all the time encouraging himself with his scattish singing, and frequently wiping his perspiring brow with a white handkerchief kept at the end of the keyboard.

For a moment Oscar looked serious, then started a single-note solo beginning of "My Funny Valentine," playing it quietly, clearly, cleanly. Guitar and bass join as Oscar, who plays with his elbows body-close, sends his hands over the entire keyboard. Suddenly he has moved into the bass, with perfect modulation is playing a few bars of Beethoven's "Moonlight Sonata." He moves out of Beethoven back to the Valentine with little effort, and just soon enough to leave the audience wanting more. As listener Joe Horhaim said: "He always does the unexpected. You're waiting for an obvious chord, and suddenly he has done something different, and much more effective."

The memo again recapitulates Peterson's childhood, adding a few details not found elsewhere. The image of his father is harsher than that he came to disseminate in later years. It says that "the elder Peterson brow-beat and fanny-beat Oscar until he had mastered both the piano and the trumpet." Oscar referred to those days as "the hassle with Dad." The memo compounds its errors. It says that the "young Oscar knew all the finest musicians. First he admired Teddy Powell." The reference is almost certainly to Teddy Wilson. Teddy Powell was a bandleader of no great distinction. He played no instrument. He stood on a bandstand and waved his hands. "He didn't even sing," critic and historian Leonard Feather said, in reference to bandleader Bob Crosby, who played no instrument but sang in front of his band. Feather suggested that the reference may be to pianist Mel Powell. Possibly Peterson referred to Teddy Wilson and Mel Powell and the writer elided them into one name. There are other errors. One wonders what fast-moving progressions "with fine harmonies" can be. The writer obviously has no idea what a diminished chord is. He seems unaware that theme-and-variations is the fundamental format of jazz, not Peterson's own approach to it; and that the custom isn't to play the melody for "a few bars" but for one full chorus, thereby to establish the theme on which the variations will be made. He uses the term "harmonics" in place of "harmonies." Harmonics are overtones.

The memo continues:

From Tatum, Peterson learned his greatest lesson: "Art taught me to play the instrument not to let the instrument play me. So many guess with difficiencies [sic], they try to avoid them. Art forced me to work on them until they were gone." Example: Oscar used to be a right hand man. From constant work, he claims: "I've become very ambidextrous. There's no use starting a phrase unless you can finish it. You can't finish it if there are any physical limitations."

Basically, Oscar's music philosophy is simple: technical perfection and what he calls the desire "to venture out. Like with Funny Valentine, during rehearsal it suddenly came to me that there was a similarity between those chords and Beethoven's. I ventured out. It worked.

"Don't get me wrong: experimentation can go too far. There's been a lot of experimenting lately, maybe too much. But it seems to me that musicians are beginning to go back to one basic thing: It's got to swing. After all these experimental kicks, it has progressed with the experimenting. It's swing, with finer harmonics."

Most people watching Oscar Peterson lolling at the piano, excitingly but easily running his hammy hands over the keys would think there was no strain, that it all came easily. Far from it. Oscar Peterson ... practices constantly. When he leaves the Tiffany Sunday for a two-month rest, he will spend four to seven hours per day practicing.

And when he practices, it is only the classics, says he: "I play Chopin because he gives you the reach. Scarlatti gives you the close fingering. Ravel and Debussy help you on those pretty, lush harmonies. Bach gives you the counterpoint. The wonderful thing about music is that you can always further yourself."

At present, Oscar is working on a new theory of harmonics which, he feels will give him completely new freedoms. Says he, "I felt a curiosity to do more harmonically, and at the same time, I felt a limitation. So I started studying this new twelve-point system with Spud Murphy. For example, instead of thinking that from cee to dee is one tone, Spud teaches you to consider the sharps and flats. It keeps you thinking every minute, but in the matter of progressions and moving from key to key it'll be great. I'm just learning it, but it's most exciting. Every musician should know about it."

The last paragraph is mystifying. It is as if the writer has been interviewing a man speaking a foreign language, and thoroughly misunderstanding what is told him. In those days before reporters carried tape recorders, he almost certainly made notes in long hand. Perhaps he couldn't read his own writing.

It sounds as if Oscar were describing a form of serialism. Serialism, whose first important theorist was Arnold Schoenberg, is a system of composition that gives equal weight to all twelve tones in the chromatic scale, to the effect of destroying all sense of tonal centre.

In May 1988, Lyle (Spud) Murphy, then eighty years old, vehemently denied ever having had any truck with serialism. "Oh God, no!" he said. "That's awful stuff! I love *music*!" Murphy, an arranger who has trained many prominent musicians, developed what he called an equal-interval system. "It's just a method of writing. It's perfect for arrangements. But it has nothing to do with serialism."

Murphy used to go by Tiffany to listen to the trio, and Oscar started to study with him. "From Los Angeles," Murphy remembered, "he went to San Francisco. He used to fly down every week for a lesson, and sometimes fell asleep, because he'd been playing until two or three in the morning. From San Francisco, he went to Portland, Oregon, and he wanted me to fly up, but it wasn't practical. After that he studied with me by mail."

For all the peculiarities of this *Time* memorandum, it preserved some useful bits of information. The writer notes that by that time Oscar was making two tours a year for Norman Granz, one through Europe, one through the United States. JATP had just returned from Japan, which Oscar said "was really marvelous. We played packed houses, and the surprising thing is, we heard some wonderful jazz from those Japanese. Norman even recorded a little jazz singer. We'd look around and say 'Wow, where am I?'"

The memo states that Oscar at this point was earning $65,000 a year, a considerable income for a jazz musician at that time. It concludes:

> All is not hard work. According to Oscar, "I don't even mind when the audience is thin. The fact is, I just love to play the piano. But I'll tell you one thing for sure. When the time comes that it's a chore to climb on the stand then I'll quit." With that Oscar left the dollar-sized table, strode to the stand, slipped in behind the piano. He threw his heavy head back and smilingly started the simple strains of "It's All in the Game." His listeners sat silently, listening to the clean notes, the husky half-singing, watching the smiling, sweat-stained face. Regards.

These three memoranda are revealing in several ways. For one thing, there is an implicit racism in their constant identification of him as "Negro," and more specifically in the stereotyping of the intense and driven young man that he was as the "Happy Negro."

96

The writers – except Howells – seem bemused that a "Negro" should play piano that well and know the European piano literature. They have a tone of the raised eyebrow, like that of "Ginny" of the CBC in her implicit bemusement that Paul de Marky should accept Oscar as a student.

As well, Allen's report says that the elder Peterson's incessant jibes "have kept Oscar humble, self-effacing, delightful company, make him seem far more intelligent than his ten grades of schooling." The writer seems surprised at Oscar's intelligence; and of course the equation of intelligence to schooling is fallacious. What's more, Montreal High was an excellent school with an advanced curriculum. A grade 10 education there gave a student a better background than a couple of years in some U.S. universities.

Finally, there is the constant reference to him as "Oscar," which seems to indicate not so much racism as an inherent condescension, rooted in the ignorance of all three writers, towards jazz itself. Had the writers been dealing with Horowitz, they would hardly have referred to him as Vladimir.

If we can sense these things through these memoranda, one can imagine – or try to – what Peterson felt in the course of the interviews from which they were drawn, and we can understand a little the anger he has held in restraint all his life.

Time is famous among journalists for the endless rewriting that goes into its production. In the case of their story on Oscar Peterson, they had a good deal of error to work with. The story came out twelve days after writer Allen (or Writer Allen, as *Time* would say) filed his report. It bore the peculiar headline *Swing, with Harmonics*. Since it was an important exposure for Peterson when his career was cresting, it is worth quoting in full:

> At the age of 28, a Montreal Negro named Oscar Peterson is one of the world's finest jazz pianists. As a touring star of the troupe called Jazz at the Philharmonic (Time, March 2), he has fascinated audiences on three continents, won *Down Beat* magazine's "best piano player poll" [*Down Beat* had no such poll; it did have a general poll on jazz] four years in a row. Last week, at Los Angeles' Tiffany

97

Club, he settled his huge (6 ft. 2 in, 250 lbs.) bulk on the bench, spread his long, spatulate fingers over the keys, and gave his doting audience a typical sample of piano à la Peterson.

Each tune, *e.g. The Surrey with the Fringe on Top*, began with a fast, straight-forward version of the melody, then, after a few bars, swung into Peterson's impromptu variations – interlaced arabesques, rhythmical counterpoints, stream-of-consciousness insertions from other tunes – then back to the original melody. Throughout, Pianist Peterson accompanied himself with his own scat-singing, in the pauses mopped his sweating brow with his handkerchief. Throughout, for all his jet-propelled technique, his fingers frisked the keys with the precision of a hell-bent Horowitz.

Tatum for Fancies. Such mastery of the keyboard did not come easily to Peterson. His father, a music-loving porter on the Canadian Pacific Railway, sat him on a piano stool when he was five and told him to start practicing. From then on, whenever Papa Peterson left on his railroad trips, he laid out practice schedules. If the practicing was not done on his return, Oscar "caught hell." Oscar began to get professional engagements in his mid-teens, but his father never let applause and paychecks go to his son's head. "You're not going to take money for that, are you?" he would snort, whenever Oscar showed signs of undue pride.

Peterson found his own style only after studying others'. His first hero was Teddy Powell. Then he focussed on Nat "King" Cole. Eventually, in 1939, he heard Art Tatum, the man Oscar calls "the greatest living instrumentalist of them all." Tatum's flying keyboard fancies knocked the budding Peterson completely off balance: "I couldn't play a note after hearing Art that first night. I gave up the piano for three weeks."

Chopin for Reach. Now thoroughly recovered from his temporary paralysis, he has gone a long way toward outdoing Tatum. One of his particular fancies is to blend in phrases from a completely different piece – such as snatches of Beethoven's *Moonlight Sonata* in the middle of *My Funny Valentine.* [Jazz musicians had been doing this since the dawn of the art; it is a form of humour.] "I like to venture out," he says. "Like with *Funny Valentine*, it came to me that

98

there was a similarity between those chords and Beethoven's. I ventured out. It worked.

"Don't get me wrong. Experimentation can go too far. But with all the experimenting that's going on these days, it seems to me musicians are beginning to go back to one basic thing: it's got to swing. Of course it isn't the same swing, because it has progressed; it's swing with finer harmonics."

After he swings out of the Tiffany this week, Oscar will return to his family in Montreal. There he will spend four to seven hours a day practicing the classics. Why the classics? "I play Chopin because he gives you the reach. Scarlatti gives you the close fingering. Ravel and Debussy help you on those pretty, lush harmonics. Bach gives you the counterpoint."

The *Time* story is fascinating, even in its errors, for what it tells us about Peterson and what it unwittingly reveals about the implicit, subtle, and pervasive racism of America at the time. Indirectly it reminds us just how ahead of his time Norman Granz was in challenging it.

They also tell us that Granz had indeed heard about Peterson as far back as 1945. That he was unimpressed with the cranked-up boogie-woogie records on Canadian RCA is a tribute to his taste. Memory was fresher when *Time* first interviewed him about Peterson, and his own statements to the *Time* researcher contradict the legend in their indication that he did not hear Oscar accidentally as he was leaving town but actually had gone to Montreal specifically to observe him, though he may indeed have heard him on a taxi radio on his way *into* the city from Dorval Airport.

One more point about the *Time* reports: Peterson's fingers are not spatulate. They are, on the contrary, beautifully tapered. His hands, far from being hammy, are instantly noticeable for length, grace, and elegance of shape. If a god of music decided to create hands perfectly designed for playing the piano, they would look like those of Oscar Peterson.

CHAPTER 8

RAY AND HERB

Oscar met Art Tatum for the first time one night in the early 1950s, not long after formation of the trio with Ray Brown and Herb Ellis.

One of Ray Brown's heroes among bassists was Oscar Pettiford, and from time to time the other Oscar would whisper to him during a tune, "Watch it now, Oscar Pettiford's out there!" And Ray would say, "Hell with him, I'm going to stomp him." And Ray on occasion would tell Oscar Peterson that Art Tatum was in the house, which of course he never was.

The trio was booked into a Washington, DC jazz club called Louis and Alex's, long since disappeared. On the third night of the job, they were in the middle of playing *Airmail Special* when Ray said, "Watch it, Art's out there."

"Hell with him," Oscar said. "He's got to contend with me."

"No," Ray whispered in an urgent voice, "this time he really *is* out there. Look over at the bar!" And Oscar looked. And Tatum was indeed there. Oscar ended the tune, and the set, as quickly as he could, frozen at the man's presence.

Ray took him over to the bar and introduced Peterson to Tatum. They shook hands and Tatum said, "Ray, you brought me one of those sleepers, huh?" "I was totally frightened of this man and his tremendous talent," Oscar said long afterwards. "It's like a lion: you're scared to death, but it's such a beautiful animal, you want to come up close and hear it roar."

Tatum asked Oscar and Ray to go to an after-hours club with him. When they got there, Tatum told him to play. "Forget it," Oscar said. And Tatum told him a story, one Oscar has repeated many times for the moral and aesthetic point implicit in it.

Tatum told him, "Listen, there's an old man in Kansas City." (In some versions of the story that Oscar has recounted to writers, it's an old man in New Orleans.) "He knows only one chorus of the blues. The man can't play the second chorus. And every time I'm there I go to hear him because nobody plays the blues like him. Everyone has something to say in music – if he has *some* talent and has the discipline to master even one chorus." And Tatum said he'd give anything to be able to play that chorus of the blues the way that old man did.

Oscar went to the piano and played two choruses of *Tea for Two,* a tune with which Tatum was strongly identified. He played it very cautiously, he says. Then Tatum told him, "I'm an egotist. As long as I'm alive, I don't figure I'm going to let you have it. But you have it and you're next after me."

"Then Art played," Oscar remembered. "It fractured me."

After that Peterson and Tatum became close friends, but, Oscar says, for a long time he had a fear of playing in front of Tatum that amounted to a phobia. One day Tatum said to him, "You can't afford this. You have too much going for you. If you have to hate me when I walk into the room, I don't care. I want you to play."

One night Oscar was playing at the Tiffany in Los Angeles. In the midst of a set he heard Tatum's voice, "Lighten up, Oscar Peterson." And the fear left Oscar.

Oscar joined Jazz at the Philharmonic in 1950. His second JATP tour closed at the end of 1951 at the Russ Auditorium in San Diego, California, where he was interviewed by Don Freeman, a stringer for *Down Beat* and in later years a prominent syndicated television columnist. Oscar said to Freeman that, on that first tour, "I was a rookie, a kid of twenty-three. I was like Mickey Mantle starting with the Yankees.

"I had heard about these big names for years and now I was playing with them. In the first place, I didn't know how they'd take me – a kid from Canada with the big buildup. I knew I could play a little, but this was the big leagues.

"To tell the truth, I wasn't relaxed very much. I couldn't, not being sure of myself, or of how the musicians and the public would acccpt my work. Thc first tour was pretty rough, for just that reason.

"And now it's altogether different. I have confidence in myself because everybody clsc has confidence in me. What's more, I'm playing a lot better, too. I know where I stand."

If he went through the shock of meeting and working with his idols, he also, by all evidence, went through a cultural trauma on touring for the first time in the United States, where the racial discrimination was not tacit and non-violent, but entrenched, obvious, accepted, and brutal. Lil Peterson told a *Maclean's* interviewer that sometimes the white musicians he was travelling with would have to bring food out to a car for him; or, she said, "he would have to stand at the back of the restaurant and they'd pass it out the kitchen door."

"I couldn't eat that way," Oscar said. "Travolling in tho South, it feels like you're not just in another world, you're on some other planet."

"Once," Lil said, "you had to play with a tire chain at your feet, to protect yourself in case anyone in the audience came over the footlights to attack you."

In March 1988, as he reread this quotation from *Maclean's*, Oscar speculated that the interviewer might have misunderstood Lil. "I wouldn't know what to do with a tire chain," he said. But, he added, at lcast onc mcmbcr of thc JATP tcam kcpt a bascball bat nearby onstage in the South.

Travelling through the South with Ray Brown, Oscar got a lesson in the difference between the quiet racism of Canada and the morc brutal American variety. Oscar was driving Ray's car, a Cadillac. Ray was asleep. Needing cigarettes, Oscar stopped before a diner. A police car was parked in front of it. Oscar entered and requested his brand of cigarettes from the counterman, producing a twenty-dollar bill, the smallest he had, to pay for them.

"Where did you get twenty dollars, boy?" the counterman said. Realizing how dangerous the situation was, Oscar said it was legitimately earned. The counterman gave him his cigarettes – and threw his change on the floor.

"Pick it up, boy," one of the cops said, his hand on his gun. In one of the few instances where Oscar Peterson ever backed down, he bent, gathered his change, and left.

Years later he recounted the incident to his friends Audrey Morris and her husband, Stuart Genovese, in Chicago: he got into the car and sat silent, waiting for the police car to leave so that he could go back in the diner after the counterman. Ray woke up and asked what was going on. Oscar told him what had happened. Ray urged him to start the car and leave, and finally his counsel prevailed.

The Jazz at the Philharmonic troupe of 1952 travelled to forty-one cities in North America, then went to Hawaii, Japan, and Hong Kong, with stops on the way back in Australia and the Philippines. By then, according to the New York *Times*, it was grossing a million dollars a year, a quite remarkable figure for the time, which left Granz with a profit of $100,000.

"The faintly brooding impresario," Gilbert Millstein wrote in the *Times*, "does not pretend to despise money (he was once, by his own account, the most proficient board marker, or quotation writer, on the Los Angeles Stock Exchange and nourished serious intentions of becoming an economist), but he displays a tendency to treat it as though it were something to spend. Thus, he permits himself to indulge a fairly recent taste for Savile Row tailoring and for frequent dinners at an outstanding restaurant called Le Pavillon; he also pays the highest wages in the band business to give the public the kind of jazz he likes best. 'If I score,' Granz said, 'I think people should score with me.'"

Curiously enough, Granz told Millstein he wanted to get out of the band business and run a restaurant like Le Pavillon.

That same year Granz made an album that surprised a great many people – *The Astaire Story*, in which the dancer and actor Fred Astaire sang thirty-four songs with which he had been associated in the course of his career. In some tracks, he danced to the music of the accompanying group, which included Oscar Peterson, Ray Brown, Alvin Stoller, Barney Kessel, Charlie Shavers, and Flip Phillips. The album was severely panned by critics, particularly Douglas Watt in the *New Yorker*, and Granz, as was his custom in those days when confronted by comments in the press that offended him, sent a denunciation of Watt to *Down Beat*, which printed it in the February 11, 1953, issue. Granz said that if Watt had liked the album, it "would have been a complete failure."

That same year, 1952, Granz suggested that Oscar move on from the duo with Ray Brown and form a trio.

There are two classic trio formations in jazz: piano, bass, and guitar; and piano, bass, and drums. The piano-bass-guitar structure was discovered more or less by accident by Nat Cole, when the drummer in his quartet failed to show up for work and Cole found he didn't really need him. Used skilfully, the guitar itself is an effective rhythm instrument. Various groups were modelled on Cole's, including the Page Cavanaugh Trio.

At first, Peterson went to the piano-bass-drums format, adding drummer Charlie Smith. This trio was never recorded. But soon Oscar decided to turn to piano-bass-guitar. At first Irving Ashby, who had worked with Nat Cole, was the guitarist. Then Granz arranged for the Oklahoma-born guitarist Barney Kessel to join them. Kessel, who disliked travelling, agreed to spend one year with the group.

"Barney came," Oscar recalled. "I'll never forget. Having an opposing force, so to speak, creatively, shocked me. I mean, he came *at* me. He came in hungry to play, and the first night Barney Kessel nailed me to the cross twelve ways to Sunday. He really did. I mean, I was in shock. He was so avid. And I couldn't get myself set. And Ray, of course, was instigating. Ray said, 'I didn't want to say anything, but you're kind of getting your ass kicked tonight, right?' And I said, 'Yeah, and you know something? I can't do anything about it. But I'll be back.'

"I remember Barney's comment that night after it was over, he said, 'Oscar, you know, that's better than sex.'"

Kessel stayed a year, as promised, and then Oscar had to find his replacement.

One of the trios based on the Nat Cole instrumentation was the Soft Winds: Lou Carter, piano; John Frigo, bass; and Herb Ellis, guitar. They had constituted three-quarters of the rhythm section of the Jimmy Dorsey band. Ray Brown heard the trio in a Toronto bar called the Zebra Lounge and told Oscar about it. Oscar made a trip to Buffalo to catch another of its engagements and sat in. The Soft Winds, a superb group years ahead of its time, was having trouble making a living, and Peterson offered Ellis a job.

Fair-skinned red-haired Mitchell Herbert Ellis, of Scottish-Irish ancestry, was born August 4, 1924, four miles south of Farmersville, Texas, a town of two thousand souls forty miles northeast of Dallas. He early acquired a harmonica, then a banjo, and finally a guitar, along with a small amplifier purchased from a Sears Roebuck catalogue. He studied music at North Texas State University – then primarily a teacher's college and now a major training ground for jazz musicians.

His first encounter with the guitar work of Charlie Christian had the same effect on him that Oscar's encounter with Art Tatum had on Oscar. Three of his schoolmates became noted jazz musicians – Jimmy Giuffre, Gene Roland, and Harry Babasin. They told Herb he had lots of skill, lots of technique, but his music was meaningless, and they made him listen to Christian's records with Benny Goodman. At first Christian's playing meant nothing to Herb, who later recalled:

"They said, 'You haven't got the message yet. Listen some more.' So I listened some more. I don't know whether it was the same day or the next day, but it wasn't a long time, and it really hit me, like a spiritual awakening. How much depth he had. And how scummy I sounded. His playing sounded deep and mine sounded shallow. I was very upset, very distraught. I put the guitar underneath the bed, and said, 'That's it. I've just got too far to go.' It stayed there about one day. Then I got it out. Now I went from all notes to no notes. Each note had to drip with emotion, and be sent from heaven. I went from one extreme ridiculously the other way. So that's how I got some direction."

Ellis never was graduated from North Texas State. He went on the road with one of the territory bands – as they were known in those days – next with Russ Morgan, then with Jimmy Dorsey, and finally with the Soft Winds.

"Oscar remembered me from hearing me in Buffalo," Ellis said in the summer of 1985. "He's got perfect memory, total recall. So he asked me to go with him. So I went to New York, to hear them play. It was awesome. They didn't have nearly as many arrangements as they did when I had been with them a while. But they had a lot of them and I could hear how hard it was going to be. But I just said, well, I'm gonna give it a try."

Oscar said, "Barney was very linear, and Barney was a shout master. Herb had that too, he could shout behind you on solos. But his was a different approach totally from Barney's. Herb came in with this quiet backup rhythm, time that you could just sort of sail along with. And then he and Ray got into this thing, it wasn't patterns they were rehearsing; they had all these avenues they could go down, they could pull any switch they wanted on you. It was a very poignant era for all of us. I remember him saying, 'Oscar, I don't claim to play like Barney Kessel. I'm not necessarily one of those players. I can play, but I'm not that heavily into the linear thing.' The funny thing is I remember thinking to myself, 'You may *think* you're not that kind of a player, but you're in for a shock by the time you leave this trio.'

"The rhythm thing Herb already had – an intuitive sense of time that very few people have. Where he developed was on the trio things that I called on him to play, which were really difficult. He'd be playing something linear and he'd have to join me harmonically with a cluster, and move the clusters around with me, and he increased his technical ability – not just technical, that's a bad word – he increased his musical capability on the instrument, and I think his solo ability increased. There was one strength that we had that was never questioned, and that was dynamics."

Ray Brown said, "Herb and I rehearsed all the time. Rhythm. For a trio that didn't have any drums, we had it all. Herb and I roomed together and we played every day. Not just the gig. We played golf in the morning and guitar and bass in the afternoon, and then we would shower, take a nap, go to dinner, and to the gig. We had it together."

Ellis continued: "I was there until 1958. Six years. That period was one of the highlights of my life and my career. The challenge that Oscar put on me and put on Ray and put on himself. So you couldn't have any qualms about it, he made it as hard for himself as he did for everybody."

Ray Brown recalled that Oscar would say, "Can this be done on the instrument?" And Ray would say, "I don't think so." And Oscar would say, "Well I think it can." And Ray would end up doing it.

"You'd end up doing it," Herb said, "after a lot of sweat and practice. And Oscar would say, 'See, I told you.' It was very difficult, but the rewards were well worth it. Because we reached musical and emotional heights that you don't reach very often. We reached some musical peaks that I doubt I will ever attain again. It was a trio where we were totally involved with each other, musically and personally. There was a lot going for it."

Oscar said, "I used to say to the guys, 'At our worst, we have to sound better than the best guys out there.' It was a piano era, wasn't it? With Shearing, Garner, Wilson, Horace Silver. Bill Evans hadn't arrived yet. Somehow we became in that shuffle what I called the crutch group. And I mean at the door. At the beginning, we may not have sold out the room every night. But whenever we came to town, we established a level that only got better. And the level of the next visit, you could rest assured it would more'n likely be higher.

"But the funny thing is that the money never went that way. For whatever reasons. There was Erroll, George Shearing, and Dave Brubeck. Ahmad Jamal was just beginning to happen. There were four. For some reason, the night-club owners would say, 'Gotta have the trio back, gotta have the trio back, love Oscar.' Norman said, 'Never mind loving Oscar, pay him.' We couldn't break whatever the price barrier was. That was in a lot of clubs. Norman kept saying, 'I don't know what it is.' Erroll had his hot records. Erroll was one of my favourite people, and Norman loved him too. Norman said, 'Regardless of what he does on records, it doesn't diminish what you do. And you sell out all the joints.' I was equalling Erroll's records in clubs, and in the case of the London House, I surpassed it.

"If you want the truth on where you stand, ask the help, don't ask the owner, ask the help. They turn in all the tabs. I got tired of the help in various clubs saying, 'You better be getting top money, because we don't do this kind of business.' That brought on a reaction from Norman. We obviously quit playing certain clubs. He just said, 'Okay, pass, it's not worth it to us. We'll do concerts instead.' And I took on, I guess, a certain aggressiveness such that I decided I was going to wipe every piano player around, if that was the only way I was going to get my just due. And I went for broke. I played some sets in the London House and other clubs where Ray and Ed or Ray and Herb said, 'Jesus Christ, I don't know what you're trying to prove.'

"I was proud of my trio, I was proud of all of those trios. I thought we had the steam. And we did have it. What was exciting about our groups ... Yeah, they were pressure groups. I kept the pressure on them.

"And because of keeping the pressure on them, it made for a belief and an approach in the group whereby everyone became self-sufficient creatively. Ray Brown believed in what he was doing, so much so that Ray Brown made himself into what he is today in the movie studios and recording field."

Ray Brown said, "To play with and for Oscar Peterson is very demanding. It doesn't take very much to upset Oscar on a stage. He and I would get into it once in a while, if he had anything to bitch about. Herb and I spent too much time honing up for him to have anything to bitch about. We were keeping that group damn near waterproof. Herb and I tightened it up to the point where it was waterproof.

"We were opening one night for Basie. Oscar said, 'They got more guys, but that's all. They're not taking nothin' from this band.' That's the way he thought. To hell with Count Basie's orchestra. You understand, they were our closest friends in the world, but on the bandstand, Oscar takes no prisoners."

Oscar said long afterwards that he was surprised he had lived as long as he had. "I was pushing it hard, bodily and musically. I don't think people realized how hard we were playing. I remember one night in Baltimore, it sticks out in my memory, when we had the challenge going. Ray and Herb came in and said, 'We're going to get you tonight.'

"So I said, 'No no, you had it last week, you were hot as a pistol last week.' I just did my bulldog act. Ray said, 'Which of us is going to get him tonight, Herb?'

"Herb said, 'I think I'll take him.' So I did my loudmouth act, and said, 'It's just another week.'

"So we opened up Monday and I went for broke, and I really had me a night. And by this time they started looking at me kind of strange. They said, 'Well he lucked up on that, he can't go for it again.' Ray said, 'I'll get him tonight, Herb, you can take it easy. I know where his weaknesses are.'

"So we went on and I had *another* night. Suddenly it got to the point where there was no more competition. They began egging me on to see if I could keep it up. Ray said, 'Well this is Tuesday night, I gotta give it to you, you did it for two nights, you can't keep that up for the rest of the week.' And of course I was doing the Jack Armstrong act by now. I say, 'Yeah I can. Ain't nothin', no big deal.' And I did. I kept it going until Friday. And then Saturday night the noise wasted me. One of those famous Baltimore clubs."

Oscar gave a low whistle of incredulity at the memory. "The place was full of all the guys with the hats and the dark glasses. Whoever. Pimps. The 'Hey wha's happ'nin', baby?' kind of crowd. During the week we had the listeners. And although Ray and Herb were challenging me, they were playing *for* me, and I could hear everything they were doing. But I just couldn't get a handle on it that night. That's the kind of relationship we had in the group. Ray and I became very tight from the outset, because don't forget, we were a duo. We lived together, we roomed together.

"I remember another thing. I was in the middle of a TV series in London, and we had a gig with the Buffalo Symphony that we couldn't get out of. Symphonies are scheduled way in advance. And Norman was saying, 'Well, we'll move that.' When the BBC series came up, he said, 'You've got to do the series, I want you to be seen.' And he was right. Except that this Buffalo thing kept looming bigger and bigger and finally he said, 'We've got to do it.' I was on tour at the time, and we were taping two days a week. I did a concert, I came in and rehearsed and did the TV show the next day, jumped on the Concorde, flew to New York, took a connecting flight, flew into Buffalo, played the concert, got back to the airport the next morning at six o'clock, flew back into New York, grabbed the first Concorde, went back into London, and was back in the studio."

But the pressures on the group from Oscar's unflagging will to excel led to explosions. One night at the London House, Oscar came off the bandstand after a set in a conspicuous cloud of discontent. Ray said to him, "Just what do you expect of this group?"

"Only a little music," Oscar said.

Oscar had tapes of the evening's work, and in the small hours of the morning he began to listen to what they had done. He called Ray, who was staying with his wife at the Croydon Hotel. He told Ray, "*Sweet Georgia Brown* was just great!"

Ray, according to Oscar, said, "We knew that last night," and hung up on him. Ray's version is a little harsher: "I said, 'Fuck you!' Bam! And slammed the phone down."

"Many times," Oscar said, "the things I disliked about my work stemmed from the very thing that I've gotten into in the last so many years, thanks to Norman and Duke – solo piano. I became too involved with what I was doing and didn't listen to my group. That's my criticism of me at times. I'd get into something and they were in it with me and I'd get so inside of the thing I was doing that I would subconsciously negate the presence of the group. I don't say I didn't play with them, obviously. But it didn't come off the way it should have, it didn't knit the way it should have, because I was so intent on doing my particular thing at that time. I accounted that as not reacting to my group properly. And it used to bug the hell out of me. Different times we'd tape ourselves, and I'd hear these things go by and I'd say, 'God *damn* it, they did *that*, they had that going there, and I didn't take advantage of it!"

Oscar's – and the trio's – career climbed sensationally. He toured Europe with Jazz at the Philharmonic in 1952, 1953, and

1954, and he has done so every year ever since. He made his Japanese début in 1953. He won the *Down Beat* reader's poll as best pianist for the first time in 1950, then in 1951 through 1955, 1959 through 1963, 1965 through 1967; he won the magazine's International Jazz Critics' Poll in 1953. Interestingly, he has never won the latter poll since.

Peterson, Brown, and Ellis were extraordinarily devoted to each other. And they were notorious for their practical jokes.

"You didn't hear the story, did you," Herb said, "about Ray Brown and me dyeing our hair opposite colours? This was out here in California. We had a day off. Ray and I played golf, which we did frequently. On the way home from the golf course, late in the afternoon, we were walking from the bus, and we passed a drugstore. And there was a new thing in the window. It said, 'Dye your hair any color, and if you don't like it, you can shampoo it out immediately.' I said, 'Hey, I got an idea. We'll buy some red dye and black dye. I'll dye my hair black and you dye yours red, and we'll call Oscar over to the apartment, and there'll be a lot of fun.' Ray said, 'Okay,' but he looked at me as if I manufactured this stuff, and he said, 'Are you sure this shit's gonna wash out?' I said, 'I don't know. That's what it says.' He said, 'It better.'

"It's late in the afternoon, and we dye our hair. Ray's is this flaming, sickening light red, and mine was jet black. We call Oscar. We said, 'How you doin'?' He said, 'Fine.' I said, 'We need to see you.' He said, 'Wha'dyou mean, you need to see me? You saw me last night, you see me every day. I'm on my way out to dinner with some people.' I said, 'Well there's something we gotta talk about.' He said, 'Well, we'll talk about it tomorrow.' I said, 'Well this can't wait till tomorrow. We gotta talk to you, man. It's semi-serious. Why don't you just drive by on your way out?' He said, 'What's the matter with you guys?' 'Just come by,' I said. He said, 'Okay.'

"Ray's in a chair, reading the paper, Oscar knocks on the door. I open the door, and he says, 'Hey, Herb, hey, Ray. Well, what do you guys want?' Looking right at us. He didn't crack a smile. He said, 'What did you want?' Ray said, 'Don't you get it?' He said,

'Get what?' He said, 'You guys detained me from my dinner.' He said, 'Get out of here. I'll see you tomorrow.' Next day we told him about it, and he maintained for a year that he never noticed anything. Now that's control, isn't it?

"Oscar would untune a guitar string during intermission, and get your attention when we went up to the point where you wouldn't even touch the guitar. He could do that. He could keep you talking like that, and then it would be, here we go. Or sometimes he would look like he was retuning it, and then he would start the tune in another key, up a tone or half a tone down.

"In 1953, the first big jazz tour ever in Japan, Jazz at the Philharmonic ... It started with Norman and Oscar playing a joke on Ray. Ray and I were in the wings. We played with Ella Fitzgerald. We played with everybody. Ray was standing backstage, waiting to come on with Ella, and Norman introduced us all, with Ray last, right before Ella. And Oscar had tuned Ray's G-string down, a *lot*. Then he got Ray's attention while Norman was announcing, some way he kept Ray from hitting the strings. And then Norman introduced Ray Brown and then Ella, right on top of it, so we walked out, and bang! counted off and hit. And Ray started to play, and the string was just loose, dunk dunk. And Ella wasn't reacting too nicely to this. And she's giving him a lot of rays back there. And Ray looks over at Oscar, and Oscar and Norman are just guffawing. And Ray said, 'Okay, all right.'

"Ray can take a practical joke, but he's not one to play it on, because he can really pay it back. Ray went out between shows. There's a game over there called pachinko, and if you win you get a lot of little steel balls, and when you have a hundred, you turn them in and you get packs of cigarettes or whatever. Ray played and won a lot of little steel balls, which he put in his pocket. So now we came back. Oscar, during that show, his hands were hurting a little bit. First time he made his entrance was when we did the ballads part. So he walks out to great applause. Bill Harris is walking out from the other wing to play his trombone solo. It's dark and I see Ray lean into the piano. I have no idea what he's doing. He's scattering these little steel balls right across the strings. It's Bill's ballad, so he says, '*But Beautiful.*' Oscar starts to take the intro, and every note is brrr, brrr, brrr, it sounds like a whore-house piano. He knew that Ray did it and he's taking the steel balls out of the piano and flinging them at Ray and they're hitting the bass. And Bill Harris is suffering out there. So we finally wade through that. And Bill Harris comes over to the piano and says to Oscar, 'One day, one day.' And nothing happened during that tour. Not till we got to Rome the next year, the Rome Opera House.

"In those theatres over there, they serve Cokes and booze and beer and everything backstage. You can order them. Bill Harris overheard Norman talking to the trio before we went on. Norman asked Oscar to sing. Oscar was very hesitant. Norman said, 'Sing something. To them it's a foreign language. It'd be just right for you.' So Oscar said, 'Okay, I'll sing *Tenderly*.' So Bill gets the waiter and gives him some lire, and gets one of those big trays, and piles it up with glasses and empty bottles, and puts it up on a ladder, and just waits back there. Oscar starts, and it's *quiet,* man. I remember it was one of those true dramatic stages that slant down, a raked stage. Norman is standing right in the back, you could just see him. He's loving the trio. And Oscar, he was kind of nervous, he goes, 'The evening breeze … caressed the trees … tenderly,' and when he goes 'tenderly,' Bill Harris gives a push, and crash! Oh! It went on, for *ever!* Crash! Bang! And it went on, and on, like it was never going to stop.

"Bill Harris ran upstairs so he could come down like he just heard this crash. He said, 'Norman, do you realize there's an artist playing out there?' And nobody copped out on him. For a long time. Because Norman was so mad. Nobody told on him."

"There was one I used to pull," Oscar said, laughing at the memory. "I thought this was a stroke of genius at the time. I'd go roaring up to the stand. I'd suddenly say, 'We're on.' The first thing they'd say is, 'He's going to tune our strings down.' I'd put my hand down on the guitar but I wouldn't touch anything. I'd say, '*Seven Come Eleven*,' beginning of the tune. And Herb would say 'God damn it,' and the first thing you'd know he'd detuned himself.

"They did some things to me that evened that pretty good. We were at the Rouge Lounge in Detroit, Ed Sarkesian's place. I came in for this matinée. We played the first set and we got ready to play the second set. I went up to the piano and I said, 'Okay, let's do *Love You Madly*.' And I counted it off. And I started to play. All of a sudden some of the notes wouldn't work, they wouldn't go down. I said, 'What the hell's going on?' Ray was saying, 'Come on, get it together, will you?' And I said, 'Ray, there's something wrong with the piano!' And he said, 'Come on, don't give me that, you just finished a set.' And I started to panic. They had taken that see-through tape and taped three keys here, then missed nine and taped some more. Finally they started to break up, and I knew they'd done something. It was the first and only time it's ever been done to me. They got me. But I used to get them regularly."

Once, during a JATP intermission, Oscar and Bill Harris reversed the mouthpieces on the trumpets of Roy Eldridge and Dizzy Gillespie. The entire troupe was to assemble onstage for the finale – Ella Fitzgerald, Roy, Dizzy, Flip Phillips, Harris, and the trio. "When Roy and Dizzy came out onstage, late as usual," Oscar said, "Dizzy picked up his horn and blew. Nothing. Absolutely nothing came out of his horn, it was unbelievable. He told Roy to play. And Roy came out with this horrible sound. He went crazy, and he was yelling, 'But it wasn't me, I swear, it wasn't me!'"

Almost from the beginning, Peterson was a sort of straw boss of Jazz at the Philharmonic – music director, trouble-shooter, and general foreman, assigned by Granz to take charge. Thus many of the figures Oscar revered, Coleman Hawkins and Roy Eldridge among them, came under his direction. For the most part it was an amiable and happy arrangement, though at times there were problems, and Oscar's will served him well. Whenever one of the troupe went to Granz with a complaint about the behaviour of someone else in the company, Oscar recalled, laughing, Granz could be heard backstage calling out, "Oscar!" And Oscar would have to take care of it.

Buddy Rich was widely considered the greatest drummer in jazz history. Born Bernard Rich to parents who were in vaudeville, he had been a professional from the age of five, when he was billed as Baby Traps, the Drum Wonder, and travelled all over the world. He was the consummate show-business professional – a gifted tap dancer, a capable singer, and a man of quick and memorable wit. Asked during the early days of the Beatles what he thought of Ringo Starr, he said, "I don't think of him." On being admitted to hospital for the last time, he was asked by a nurse if he was allergic to anything. "Country and western music," he answered.

To drummers, his playing had an almost mystical quality, particularly if viewed from behind. He did not raise his hands high above the drums in flailing motions. And his arms seemed to be moving more slowly than the sounds he was producing. Furthermore, when his sticks hit the head of his snare drum, they produced sound at a volume far greater than the apparent weight of the stroke. And – you can ask drummers about this – the sound seemed to rise *before* the stick hit. He was an incomparable technician whose cymbals and foot pedals and tom-toms seemed like extensions of his own small and wiry body, he moved with effortless command and control, and as his hands came down in that seeming slow motion there was a last-second break of the wrist that accelerated the stick. This no doubt contributed to the strange intensity of his playing. Even Buddy seemed a little puzzled by it. He once told an interviewer, "It's as if the man upstairs said to my hands, 'Be fast,' and they were fast."

He had had a remarkable career with the bands of Artie Shaw, Tommy Dorsey, and Count Basie, all of whom attested that their bands never before or afterwards had the same drive, sound, and swing that Buddy gave them, and, when the big-band era entered its waning days, he became one of the featured performers in the Granz company, along with another great drummer, Gene Krupa, who also used to shake his head at Buddy's mastery.

Buddy Rich was fast and funny, and could be delightful company. He also had a fiery and touchy temper and an egomaniacal appreciation of himself that was alloyed to an almost naïve honesty. When, while hosting Johnny Carson's *Tonight Show*, Sammy Davis

Jr. gushed that Buddy was the greatest drummer in the world, Buddy said, "That's true," and meant it.

He was a spendthrift and often didn't pay his bills – and often didn't pay his musicians either, when he was leading his own bands. At one point, Oscar recalls, Buddy drove to Granz's office in the new Jaguar he had just purchased. He didn't have enough money for gas. Granz, always known for paying musicians well, was getting tired of doling out funds to Buddy and turned down this latest request for an advance. Buddy threw a tantrum as only Buddy could and said he was going to kill himself. With an accommodating gesture, Granz opened a window for him, and Buddy left in a rage.

Oscar used to call Buddy "The Gorilla" and teased him that he should be kept in a cage and turned loose only when he was needed to play.

Now, the term *time*, as used by jazz musicians, is somewhat evasive of definition. Confronted by writing about jazz, editors of "classical" music publications will often try to change it to "timing," which is not what it means. The problem is that the term is inapplicable to classical music, which puts no comparable emphasis on rhythmic pulse. "Time," in jazz, means a compound of things, among them: a very accurate and steady sense of the pulse; an ability to place notes subtly off the centre of that pulse without losing it; a sense of which notes to stress in relationship to the main rhythm to make the music swing; and a highly tuned feeling for the length of an improvised phrase so that it works out in a placed coordination with the music going on around it. Good time is one of the most prized attributes a jazz musician can have. Probably no other drummer ever had the elegantly perfect time of Buddy Rich, and he took a justified pride in it.

Oscar, as the de facto leader of the group, would be required to kick off tempos for the tunes. And some of the older masters with the Granz company, including Roy Eldridge and Coleman Hawkins, liked tempos at a medium pace that would permit them to show their abilities to best advantage.

117

Buddy, however, would move them up to where *he* wanted them, and where, presumably, they showed *him* to best advantage. Collectively they could have overcome a weaker drummer, but not Buddy Rich, and they would be forced to play at his tempos. Hawkins and Eldridge and others would complain to Granz or Oscar or both, and finally Oscar confronted Buddy.

Buddy denied the charges. "I'm only playing the tempos you're counting off," he said.

"You really think you are?" Oscar said.

"That's right," Buddy said.

Oscar became earnestly polite. "Then I apologize, Buddy," he said. "I'm really sorry. I really didn't realize that you had this problem. You've got rotten time."

One of the most gifted of the saxophonists with JATP was prone to sullen moods, and when one of them was on him he would stand behind Ella Fitzgerald and play scales unrelated to what she was singing, in what saxophone players call "practice tone," a dead, colourless sound, sometimes referred to as "the tone that came with the case." Ella would be disconcerted and complain to Granz. Granz's voice would ring out backstage after a concert: "Oscar!" And Oscar finally took up this issue, too, telling the saxophonist to discontinue these distractions. The latter said, "Who, me? I'm not doing anything."

"Really?" Oscar said. "Then I see what your problem is: you've got bad intonation."

One of the most important soloists to travel with JATP was Lester Young, a wonderfully lyrical player whose influence on Stan Getz, Zoot Sims, Alan Eager, and a host of other tenor saxophonists, as well as the early Charlie Parker, makes him one of the music's most important innovators and influences.

Lester Young was one of a kind, an other-worldly, poetic soul who had risen to prominence in the band of Count Basie. Even there, he was a sort of odd man out because of his soft, singing tone as opposed to the heavier, darker, more muscular sound of Coleman Hawkins, which was considered the True Faith of tenor playing. Drafted in World War Two, Lester Young, known as "Prez" – president of the tenor saxophone; the nickname was given to him by Billie Holiday – underwent incessant humiliation from sergeants, finally was sentenced on a trumped-up drug charge to the stockade and further brutalization, and came out of the army a more or less broken man with a heavy drinking habit.

Very intelligent and intuitive, he was an idiosyncratic figure in a pork-pie hat perched in a forward tilt above sleepy eyes set in an almost Asiatic face, with a lazy, slouching walk and a delicate, effeminate manner of speech that led some to speculate – inaccurately – that he was homosexual. There is evidence that Prez was in love with Billie Holiday.

He was noted for a verbal inventiveness that rivalled his musical creativity. He originated any number of expressions that became part of the arcane parlance of the jazz musician, including "feeling a draft," the term he used for sensing racial prejudice in a situation. It has long since come to mean feeling hostility of any kind and has passed into the general American vocabulary. To a certain famous and unpleasant and very short night-club master of ceremonies who was prone to shake down jazz musicians for a bribe *not* to botch his introduction of them, Prez said, "Get away from me, you half a motherfucker."

He had the habit of inventing nicknames for people, often of arresting vividness. He referred to Ray Brown as Lawyer Brown, which any of Ray's friends will agree is extremely apt. He also liked to prefix names with the form of address "Lady," and he called Oscar Lady Pete. He called himself Dr. Willis Wiggins.

His health was, by now, obviously failing. Some say he never recovered from the abuse he suffered in that army stockade. He had ruined his system with alcohol. Food had lost all flavour, and he had in consequence lost interest in it.

Oscar remembers: "He was loved. He was idolized. Illinois Jacquet and Flip Phillips would get up and give him bus seats. Jacquet can be very bullish, and he'd say, 'Hey Prez, come on, here's your seat, right here.' Guys stood in restaurants trying to get him to eat. I went with him one day, and he ordered a sardine sandwich with ice cream! We said, 'Whatever you want, Prez. Eat.' He said, 'You know what I think I'd like? Me Lester, you Lady Pete? Have me some *sardines*. And some ice cream.' I thought, 'Good Lord!' But anything to get him to eat at that point."

The pianist Bobby Scott, who travelled in 1955 with JATP as a member of the Gene Krupa Quartet, remembers him with deep affection, observing, "He had the oddest, gentle way of saying 'motherfucker.'" Young's nickname for Scott was Socks, short for Bobby Socks, because he was only eighteen.

Scott wrote in an essay about Prez, "His brand of story-telling was littered with so many 'motherfuckers' that it was shushed down, and out, when we found ourselves in the company of the general public. But when we travelled in quarantine, he was allowed to stretch out, and never since have my sides ached so much.

"He would have mock fights with Roy Eldridge and other 'shorter' fellows who would grab his arms as if to do him up. 'Midget motherfuckers!' he would cry out in pretended desperation. 'Lawyer Brown, Lady Pete! Socks! You gotta help me with these midget motherfuckers!' Only Prez could carry it off. For minutes afterwards, he'd mumble to himself, still in his fiction and dramatic mockery, 'Those ... *midget* ... motherfuckers!' And he would say, 'Socks, I could take 'em – one at a time! But the midget motherfuckers gang up on me! They gang up on ol' Prez!'

"I can hear him again, hear the fake dramatic pauses, the ham acting, the truncated exclamations he was known for and, most of all, the disarming sweetness."

Scott and others remember an incident that made more than the musicians laugh – the audience got in on it too.

Oscar again: "If the rhythm section was steaming, it was part of Prez's thing when he came onstage to feign disorientation. Particularly if the soloist who preceded him had been steaming, he'd come out and it would be like, 'Hmmm?' I remember him holding his chin. I vividly remember this. This night, he came over toward the piano, and we were *into* it, whatever it was. We *had* it. And he said, 'Where you motherfuckers at?'"

He said it right into the microphone inside Oscar's grand piano.

Scott recalled: "The audience's laughter sounded like Niagara Falls.

"Norman Granz told Lester to stay after the concert. I found him sitting cross-legged, his face as forlorn as the head of a cracked porcelain doll.

"'What are you waiting for, Prez?' said his worshipping eighteen-year-old friend.

"His eyebrows raised, in acknowledgement of his faux pas. 'Lady Norman's gonna give me a reading.' He winked. 'I bought it, Socks,' he said, as I walked slowly off the stage, looking back and thinking how much he seemed like a kid kept after school."

Oscar Peterson was thirty at the time, Lester Young was forty-seven and slowly dying – two years later he was gone. The incident happened in the Montreal Forum, a few blocks from Oscar's birthplace.

In November of the following year, 1956, Oscar was playing an engagement in San Francisco when he received a call from the trumpeter Harry (Sweets) Edison in Los Angeles to advise him that Tatum was dying. Edison asked him to fly immediately to Los Angeles, saying he would meet him at the airport. Oscar asked the proprietor of the night-club to let him cancel that night's performance, his last, but the club owner held him to their contract. Oscar fulfilled the contract and caught a late-night flight south. No sooner had he checked into a hotel when he received a second call from Edison, telling him Tatum was gone. Oscar, bereft, told Edison he would stay for the funeral. Then he received another call, this one from his sister, telling him that their father had just died of a stroke, and he flew home to Montreal for that funeral.

"In one week I lost two of the best friends I ever had," he said.

On the wall of Oscar's studio in the basement of his home in Mississauga, there is a photo of himself, Vladimir Horowitz, and Art Tatum.

CHAPTER 9

ALL THE POSSIBLES

If Norman Granz's opposition to racism had cost him a commission during his army days in Texas, it seemed during a JATP visit to Texas that it might cost him his life.

Segregation in Houston was rigidly enforced, but it was an apartheid of custom, not law. Granz knew this. He rented a hall that was owned not by a corporation or an individual but by the city, and hired his own personnel for two concerts, the first at seven p.m., the second at ten. He gave this instruction to his ticket sellers: "You will tell people that these concerts are not segregated. If anyone doesn't like it, you will return their money, and you will not assign them other seats." To assure the peace of the evening, he hired a number of off-duty policemen as security guards.

Just before the first concert began, he noticed three strangers backstage, men in business suits. He told them that only people on the concert staff were allowed backstage during performances and asked them to leave. They said they were off-duty police detectives who just wanted to listen to the music and showed him their credentials. For once Granz relaxed his rule. He told them they could stay.

While Oscar was onstage performing during the first concert, Gene Krupa, Illinois Jacquet, and Dizzy Gillespie gathered in Ella Fitzgerald's dressing room, laughing and telling tall tales. Someone pulled out a pair of dice, and a dollar game of craps promptly sprang up. The three detectives entered the room and told them they were all under arrest for gambling. Hearing the tumult this proclamation inspired, Granz came running. The cops told him that he too was under arrest — for running a gambling game.

One of the detectives entered Ella's bathroom. Granz, well aware of the police tactic of planting narcotics on jazz musicians, followed him.

"What are you doing?" the detective said.

"Watching you," Granz said.

The cop drew a gun and pointed it at Granz. "I ought to kill you," he said.

Granz is said to have faced the gun with icy calm. "It was not with icy calm," he said with a slight smile as he recounted the incident. "I just didn't say anything. I did realize there were witnesses, but there were also two other cops. I suppose if he had shot me they'd have come up with some story."

The detectives said that they were taking everyone down to the court-house. Norman said, "All right, but before we go I am going to walk out on that stage and tell three thousand people that they are not going to see the second half of the concert, and you are then going to have a riot. And they will be leaving and they'll walk right into the other three thousand who are waiting to get into the second concert."

The detectives agreed then to wait until the two shows were over. Then Granz, Gillespie, Jacquet, Krupa, and Ella Fitzgerald were taken to a court-house and charged with gambling. "Curiously enough," Granz said, "there were newspaper photographers present. That's when I knew they'd set us up to smear us."

The judge ordered that bail of $10 be posted for each of the five persons arrested. Granz put up the $50 and the JATP group left. "Ella was fit to be tied," Norman said.

As with traffic offences, the system assumes that no one will waste the time and money necessary to fight a minor charge, and the forfeited bail becomes in effect the fine. But when the members of the JATP group arose the following morning, they found their pictures in the newspapers with the story of their purported backstage debauchery. It was in part Ella Fitzgerald's humiliation at this exposure that determined Granz's course of action.

"I decided to do what no one in his right mind would do," he said. "I decided to fight them." He called his lawyer in New York and told him he wanted the best lawyer in Texas. His lawyer urged him to forfeit the bail and forget it. So did the Texas attorney he engaged.

When the case in due course went to court, the presiding judge threw out the charges. With legal and other expenses, it had cost Granz more than $2,000 to get the $50 back. His satisfaction came in the newspaper accounts, one story in particular: a reporter wrote that in view of their behaviour in this unseemly incident, the Houston police should have as a crest a chicken rampant on a field of yellow.

By 1953, when Herb Ellis joined the Oscar Peterson Trio and thus Jazz at the Philharmonic, JATP had grown to enormous proportions. In a 1954 *Saturday Review* article titled "Pandemonium Pays Off," Whitney Balliett said that Granz was the "first person who has ever been able to successfully mass produce jazz." Granz, he noted, "owns and operates a record company that has mushroomed so violently in its first year it has had to be split into two companies to accommodate overworked distribution facilities."

The worth of the Granz enterprises at that point was an estimated $5 million. Those are 1954 dollars, it should be remembered, and in the jazz world the figure was astonishing. There were eleven musicians, including the Oscar Peterson Trio and Ella Fitzgerald, in the JATP company. The group that year played seventy-five concerts in fifty American and Canadian cities; twenty-four concerts in Japan, and fifty concerts in twenty-five European cities; 400,000 persons paid from $2 to $4.80 for seats. The two Granz record labels, Clef and Norgran, had released more than two hundred albums, and in one month alone of that year, twenty-five of their albums were shipped to record stores. Indeed, 50 per cent of all the jazz records being released at that time came from the Granz companies. "And," Balliett noted, "Oscar Peterson, the 29-year-old Canadian pianist, who has virtually been handmaidened into fame by Granz and has since become the Granz house pianist, now has 16 albums to his credit."

In addition to running his record companies and booking JATP, Granz was the master of ceremonies at all the JATP concerts, speaking in a soft voice with dentalized *t*s and *d*s. "I go crazy at concerts," he told Balliett. "I lose my temper every five minutes. I yell at everybody. I'm rude to people who pester me. Every concert has to go perfectly. If somebody goofs he pays for it."

Balliett left a vivid image of JATP in his *Saturday Review* piece: "This concentration on jazz as a solo art has brought off some weird musical achievements. One is a regularly featured trumpet battle – Roy Eldridge and his old pupil Dizzy Gillespie will be the participants this year – in which two trumpeters squeal at each other like a brace of stuck pigs. Another is a blinding, deafening drum battle, that invariably jellies the stoutest audience. If this be pandemonium, Granz makes the most of it. Most of the musical materials are banal, being restricted to the blues at a variety of tempos, and to such weary evergreens as *How High the Moon*, and a handful of Gershwin tunes.

"From close observation Granz feels that the average age level of his audience has increased in the past nine years, and that it is now somewhere between 21 and 28, which is probably a rather casual statistic, judging by the oceans of heated teenage faces one can find at any Granz concert. One might at first describe these audiences as the spiritual offspring of the sprites who jitterbugged in the aisles and on the stage of the Paramount Theater in New York in the late '30s when Benny Goodman first came to town. But at second glance these present-day audiences are of a different and more warlike tribe. They rarely move from their seats, yet they manage to give off through a series of screams – the word 'go' repeated like the successive slams of the cars on a fast freight – blood-stopping whistles, and stamping feet a mass intensity that would have soothed Hitler, and frightened the pants off Benny Goodman.

"Granz the jazz lover is predominantly visible through his studio recording sessions. In these he has been responsible for a polite amount of excellent jazz, as well as a great deal of musical mediocrity. Granz officiates at every recording date, and ominously announces this fact on every record label and record sleeve with, respectively, the words 'Recorded under the Personal Supervision of Norman Granz' and 'Supervised by Norman Granz'. He also composes all the liner notes for his albums, which have become noted for barrages of adjectives and their lack of information. Although Granz ... claims that he never dictates to his musicians, much of what emanates from his recording studios has come to have a distinct flavor. This flavor, as an observer recently pointed out, is reminiscent of good roast beef that has been left in the icebox too long. For, in spite of the fact that their personnels are often laundry lists of jazz royalty, many Granz records are, peculiarly, boring and cold. One reason for this may be that a good number of the musicians who appear on Granz recordings are also members of JATP, and, because of the nature of the music they must play seven months out of the year on the concert stage, have gone dead. And if the requirements of a touring job with Granz often make his musicians artistically laconic, these requirements have also seriously stunted the musical growth of such talented men as Flip Phillips, Oscar Peterson, Charlie Shavers, and Buddy Rich.

"When Granz inaugurated this year's JATP tour on September 17, in Hartford, he had on his payroll 11 of the best jazz musicians money can buy. He is paying them salaries that start at several hundred dollars a week, and range up to $6,000 a week for Ella Fitzgerald and $5,000 a week for Oscar Peterson. In addition to the European tour, which will take place in the spring, and the fall tour of the U.S. and Canada, JATP will take a brisk swing through Australia, as well as Japan and Honolulu. Granz has also promised that he will release a minimum of 120 LP albums in the next 12 months. To at least half a million potential customers around the world, Granz will be doing for jazz what another prestidigitator, P.T. Barnum, did for midgets."

Granz told a *Time* magazine reporter that one reason for his success was that "I give the people in Des Moines and El Paso the kind of jazz they could otherwise never hear." He also said he had learned as much as any man alive about "scaling a house," that is, deciding how much to charge for each seat. "I've got a sixth sense about it," he said.

Two years later, in early 1956, Granz founded a new record company, which he called Verve. His intention was to make it a popular-music label, with his jazz product continuing to be issued on his Norgran and Clef labels. In addition, he set up a label called Down Home to issue traditional jazz. But all this proved too ponderous to administer and he amalgamated all his recording activities under the one label name, Verve. And many of Oscar Peterson's best records were made for Verve.

Granz produced the best known of the Peterson–Ellis–Brown trio recordings for Verve at the Stratford Shakespearean Festival in Stratford, Ontario. Recorded August 8, 1956, it still is considered a classic by musicians.

All the albums by that trio are in monaural sound, since the age of the commercial stereo disc had not arrived. Curiously enough, some stereophonic tapes of the trio do exist. In 1954, when the trio was playing a night-club in Los Angeles, Oscar's old bandmate Gerry Macdonald, he of the spinning sidecar, turned up. By then Macdonald was a recording engineer and designer of equipment. He was already experimenting with stereo tape recorders. He asked Oscar if he might tape the trio with one of his prototypes. Oscar granted permission. Macdonald taped dozens of hours of that trio, night after night. The tapes now repose at his house in Long Island, a remarkable documentation of a brilliant musical group.

Ellis had, and has, a way of using the guitar percussively that gave the group the kind of drive that normally only a drummer can provide. He and Peterson were both so skilled at the use of voicings that these two harmonic instruments, piano and guitar, never clash. The integration of the group is astonishing. The tapes should be and no doubt would be issued publicly except for one thing: the piano, like most night-club pianos, was bad – tinny and out of tune. Were it not for that, these would go down in the discographies as some of the finest recordings Oscar Peterson ever made – and the only recordings of that trio in stereo. Nothing on the issued recordings captures the power of that trio the way those suppressed tapes do.

"When that trio had the lock-down going," Oscar said, "it was a unit nobody could interfere with. Ray and Herb did something that a lot of players don't do. They played together in the daytime, apart from the gig. They sat down and actually practised harmonic movement. And not set-up. They didn't say, 'On bar four we're going to do this.' They practised *possibles*. All the possibles, all the alternatives. And whatever triggering mechanisms they had – and I wasn't allowed in that club – they could go any given way at any given time. It was just automatic with them. And I could sense it. They had a way of letting me know they were going in such a way, at times. And other times Ray would turn and say – this was his famous line – 'See if you can hear this.'

"The other thing that that trio had, which people may or may not have realized, was a tremendous linear suppleness. We could play lines together like nobody else could play lines together. We could run lines against each other, and it was because we had such a great understanding of each other's playing. And we could run these lines in such a way that at times, depending on where we were on the instruments, it was almost impossible to tell which instrument you were hearing."

There was one unhappy note in the group – Herb's drinking. "Norman Granz," Herb said, "was very understanding at that time when I was struggling with booze. The problem had hit me and I really didn't know I had a problem. We didn't know about alcoholism, he didn't know, Oscar didn't know. But he knew that I missed the plane to Europe and some incidents later ... I was a periodic-type drinker. And Norman and Oscar must have known innately that I wasn't a bad guy. That the sickness, when I would drink, would make me do those things. Norman stuck with me. He told Oscar, after the second time when I fouled up with that group, 'You know, I don't want to get into your business, it's your group, but I wouldn't get rid of him.'

"I'd get so sick. We'd have time off and I'd start to drink. I never drank on the job. When I was with them, I hardly ever drank. But we'd have some time off, I'd start to drink, and it would be okay for a few days, and then it would get the best of me. One time I got so sick in New York that I just couldn't make the plane. I couldn't get the passport, I couldn't get the transformer I needed, I just got so screwed up, so sick ..."

Oscar was staying at the Algonquin Hotel in New York, almost always his residence in that city. "When we were going to Europe," Granz said, "we'd all get together in New York two or three days in advance. I always stayed at the Algonquin because they had never discriminated against anybody. I had even lived there for a while."

"I was staying with my mother," Ray Brown remembered. "She lived up town." To black Americans, that term, applied to New York City, means Harlem. "Herb used to come up there and eat dinner with me damn near every night. Oscar would come up once or twice a week. My father was a chef. Oscar ate so much, my father just liked to watch him. They were great buddies.

"I think what happened is, Herb got up that morning and he went out and got a couple of drinks, then got scared that he was going to blow it. And he called my mother. I was in another room still asleep. She didn't want to wake me up. She asked Herb if it was vitally important. And Herb, in his nice way, even though he was having a panic, said, 'No no, I'll call back.' If I'd gotten that call, I could have gone and gotten him. I couldn't jump on my mother about not waking me. She had no idea, she didn't even know about Herb's drinking, he never took a drink at our house."

On the morning of the flight to Europe, Oscar descended to the lobby to pay his bill. His luggage was stacked near the front door. Ray was waiting for him. Ray said, "Have you seen Herb?"

Oscar said, "What do you mean, have I seen Herb? That's your buddy, your roommate."

Norman Granz was immediately concerned. He and the hotel manager went up to Herb's room and found it empty. He descended to the lobby and told Oscar, "It looks like you're without a guitar player."

Oscar said, "Norman, come on."

Granz told the hotel manager to find someone to look for Herb and left the guitarist's ticket with him, in case Herb should show up. The JATP company departed by limousine for Idlewild Airport. Oscar still, unrealistically, believed Herb would somehow join them. But as they got closer to the airfield, he could feel the pit of his stomach falling. Oscar, Ray, Norman, and the rest of the company boarded the airplane.

"I kept looking at the door," Oscar said. " 'Cause, you know, we were *ready*, as that trio always was. Ray was really drug. Not that I wasn't. But it took a lot out of Ray. When they finally closed the door, they closed part of me outside. Then of course, the worry, 'Where is he, what is he doing?' So then I consulted with Norman, and Norman said the only thing we could do was to get a detective agency, try looking. I forget how they found him. Somehow somebody found him."

As the group toured Europe, Ellis, in New York, turned himself into Alcoholics Anonymous, and they put him into a hospital to dry out. When Granz and Peterson finally found out where he was, they called him and told him to join them.

"And I did the wrong thing," Oscar said. "I helped do the wrong thing. We couldn't wait to see him. The first thing that hit me was how thin he was, how emaciated. I didn't know that much about alcoholism. The first night, if I remember correctly, I think we were off, in Hamburg. The first thing we did wrong was we went to a beer garden. I really didn't know the seriousness of alcoholism, because I was encouraging him to have a beer. I didn't know that much. It was my first crunch with it. I was just so glad to see him. Just dumb. I remember in this beer garden, they were serving these big steins. I said, 'Come on, Herbie, have a beer.' And we started drinking beer. I was just so glad to see him. It didn't seem to bother him, he didn't get stoned or anything. And he finished the tour. After that he disappeared another time. I remember I was in L.A."

"It happened a year or so later," Herb said. "Nobody knew where I was for a month. I only knew I was in New York, just surviving from drink to drink and day to day. I couldn't make any moves, because if I'd stopped I'd have gone into DTs or shock or something. I didn't know that, of course. I even made Walter Winchell's column. 'Where is the red-headed guitar player?' Because nobody knew where I was. My folks didn't even know."

"By this time," Oscar said, "I had consulted with AA and they had sort of chastised me about my babying him and catering to this weakness," Oscar said. "And they made me understand that I wasn't doing him any good. I called him when they found him in New York and he called me back. And he said, 'Oscar, I've let you down.' I said, 'No, Herb, you've let yourself down.' And I went that way with him. He said, 'I don't know what to do.' I said, 'Herb, you know what to do.' From then I got a little heavier with him, which they told me I should. He said, 'Oh, I'm not going to be able to …' I said, 'Herb, I don't want to hear it. You owe me. Never mind owin' yourself, you may not want to own up for that one, but you do owe me. So get on a plane and get out here.' He said, 'I didn't think you'd want me back.' I said, 'I don't want to go through all this. Get on a plane and get out here.' And once he got out there, we started talking. There was no scolding, I don't mean it like that, nobody can ever scold anybody. I just made him understand that it was hurting us almost as much as it was hurting him. And I think he finally bought it."

Ellis became a committed member of Alcoholics Anonymous and quit drinking.

In 1958, tired of travelling, and with his wife, Patti – whom he had married while he was with the trio – now pregnant with their first child, Ellis reluctantly resigned from the group and settled in California to work in the recording studios and raise his family. One of the last gigs the Peterson–Brown–Ellis trio played, curiously, was in Hamilton. On July 25, 1958, the *Spectator* carried the four-column headline 'Oscar Returns, Without a Grudge' and a story that began, "Oscar Peterson returned in triumph last night to the town where just seven years ago he had trouble getting a haircut. Back in 1951 … he made headlines in The Spectator and all across Canada when he alleged a Hamilton barber refused to cut his hair because he was a Negro." One change in the intervening years was that the paper had begun to spell Negro with an upper-case N. "No," the story quoted Oscar as saying, "I don't hold any grudge against this town."

And it noted that he was "fresh from his seventh annual concert tour of Europe with his trio, which includes Herb Ellis on guitar and Ray Brown on bass."

Other changes were coming about in the working life of Oscar Peterson. Norman Granz closed down North American tours of JATP after its 1957 season, though he continued to take it to

Europe. He took up residence in Geneva, Switzerland, and moved his substantial art collection – which included a great many Picassos – to his home there. He concentrated his show business attention on managing the careers of Oscar Peterson and Ella Fitzgerald.

"My feeling," Granz told John Tynan, then West Coast editor of *Down Beat*, "is that jazz concerts, as I've laid them out, will never be the way they were.

"As impresario and as fan, I feel at this point that all jazz concerts, by the very nature of the artistic demands made on the musicians, must inevitably begin to repeat themselves. Jazz just hasn't produced enough musicians to make such concerts possible any more."

Granz again complained about his treatment by the press. "I felt the undue accent on my business acumen was somewhat out of line in most of the stories about me," he said.

"One story on me I disliked *very* much appeared in the *Saturday Review*. Whitney Balliett wrote it.

"To me, the all-important aspect of my work is the obvious use of jazz in fighting sociological problems. This aspect hasn't been given nearly enough attention so far as I'm concerned."

He also said to Tynan, "Some musicians may not like me, they may not want to work for me. But nobody, not even those who may feel like that, can say they don't respect me."

"God, those were exciting days with Oscar and Ray," Herb said. "Hoo! Did you ever see us? The Stratford album comes about as close as anything to what we sounded like. Oh, they were great days." He had tears in his eyes.

It was Ray Brown who had recommended Herb to Oscar. Ray Brown would recommend his replacement as well – not another guitarist, since Ellis was irreplaceable, but drummer Edmund Thigpen.

Excepting Daniel Peterson and Norman Granz, no man has played as important a role in the life and career of Oscar Peterson as Raymond Matthews Brown.

CHAPTER 10

RAY AND ED

The foundation of any jazz group, its very underpinning, is the bassist. He provides the bottom of the harmony out of which the other players construct their improvisations, and he keeps the time, the centre of that rhythmic pulse essential to the music if it is to be definable as jazz. Great bass players are treasures, unnoticed as a rule by the casual listener but valued beyond measure by fellow musicians. And at that time in jazz history, Ray Brown was valued beyond all others.

"This business of who is best on an instrument is a lot of nonsense," one bass player said then, "and most of the time it's impossible to say who's best. The one exception is bass. There's no question about bass. Ray Brown is the best there is. He's so far ahead of everybody that there's simply no comparison. He's a tall man in a crowd of medium to small men. That's how he stands out."

Wherever the Oscar Peterson Trio travelled, the pianists and bassists would come from afar, and you'd hear later that this bassist or that had been up in Ray's room, picking up a few pointers, for, as Oscar says, bass players are clannish and peculiarly supportive of each other. Or that Ray was hanging out with the premier bassist of the New York or Los Angeles Philharmonic or the Chicago Symphony. The question was, who was taking lessons from whom?

"Well," Ray said, "let's just say that I'm either studying with them or hanging out with them, talking about the instrument. The average bass player today is pretty well studied, with few exceptions. It's a much more accepted thing than it was when I was coming up as a youngster.

135

"I consider that the greatest assets a bass player can have are good time, good intonation, and a big sound."

Ray embodied all these virtues. His time was not merely good, it was so profoundly firm and grounded that it seemed like the heartbeat of all jazz. His intonation was so accurate that it would make your ears pop. And his sound was more than big, it was enormous. It could cut through the laughter and talk of the noisiest night-club or boom out through the murkiest jazz-festival sound system.

Characteristically, Ray attributed the sound to the instrument he owned, a bass he acquired in 1947, two years before he met Oscar Peterson and co-founded one of the most enduring friendships in jazz. "I've had it legitimately appraised three times," he said in 1961. "I mean I paid money to have it appraised. Two experts said it was an Italian bass, and one said it was English. It's also been called Scotch. It doesn't matter, really. I'm not one of those pedigree followers. If it gets the sound I want, that's it.

"Actually, it's not the best bass for solos, but it's such a gas for other things. I could get a lot more speed on a smaller instrument. But my heart lies in that sound."

This evaluation should be taken with caution. Though that great dark wooden instrument was all he said it was, he has been heard getting virtually the same sound out of a $125 Kay student-model bass when he was teaching a class at Peterson's Advanced School of Contemporary Music in Toronto.

"I used to think," he said, "that if you studied you'd naturally stay in tune. But it's ... it's something besides knowing where the notes fall that makes some bass players play more in tune than others. It's some little inner thing. One of the most in-tune bass players I've ever heard is George Duvivier.

"Frankly, I credit Oscar with a lot of my development. He always gives you a little more than you think you can do. He'll say, 'Is this possible on the instrument?' It's been a spur and a challenge to me.

"Most people who think about bass or bass players think about solos. They tend to measure the greatness of a bass player according to the way he solos. But to me, the major, the primary function of bass violin is time.

"There have been a lot of different concepts in the last decade, and a lot of experiments made on the instrument and in conjunction with other instruments. And there has been a tendency to get away from basic time. But I don't think bass can ever get away from time.

"And I'll say this too: bass is a two-handed operation. A lot of people think it's a matter of pulling the string. But you have to match the pressure of the left hand to the pull of the right. A lot of guys will pull hard with the right, but the left will be weak in comparison. Matching the hands – that's one of the secrets of a good sound."

The matched hands of Ray Brown entered the world in Pittsburgh, Pennsylvania, on October 13, 1926. At that time, in Montreal, Oscar Peterson was fourteen months old. Ray's father was a cook during the boy's youth, and cooking has always been one of Ray's hobbies.

Ray, too, was required to take piano lessons in childhood, but there was this difference between his training and Oscar's: his father didn't want him playing Bach and Liszt, he wanted Ray to play like Fats Waller, and, later, like Art Tatum. "That was asking a little too much," Ray said. "But that's not the reason I gave up piano. I just couldn't find my way on it. It just didn't give me what I wanted.

"Besides, I was in a high school orchestra and there must have been fourteen piano players in it. And twelve of them were chicks who could read anything in sight."

He took up trombone. His father said he couldn't afford to buy Ray an instrument. There was a bass available at school.

"I played that school bass for two years. I used to take it home weekends. The teacher used to think, 'That Ray Brown, he's really serious, the way he practises.' He didn't know I was making gigs on the school's bass. But then they ran my picture in the paper, in connection with some job I had, and the teacher saw it. They stopped me taking it home, right there. My dad gave in and bought me a bass."

For a time he worked in what were called in those days territory bands. He played in the band of Snookum Russell shortly after two other major jazz figures left it, trumpeter Fats Navarro, who died young after a brief and brilliant career, and trombonist J.J. Johnson.

The Russell band played Miami. "Three other guys and I began plotting to get to New York and try our luck," Ray said. "But the night before we were to go, everybody chickened out, leaving me with my bags all packed. So I said, 'The hell with it,' and went.

"I got to New York, took my bags to my aunt's place, and the very same night had my nephew take me down to show me where 52nd Street was.

"That night I saw Erroll Garner, Art Tatum, Billie Holiday, Billy Daniels, Coleman Hawkins, and Hank Jones. I'd known Hank before. While we were talking, he said, 'Dizzy Gillespie just came in.' I said, 'Where? Introduce me! I want to meet him!'

"So Hank introduced us. Hank said to Dizzy, 'This is Ray Brown, a friend of mine, and a very good bass player.'

"Dizzy said, 'You want a gig?' I almost had a heart attack! Dizzy said, 'Be at my house for rehearsal at seven o'clock tomorrow.'

"I went up there next night, and got the fright of my life. The band consisted of Dizzy, Bud Powell, Max Roach, Charlie Parker – and *me!* Two weeks later, we picked up Milt Jackson, who was my roommate for two years. We were inseparable. They called us the twins. Milt and I did some *starving* to death together at times. Milt introduced me to my wife, Cecille. They'd been kids together.

"After I'd been with Dizzy about a month and figured I had everything down, I cornered him after the gig and said, 'Diz, how'm I doin'?' He said, 'Oh – fine. Except you're playing the wrong notes.'

"That did it. I started delving into everything we did, the notes, the chords, everything. And I'd sing the lines as I was playing them."

"Ray's always been that kind of guy," Dizzy Gillespie said. "Very, very inquisitive. On *I'm Through with Love,* we get to one place where the words go 'for I mean to care' … Right there, that word 'care.' The melody goes up to an E-flat, B-natural, and G-flat, and that sounds like an A-flat minor seventh chord. *Sounds* like it. So I told Ray, 'Now, Ray, you're making A-flat there.' He say, 'But you're making A-flat minor seventh.' I say, 'No I'm not.' He say, 'Show me.' So I take him to the piano and play D, and there's the same note up there in the D. And he say, 'Aha!' But I had to show him.

"He'd have done it anyway, because I'm the one playing the solo. But Ray always wanted to know *why*."

"Ray," Oscar said, half laughing, "has an insatiable desire – insatiable, absolutely insatiable – to find the right note at the right time. I'm not just saying that about one playing. I know a lot of players that'll say, 'Hey, wait a minute. There's a better change we can use there.' Then they'll say, 'Hey, there it is, that's a better change.' For Ray, that's okay for this playing. The next time around, you'll see the eyes going, and he'll approach that same spot, then all of a sudden he'll lay something on you, because all of a sudden he hears a better placement of that particular harmonic sequence."

This is evident in the beautiful lines he would play underneath everything Oscar Peterson played, whether in the trio with Herb Ellis or that with Edmund Thigpen – and for that matter in every record he ever made. But it was with the Peterson trio that he was really able to glow, sometimes skipping on the harmonics (harmonics are delicate bell-like overtones obtained on stringed instruments by barely touching the string with the left hand at certain critical locations at the moment the string is plucked or bowed and instantly pulling the finger away) or just "walking," his feet sinking into the earth like some sort of Paul Bunyan of music. So close was the rapport between Brown and Peterson that Ray's notes sometimes sounded as if they were being produced by a sixth finger on Oscar's left hand.

Oscar once described him as "the epitome of forethought. Sympathetic forethought." "Ray Brown," he said in 1986, and fell into a long silence, musing on a thirty-seven-year association. "A very, very difficult talent to describe. Because his talent has the kind of depth … It's not just intuitive. His talent is almost ethereal. The thing that he has you can't describe. I believe that Itzhak Perlman could pick up any violin, and it's a $19.95 job, and I don't think many of us would be aware of it. Buddy Rich has that thing too. I've seen Buddy Rich sit down at a set of what I call soggy drums, and make them sound like his. Ray has that kind of talent. He is a walking sound. Ray has a sound that he walks around with that he can't even describe, within himself. I don't care what *he* says. The fact of having the instrument under his hands makes him approach it that way. There are very few people like that. I think Dizzy's like that with a horn. Ray has that.

"And the other thing that Ray has is an innate mechanism, something within himself, that will adjust him to any situation; and consequently he will adjust that situation to what he thinks it should be. Ray has that mechanism within him, like a tuning fork, that keeps him straight. It's so well built into him that he can infiltrate another situation – ask any players who've played with him – and put it on the same venture that he's on. This is unknowing on his part. Totally unconscious. The times when it doesn't work is when he forces it. If he comes in and just plays the way Ray Brown plays, everything sort of adjusts to it.

"Ray can be bad for certain piano players. He is so strong that they tend to lay back on him. I've heard various players with Ray. I think the reason I worked with Ray and can still work with Ray is that I attack Ray – or challenge him. That's a better word. I challenged him at every level, just as he's challenged me. But that's the whole idea of playing. The big mistake some pianists have made playing with Ray is that they figure, 'Oh now I've got it, I've got the foundation, all I have to do is sort of sit on it.' And the first thing you know is the foundation has flipped and you're crushed. So consequently I tried to stay on top of Ray, and he'd say, 'Go ahead, you press all you want, I'm gonna be there.' And that was a good feeling between us. There was resistance and then there was the forcing and then the resistance and then the cohesiveness. You have to have disagreement to have agreement."

Peterson has said repeatedly that he and Ray are as close as brothers. And when Herb Ellis left the trio, it was Ray who selected his successor.

Oscar had decided against trying to replace him – he considered
him irreplaceable – with another guitarist. He changed the format
to that other classic trio instrumentation, piano, bass, and drums.
He hired Gene Gammage, who played drums in the group for a
few months of 1958, and then Edmund Thigpen. Thigpen, whom
John Tynan of *Down Beat* dubbed "the thinking man's drummer,"
introduced a new coloration into the group, which was by then
recording for the third of Norman Granz's labels, Verve.

Edmund Leonard Thigpen was born September 28, 1930, the son
of Ben Thigpen, a superior drummer known best for his work in
the Andy Kirk Orchestra.

His mother, after she and his father separated when Ed was five,
moved to Los Angeles, where Ed grew up and went to high school.
The woman Ed describes as his "sister," Beverly Watkins, a San
Fernando Valley high school principal, gives us an insight into his
childhood. His mother died when Ed was twelve. Ed was boarded
out with a family who could not abide his interest in drums. "There
were four children in our family," Beverly said. "My father liked
people, he liked people around him. But he didn't go out much. He
couldn't even drive. We didn't own a car."

There are certain rhythms and inflections in her speech that are
identical to Ed's. Whether they are particular to certain parts of
Los Angeles, to that neighbourhood, or to that family, would be
difficult to determine.

The neighbourhood was not a ghetto. Blacks had begun to move
into it, but the Anglos had not begun to move out. "Nobody
moved," Beverly said firmly. There were Italian families and Mex-
ican families as well. It was a good, solid, middle-class working
neighbourhood. "Families were very tightly knit," Beverly said.
She was a beautiful woman at this point in her fifties, quite distinguished in bearing and appearance, very light-skinned, of Cre-
ole descent, her name at birth Guero, pronounced gay-ro, probably a variant of a French or Spanish spelling. Her mother had
remarried and the step-father of whom she spoke with such affection was named Collins, Tony Collins. "When there are four kids
in a home," she said, "one more doesn't make much difference. I

remember Ed brought his little drum set over to our place, and he used to practise there.

"I think he saw in our household what he felt he was missing. My mother never worked outside the home, and she was always there when we came home from school. And you know, a young boy with a drum set, that would drive most people crazy, but it didn't bother her.

"He was pretty much like he is now – very positive, very active, very much in love with life itself. He was the kind who would say that the glass was half full, not that it was half empty, even then. He's always been a giving person. He always sees where he can share."

In 1951, Ed joined the Cootie Williams band at the Savoy Ballroom in New York. He was in military service from 1952 to 1954, first as a drum instructor at Fort Ord, California, later with the Eighth Army Band in Korea. After his discharge, he returned to New York and worked with Dinah Washington, the Johnny Hodges band, Gil Melle, Jutta Hipp, and Toshiko Akiyoshi, and recorded with many of the best young players of his generation. He worked with Lennie Tristano, then with the Billy Taylor Trio.

"In 1958," said Taylor, who in addition to being a fine pianist is considered one of the major scholars of jazz and its history, "I was musical director of a show called *The Subject Is Jazz* on National Public Television. At the end of the thirteen weeks, I was asked by the producers to make a prediction: where is jazz going? I said, 'There's a young man who's just recorded a piece written by a friend of mine. I'm not good at predicting, but I believe this is one of the directions that jazz is going. George Russell has just written this piece called *Billy the Kid* and the soloist is Bill Evans.' I said, 'We don't have sufficient time to rehearse a work of this difficulty, so why don't we bring in the guys who did the record?' So we brought the band in and for some reason the drummer on the record date couldn't make the TV date. So Ed Thigpen, who was my drummer, read the son of a bitch at sight! I mean, sight read the son of a bitch! And played the hell out of it. He's one of the damnedest musicians on earth."

Just before Christmas of 1958, Thigpen advised Taylor that he had had an offer from Oscar Peterson. Taylor urged Ed to take the job, and leave with his blessing, since it would constitute a major advance in the drummer's career.

"I joined Oscar and Ray January 1, 1959," Ed said. "I had been called earlier in '58 for the job. It was a matter of how much bread. It seemed I asked for a little bit too much, and Norman Granz decided to get someone else, and they got Gene Gammage. I could have kicked myself. But, as they say, the Lord provided, and the call came anyway five months later.

"I first encountered Oscar in Japan. I was in Korea. I had gone down to Tokyo on R. and R., right before I came home. Jazz at the Phil was there. Naturally, I knew Ben Webster and most of the guys because of my father. And I knew Ray from New York. I was very young when I first met Ray, and he was very kind. He took me out and gave me a milk shake and sent me home.

"I started doing a lot of Prestige and Blue Note things, some dates with Coltrane, some things with Art Farmer and Kenny Dorham. I was recording just enough to get reviews every couple of months, and they were always very favourable. And I started moving up that way. And then I recorded Toshiko's first album in America, and Lee Morgan's first album. It was the young new ones coming around. Then, Ray, Kenny Burrell, and I recorded with Blossom Dearie.

"I always wanted to be with Oscar's group, even when Herb was with that band. I told Ray in Japan, 'The only thing wrong with this group is you need a drummer.' Ray said, 'Well, y'never know, kid.' I said, 'I need to play with this group. I love this group.' And they went out and proceeded to swing so hard I thought, 'Well, maybe I'll miss it, but I still would like to play with the group.' So it was four years later that I joined them. Yeah, it was a lot of pressure though. It was. Because whatever insecurities I had … I was in awe of those guys, I loved them, I really loved them, and when it's like that, you give everything you have. They were so heavy, so fantastic and, obviously, so acclaimed, that I was in awe of both of them. Ray was very kind. All the time. He just took me under his wing and saved me."

Peterson's was by this time the highest-paid jazz trio in the world. Along with the praise, Oscar had begun to garner some bad reviews. One of them was written by me, after a Jazz at the Philharmonic concert in Louisville, Kentucky – part of the same 1955 tour during which Lester Young committed his hilarious indiscretion in front of an open mike in Montreal. At that time I was music critic of the Louisville *Times*. Influenced perhaps by the memory of those RCA boogie-woogie records, I said what Peterson's detractors have always said, that he struck me as a cold player.

Four years later, in May 1959, a few months after Thigpen joined the trio, I became editor of *Down Beat*. My duties required that I make the acquaintance of prominent jazz musicians and put in protocol appearances at their performances in Chicago. A legend has grown up that you have to hear Oscar Peterson in person and at length and preferably in intimate conditions to know the scope and beauty of his work. I know that legend well. I helped start it. And I started it because it's true. I would go to hear the group at the London House. Thigpen and I became very close friends. Indeed, I became friends with all three men. But Thigpen and I developed a special relationship, one that still exists. Soon, I was going to hear the trio night after night not out of duty but out of love of its music, and of the men who were making it. Sometimes, after the gig, Oscar and I would sit up late in his hotel room, where he had a small electric piano, and he would show me things on the instrument, including chord voicings.

And the difference of philosophy between him and those who seek to play the piano as if it were a wind instrument became clear.

"I have always sought to play pianistically," he said. "I think most of the younger pianists don't want to face up to the job of mastering piano.

"Charlie Parker, of course, was a tremendous influence not only on the horns but on piano. Because so much piano playing is so linear, a great many people have thought you could eliminate it, as Gerry Mulligan did. But as far as I'm concerned, piano is too much instrument to be approached always in terms of horn lines.

"And so who are my influences? I think one *should* be influenced by a format.

"I listened to Tatum as a listener. But as a pianist, I admired the format, the approach. Art played *pianistically*. Most of the older pianists did – or do, as the case may be.

"And that's why I'm not impressed by most of the crop of younger pianists. I just don't hear what I want to hear from most of them. Consequently I can't bring myself to admire them. I admire the initial effort, but not the result.

"I can remember hearing most of the span of Art's records, and I've yet to hear something from the younger pianists that I haven't heard from Art in one vein or another."

"How about, say, Horace Silver, Erroll Garner, and Ahmad Jamal?" I asked.

"Each of these men," Oscar said, "is confined for a certain reason. Erroll because he's a stylist. We will never hear what he *might* have done if he'd studied. Horace pursues primarily the linear approach. Ahmad sticks to the type of abstract singing lines that he uses. All these men are pursuing one line of the instrument's potential."

"What about Bill Evans?" I said.

Evans had just been voted new star on piano in *Down Beat*'s International Jazz Critics' Poll. He was destined to become the most influential jazz pianist after Bud Powell, exerting in time an influence even on Oscar himself: Oscar's approach to ballads would be affected by Evans, as Evans had in his formative years been influenced by Peterson.

"About Bill it's hard to say at this point," Oscar answered. "It is like trying to judge the colour of a rose when the bud is only half opened." This was the question I put to him years later in New York, only to find he had not forgotten his Chicago answer.

"I was very close to Art Tatum. Personally. He used to tell me, 'You have the instrument, so you have nothing to worry about.'

"A lot of these pianists don't have the basis to start with. Because a man is working within one aesthetic framework, that's not to say he shouldn't therefore use the rest of the scope of the instrument. I think this is why a lot of pianists never grow. One thing that has made me, subconsciously, never want to become as hot, commercially, as Ahmad or Erroll is that I don't want to be confined to only one part of what I do. A piano can be as subtle as a French horn in the distance or as driving as the Basie band.

"When I am working, it's a challenge, not a chore. But I'm not afraid of the instrument. I love it.

"You should be able to build. You shouldn't build to a summit only to fall off. That is another thing wrong with much jazz piano. When the pianist shifts into high, often he's used up all he's got to get there.

"You know, it was not as a trio pianist that I really admired Art. He could never be subservient enough to be a trio pianist. I'm not trying to make my group piano with rhythm accompaniment.

"There is a danger in trio piano. Most of the younger men are trio pianists. It means thinking so sympathetically with the other two that you worry about washing yourself away pianistically.

"The first thing I'll decry is this sleep-walking approach to swinging piano. Most pianists don't swing because basically they don't believe the instrument *can* be swung that hard – which Erroll disproved.

"The problem is that most pianists today don't think dynamically. They start way up, and then have nowhere to go. As Lester Young used to call them, the little kiddies ... When I hear them talking, I feel a little more confident about what I'm doing.

"Pianists must be *taught*. If a man has no technique, if he has been self-taught, you'll hear it said that he has an open mind. Not true. On the contrary, he has grooved himself. But the classically trained musician has been trained to take in new aspects, new material. You're equipped with the technical tools you'll need. It is not a matter of blatant change from classical piano to jazz; it's a matter of modification. But there are inadequacies when you apply it to jazz." Clearly, he was responding to the recurring charge that he had "too much" technique. I remember cautioning him that some of his opinions about other pianists could cause resentment. "It's the way I feel about piano," he said simply.

That Oscar Peterson could be flamboyant and merely dazzling was true. But there was another side to his personality, best

discovered late at night when the drunks had gone home and only
the music lovers lingered on at the London House. This was the
time when he would play ballads, when – no longer needing to
dominate noisy crowds – he would sink into pensive sensitivity and
play with an exquisite simplicity that has been too rarely captured
on records. Midnight would come, and Liszt would sound more
like Chopin – and Debussy. It was during this time that I changed
my mind about Oscar Peterson.

Oscar's relations with other pianists have always been an interesting mixture of the critical and supportive. As far back as when he
was twenty-six, he was giving the benefit of his knowledge and
experience to other pianists. Chicago pianist Norman Simmons
told Mark Gardner in a 1960 interview for the British publication
Jazz Monthly.

"Oscar Peterson is responsible for opening the way to technical
accomplishment in my case. From some incorrect playing [stand-
ing up] ... I grew a cyst on my wrist. I met Oscar [on] my first gig
after taking off the bandages. I had nothing to which I could refer
for regaining what facility I previously had. I was playing ... with
Flip Phillips and Bill Harris at the old Blue Note in Chicago about
1951. Oscar and Ray Brown were just a duo then and I remember
Oscar was singing some also.

"In the few minutes between our sets, Oscar stopped me and we
sat at one of the tables. He said he liked my potential and wanted to
show me a couple of exercises which would help my technique. He
demonstrated about three table exercises. One sounded like a
drummer playing paradiddles, rapid and very distinct. One was a
wrist rotation which he did so fast his fingers disappeared. These
exercises turned my playing over for the next two years and I still
find that approach essential today in my practice ... He also told me
not to develop favorite fingers while playing but to play on all of
them and the weaker ones more.

"Oscar told me that no matter who I follow to the piano – him or
anyone else – 'for that moment *you* are the only piano player in the
world.' I played better on the next set."

He gave similar advice to Eddie Higgins, who led the house trio (the local group required by union regulations to appear opposite a visiting group) at the London House during the years Oscar played there regularly. Higgins, a handsome, blond young man with New England ancestry, somewhat resembled actor Richard Denning. He worked opposite the Peterson trios – the Ellis and Thigpen editions – at the London House fourteen times in twelve years of the 1950s and '60s.

In 1985, a well-established jazz pianist, Higgins described the disorientation any number of pianists have experienced in playing opposite Peterson. "Oscar and Ray and Ed Thigpen were having a particularly hot night," he said. "Even when one or another of them wasn't 'on', the trio was awesome – in my opinion the greatest piano trio in the history of jazz. And on this occasion, they were all on, and the total effect was just devastating.

"After they had finished their third encore to a five-minute standing, whistling, screaming, stomping ovation and left the bandstand, it was my unenviable task to follow them with *my* trio. I was proud of [bassist] Richard Evans and [drummer] Marshall Thompson, and we had developed a good reputation of our own among the various groups with whom we shared the bandstand in those days. But there wasn't anyone who could have followed Oscar Peterson that night. I mean, there was, I swear, smoke and steam coming out of the piano when the set ended.

"Well, I did what I was being paid to do, but with that sinking feeling you get when you're down two sets to love, the score in the third set is two–five, and you're looking across the net at John McEnroe.

"After a lacklustre set of forty minutes, which seemed like three hours, we left the stand to polite applause, and I started to look for a hole to climb into. Oscar had been sitting with friends in booth 16 – remember? – and as I attempted to sneak past him into the bar, he reached out and grabbed my arm.

"'I want to *talk* to you,' he said in a grim tone of voice.

"I followed him out into the lobby of the building, which of course was deserted at that time of night. He backed me up against the wall and started poking a forefinger into my chest. It still hurts when I think about it.

"'What the hell was *that* set all about?' he said.

"I started a feeble justification but he cut me off. 'Bullshit! If you couldn't play, you wouldn't *be* here. If I *ever* hear you play another dumb-ass set like that, I'm going to come up there personally and break your arm! You not only embarrassed Richard and Marshall, you embarrassed *me* in front of my friends, just when I had been telling them how proud I am of you, and how great you play.

"'I know we're having a good night, but there are plenty of nights when you guys put the heat on *us*, and if you don't believe me, ask Ray and Ed. We walk in the door, and you're smoking up there, and we look at each other and say, "Oh oh, no coasting on the first set tonight!" So just remember one thing, Mr. Higgins, when you go up there to play, don't compare yourself to me or anyone else. You play *your* music *your* way, and play it the best you have in you, *every* set, *every* night. That's called professionalism.'

"And he turned and walked back into the club without a further word.

"I've never forgotten that night for two reasons. It was excellent advice from someone I admired and respected tremendously. And it showed that he cared about me deeply."

Similar stories are told by pianists all over the world.

"Piano players are a product of a certain amount of intimidation, partly because of the nature of the instrument itself," Oscar said to me once. "And they do a fair amount of accompanying, vocalists and horns and other instruments. And that can be a hair-raising experience, depending on who you're accompanying and how that person feels from night to night. So some pianists get a little browbeaten, and they get this inner rage that they manage to keep dormant. And they start to think, 'I'm gonna play whatever I have to for this cat, but past that, I'm not giving him a thing.' And when they get their solo chance, they *go* for it.

"Pianists are the worst old women in the world. When they meet each other, they gossip. There's a lot to gossip about. Because of the very set-up of the instrument, there are so many ways of going wrong." He laughed. "You'll be playing your buns off with your left hand and playing a fairly good line with your right, you'll have the time together and everything, and maybe you don't pedal right. No matter how good the performance was, the pianists will say, 'You know something funny? He just doesn't have his densities together with the pedals, does he?'

"Pianists *revel* in this.

"You can almost categorize attitudes by the instruments.

"Guitar players are really clannish. They're the inside group. You can't get *into* that group, I don't care how well you play. You can come to town with the world's *worst* guitarist, and he will outdraw you in the dressing room, with the other guitarists. And if you make the mistake of going over to that room to say hello, you're gonna get frosted.

"Bass players are very protective of each other. I would find it almost unbelievable if you told me you'd ever heard a bass player say something about another bass player that wasn't good. If you look at the history of the instrument in jazz, you can see why. They were always the slaves in the early days. The public never used to notice bass players, until Ray Brown, Scotty LaFaro, Niels Pedersen, and so forth. They were always the guys who came into the group and were given one order, 'Walk!' Once in a while they'd be thrown a bone, like, 'Walk – one chorus solo.' Finally they managed to break away, because of the proficient players who came along.

"Drummers I can't account for. I'm not even going to get into that one."

"Maybe the noise gets to them," I said.

He laughed some more. "Now saxophone players tend to be very mysterious. They're even mysterious with each other. Maybe it's because they're going to go out and be combatants on the stage. They'd be in the room, talking to each other. 'Hey, man.' Very friendly, right? And you could tell there was something underneath all that. And I'd think, 'Hey, I don't know what he *isn't* saying, but whatever it is, I don't think I want to hear it.'" And he laughed again.

Oscar Peterson *c.* 1944. That summer he turned 19. He had been a member of the Johnny Holmes orchestra since 1942, and Count Basie was singing his praises to American musicians and journalists.

Playing a duet with his father. Daniel Peterson, a CPR porter who had taught himself music on a portable organ during his youth as a merchant seaman, was determined that his four children would escape their Montreal ghetto through music.

Oscar and his brother, the tragic Chuck. Chuck played trumpet with the Montreal Garrison Band during the war years, but his true love was the piano. His dream of a career on that instrument ended when he lost his left forearm in a factory accident.

By late 1947, Oscar was leading his first trio, and performing at the Alberta Lounge, close to Windsor Station, out of which his father worked. The trio, with Ozzie Roberts on bass and Clarence Jones on drums, is seen here during a CBC radio session.

The great trio with Herb Ellis and Ray Brown. Oscar exchanges a word with Ray at Toronto's Town Tavern, some time in the mid-1950s. He constantly pressured Ellis and Brown, and himself, to ever higher attainments on their instruments and as a group.

Oscar and Lil Peterson with their five children, gathered by their custom-built stereo set, in 1959. Despite the smiles, the marriage was coming under strain from the pressures of Oscar's career and his incesssant travelling.

The next trio. Ray Brown had recommended Herb Ellis to Oscar. When Ellis left the group to settle in California, Ray recommended his replacement, Edmund Thigpen, "the thinking man's drummer," as one critic dubbed him. Oscar remembers the new group as "six years of un-believable music."

In 1972 Oscar Peterson was invested as an Officer of the Order of Canada. He received the decoration from Governor General Roland Michener.

The next great guitar trio, at the Montreal Forum in 1972, the group Oscar called Pedersen, Peterson, and Pass – Joe Pass on the left, Niels Pedersen on the right. For one of his practical jokes Oscar used a synthesizer to sound like a guitar, recorded at dazzling speed things impossible on the guitar, then phoned Pass and played the tape for him, saying it was by a new young Japanese guitarist he had discovered.

With Vladimir Horowitz in Los Angeles. Horowitz played a matinée at the Dorothy Chandler Pavilion just before Oscar was due to open the Pablo Jazz Festival with an evening concert.

Oscar with a Grammy Award for best instrumental performance, 1979. He has won innumerable awards and polls.

Oscar Peterson and his manager-producer Norman Granz at a recording session. Theirs has been one of the longest professional associations, and friendships, in jazz history.

Oscar Peterson shares a laugh with singer Anne Murray just before they are invested as Companions of the Order of Canada in 1983.

At home in his studio, surrounded by synthesizers and recording equipment. Insatiably curious about such things as cars and cameras, he went into electronic music with the same intense concentration he had applied to the piano in his youth.

Back in his home town, Oscar waves to the crowd after a concert closing the Montreal International Jazz Festival.

Eddie Higgins' bassist in those London House engagements, Richard Evans – later a well-known arranger and record producer in Los Angeles – had feelings of admiration for Ray Brown similar to those Higgins held for Oscar. About working opposite Ray, he said, "It's as if your brother-in-law were going over a cliff in your new Cadillac. You don't know whether to be drugged or delighted." He smiled slyly and added, "One could lose one's cool, right quick."

"The trio with Ed and Ray," Oscar said, "that was six years of unbelievable music. Again, where you had a tightness and a cohesiveness between members of the trio. I seldom had to call tunes. I'd just say, 'Okay, it's here. One, two ...' And for some reason we'd know, if it was the right moment. As strange as it all seems. There were tremendous repertory challenges in that trio, too.

"Ed Thigpen. Ed Thigpen was ... a very reflective yet complete percussionist. He wasn't really a drummer, he was a percussionist. He had that feeling, all the time he was sitting at the drums, that it wasn't just drums he was sitting at. That's Ed Thigpen. People may or may not know it, but *I* know it. It's the way he thinks. He sees his drums as a complete, not instrument, but orchestra. Whatever he wants it to be. He approaches everything that way. To the point where," and Oscar chuckled at the memory of those years, "at times when we wanted to really get down into the gorilla bag, and he was in his reflective mood, Ray would *stomp* on him, y'know, say, 'I don't want none of that shit, you know what I want, put it up here for me.'

"Of course I never got into that with them. As much as possible, I'd stay out of the rhythm section end of it. They had to solve that. I wasn't playing rhythm, I was playing solo. And to play rhythm for a bass player ... You're not going to sit at the piano and play four.

"Ed Thigpen has a touch on the drums that you seldom hear. Jo Jones had that same thing. Ed was not the gorilla Bobby Durham was. Ed came in another door altogether. And if you mixed that with Ray Brown! At that time, there was a question of, 'Oscar can't pull all that off, it's all right to do that with the guitar, because it's light, it's up here, you can skim over the keys and all that.' When we brought in Ed, it was a chance to prove that I play the way I play, that's it. No matter who's sitting there. Unless you're going to hit me over the head with a building."

Shortly after Thigpen joined the trio in 1959, the group went into a studio to perform a marathon feat of recording.

British critic Richard Palmer noted in a 1984 monograph on Peterson's recordings that the new trio played four weeks at the London House that summer, re-recording much of the Peterson-Brown-Ellis repertoire, making 124 tracks in six days, and "throwing in an appearance at the Chicago *Playboy* jazz festival for good measure."

Many of the eight stereophonic albums that resulted from these sessions were remakes of the early "songbook" albums. No one, not even Richard Palmer, claims that they are first-rate Peterson. Indeed, the albums are cited by the detractors of Norman Granz in the argument that he has, throughout Peterson's career, heavily over-recorded his most successful artist.

CHAPTER II

TRIAL TERM IN TORONTO

In response to the constant requests from other musicians for counsel and direction, Oscar, Ed, Ray, Butch Watanabe, and composer Phil Nimmons established the Advanced School of Contemporary Music (ASCM) at 21 Park Road in Toronto, opening their doors in January 1960.

It was by no means the first attempt to teach the playing of jazz in an academic setting. Teddy Wilson began teaching improvisation at Juilliard in New York well before that. The ASCM wasn't even the first jazz school. The Berklee School of Music in Boston had been in operation for some time. Indeed, there were by this time an estimated five thousand stage-band programs in U.S. universities, colleges, and high schools, and Herb Ellis's alma mater, North Texas State University, had a full degree-granting jazz program that was turning out players and composers of advanced professional skill. But no school offered to the same extent as the ASCM the stimulation of practical regular contact with several professionals of such stature.

Oscar and Ray had been considering such a school for some time. "Finally we decided to do it," Oscar told the late Don De-Micheal, my successor as editor of *Down Beat*. "We didn't have the funds, but it wasn't just a matter of money; we were working and couldn't afford to get a building and everything until we could see what was going to happen. We were a little unsure of the format, so we set up a trial term, using some of the principles we intended to use in the full-scale thing."

A year later, the school occupied a sixteen-room house and had all the students its faculty could handle. It was a very practical school. In addition to studying with Peterson, a pianist would have the chance to play with Ray Brown and Ed Thigpen, and a bassist would gain experience from playing with Peterson and Thigpen. A number of excellent musicians are alumni of the courses, pianists Carol Britto, Mike Longo, and Wray Downes, and bassist Jay Leonhart among them.

"I give my students something to do," Oscar said, "but that doesn't mean they can't go to see Phil, Ed, or Ray. If, say, Phil gives a student an assignment, the student might come to me and ask me what I think of it. I won't *do* it for them, but I can get them started.

"And in the forums" – a term the school used for public performance before students and faculty – "Ray's going to criticize the piano player's playing from a bass player's standpoint. If I tell the piano player that's a bad voicing, it has just as much and more meaning coming from Ray. He might stop them and say, 'What was that chord? I can't find any note to play. He'll take a bass and have them play the chord, and he says, 'You got C-E-G-A-D-C-A-C – what am I going to play?'

"There's no way out. You're criticized from every possible level. It's nothing to find Ed Thigpen going after a piano or bass student."

The students were required to pay attention to the music's history, as well: Oscar would have them listen to records by the major figures in the music's evolution, including Duke Ellington, Coleman Hawkins, Lester Young, Dizzy Gillespie, Charlie Parker, and Art Tatum. Some of them would protest that they already knew the recordings, had indeed been listening to them for years.

They were unprepared for the first encounter with the man trained by Daniel Peterson. Oscar would say: "Describe the background supplied behind the trumpet solo. Didn't hear that. Can you tell whether the drummer played sticks or brushes in this part of the record? Harmonic structure? Form of the tune?" They would begin to listen with new ears.

Peterson was at the time emphatic that he was not trying to produce imitations of himself or his trio. "We're not building robots," he told DeMicheal. "First thing, we're not teaching a style. If you come into my classroom and play what I play, you're in trouble. If you come in playing anything of Erroll Garner's, you're in trouble."

The proof of his method is that none of the students he turned out – Carol Britto, Mike Longo – plays at all like him, nor for that matter do they play like each other. Longo remembers:

"He put the emphasis on two things. How to play and what to play. How to play involved your touch, your time, your tone, your technique, and your taste, what he called the five T's. I remember in one lesson he said, 'Mike, if you want a career as a player, you're going to have to have a touch that's impeccable, your time has to be beyond reproach, your tone exquisite, your technique flawless, and your taste a thing of beauty.' What to play had to do with harmonic progressions, how to develop runs, how to handle points of rest in ballads, how to put a piano arrangement together.

"If you examine a Chopin étude, the techniques I learned from Oscar are exactly the same. The left-hand techniques and textures – he put a lot of emphasis on that. Piano is piano. Art Tatum played that way also."

Oscar had given up Montreal residence more than a year earlier, in the early summer of 1958. He had been travelling to Toronto fairly frequently, not only to play engagements but to work with his close friend Phil Nimmons, who would write the first orchestration of his *Canadiana Suite*. Oscar found the night-life of Montreal increasingly decadent, with go-go dancers "and what we called the walkers, the girls who walked across the stage," replacing musicians in the clubs. "I would arrive at the airport," he said, "and Phil would pick me up at the airport and drive me to his house in Scarborough, and the grass would be showing through while in Montreal you couldn't find my house for snow." So he and Lil and the children moved to Chrysler Crescent in Scarborough, a suburb just east of Toronto, on the shore of Lake Ontario.

A fresh incident of racism occurred when Oscar bought the house. Residents of the area talked of taking up a petition to prevent the family's move there. Friends urged Oscar to go public about it, or to file suit. Knowing the law was on his side, he did nothing.

"I wasn't even worried about it," he said years later. "What could they do? You know the funny thing about it, the way it ended? They ended up using it as a selling point in the area, and they thought I didn't know. Friends of mine said, 'Are you getting a commission on the sale of houses in this area?'"

Ray Brown and Ed Thigpen had obtained Canadian residence visas and had also moved to Toronto, Ray and his wife, Cecille, taking an apartment in the Avenue Road–St. Clair area and Ed and his wife, Lois, an apartment in suburban Don Mills.

And an ugly little racial incident involving Ed and Lois briefly arose. They were refused admittance to the Edison Hotel, where Woody Herman and his small group (two of whom were black) were appearing. The story made a blazing front-page headline February 1, 1960, in the Toronto *Telegram*, whose flamboyant editor, Doug McFarlane, simply loved this kind of splashy journalism. (He had been known to write a headline and order a reporter to find a story that would fit it.)

"Barred from Bar" read the headline above a photo of Ed and Lois. The story reported that Ed had phoned earlier and been told that reservations were unnecessary. Ed told the newspaper that he and Lois had arrived shortly after midnight and met at the door a man he learned later was the proprietor of the Edison.

"He said we couldn't go in because the bar was just closing," Ed told *Telegram* reporter Frank Jones. "We said O.K., we'd go into the dining room. 'But you haven't reservations,' he told us, 'so you can't come in. Why don't you just go away and come back some other time?' he said.

"As we were leaving," Ed told the paper, "a group of white people were going in. We asked them if they had reservations, and they said they didn't. They got in without trouble.

"I went back and asked the owner why they had been allowed in without reservations.

"He said, 'Look here, I don't want any trouble. I told you you could not come in here. Now you want to know why, I'll tell you: I don't want any mixed couples in here!'"

Ed said that as he and Lois were leaving, a group of people who saw what was happening told him, "We're with you on this," and themselves turned away. A doorman told Ed: "Don't fight this. You'll lose."

The owner told the newspaper, "Sure I told them they couldn't go in – because the place was full. If we're full, we don't let anyone in – blue, yellow, or red.

"I did not refuse to let them in because the man was coloured.

"These coloured people are funny. They have a chip on their shoulder. If you refuse them anything, they always say it's because of their colour."

This of the literate poet of percussion, Edmund Thigpen, the thinking man's drummer, sensitive optimist who always saw the bottle half full rather than half empty, this brilliant musician who had sight-read *Billy the Kid*, reduced now to one of "these coloured people with a chip on their shoulder."

"Why should I discriminate?" the owner said to the *Telegram* reporter. "I'm Jewish."

Afterwards, Oscar pressed on Ed the point that the newspapers had been on his side, that the *system* did not support the owner.

Edmund told the newspaper that, in spite of the incident, he and Lois were sold on Canada and impressed by the friendliness of neighbours they had met. "I guess you meet the odd biased individual anywhere in the world," Ed said.

Twenty-six years later, neither Ed nor Oscar recalled the incident clearly. In self-protection each of them had buried it far down in memory.

At the pinnacle of his career, Oscar Peterson appeared to have everything the boy from St. Antoine could have wanted – world fame, friendship, the school he had dreamed of forming, and a happy marriage. He had acquired land on a lake in the Haliburton region of Ontario and built a summer house there. He was immersed in a hobby, namely photography – and famous for the scope and expense of his equipment. "He doesn't buy a camera," Butch Watanabe said, "he buys a complete system." And he would get rid of it as soon as something new came along, manifesting his passion for gadgetry. "I'm afraid of the cameras," Oscar said once.

"Every hour I spend with them is an hour away from the piano."

In an article published in the October 25, 1958, issue of *Maclean's*, reporter June Callwood described going to the Chrysler Crescent house as Oscar was sitting down to his afternoon breakfast with Norman, then five.

"He always waits to have breakfast with me, whenever I'm home," Oscar told Callwood. Oscar Jr., then six, approached him shyly. "You want some too?" Oscar Sr. asked. The boy nodded. "He's already eaten," Lil said, serving scrambled eggs from her kitchen. "I'll give him part of mine," Oscar Sr. said, and the boys ate with him at the table.

Oscar was then thirty-two. "He is a huge man," Callwood wrote, "over six foot one and weighing two hundred and forty; she is small, trim, and quiet. Both credit this, a manifestation of the balance of their relationship, with the success of their marriage." June Callwood is the only person who ever called Lil Peterson small.

And the article contains this curious passage of ecstatic prose: "Oscar Peterson, rated by many the best jazz pianist alive, spends his working hours in the lemon-blues world of jazz music, bowing in his tuxedo and cummerbund to applause in Carnegie Hall or the Hollywood Bowl, watching cigarette smoke drift through thin spotlights on nightclub bandstands in New York and Chicago, goading himself to perform brilliantly in the embalming environment of recording studios. He sleeps restlessly by day, rising in the full afternoon to eat breakfast, and rides airplanes between concert bookings in Europe or the Orient.

"Few careers offer so many obstacles to the likelihood of a cohesive marriage and sound family life, but Peterson has both. He lives with his pretty wife and five merry-eyed children in a four-bedroom bungalow in Toronto. His friends know him to be a loving and stern father, insisting on better behavior than most parents can exact from their children, a sensitive and positive husband whose 11-year marriage is weatherproof, and a conscientious citizen. He once astounded Montreal police by reporting an unwitnessed collision with a parked car."

There was another incident involving a car that astounded police, this time in Toronto. The story, which has been blown up to the proportions of legend among his friends, has it that he once tore the door off the car of a motorist who offended him. Oscar denies this. Yet the real story is as funny as the myth. This is Oscar's version:

He bought Lil a new Buick convertible as a birthday present. She baked a chocolate cake, which they took that evening to the home of friends for a small celebration. Oscar took the wheel as they headed home. And an importunate driver began to get on his nerves.

"This cat was doing the in and out," he recalled. "It was a two-lane road, and he was trying to pass where there wasn't room, there was oncoming traffic, so I wouldn't let him pass. And I was getting madder, because he kept trying to force me over. So finally I said, 'You know what, I'm going to fix it so that he's going to have to stop at that light at Larchmount.' I knew there was a light there, I don't know whether he knew it or not. Sure enough, he pulled up to the light. And I ran over to his car, and he quick rolled the window up and locked the doors. And I was so incensed and I'm screaming at him, and he wouldn't get out of the car. He rolled the window down and said, 'What's the matter with you?'

"I said, 'You get out of the car, and I'll show you what's wrong with me.' And in the furor, I grabbed the door handle and yanked. It was an older car, and obviously the thing was loose, and I pulled the whole thing out, it came out, the handle, the backplate, and the bolts ... When he saw it come out, he looked, 'What?', he couldn't believe what had happened. When I looked at it, I was so mad, we were in front of a shopping centre, and I threw it up into the shopping centre, and he went around me and split, he backed up and took off, *swoosh*, and Lil said, 'Come on, let's go home.'

"When we got home, we put what was left of the cake in the house, and Lil said, 'Why don't we go out for a nice quiet drive, get your nerves down?' So we went out. And then I turned down O'Connor Drive or Victoria Avenue or something. And all of a sudden, there was a police car parked at the block. I wasn't speeding or anything. It was about two o'clock in the morning. And around the corner he comes. And he runs me over to the curb. So I start to get out of the car. And he's sort of got his hand near his gun, and he says, 'I want your driver's licence, sir, but I don't want anything else but that, and be careful how you do it.'

"He said, 'Easy,' and I got my licence, and just handed it over, and he said, 'Thank you. Now would you just stand there quietly.' And he went to his car and he said something on the radio. And the next thing I know, minutes later, here come two more police cars, and all these cats get out. And one of them put the flashlight on the licence. He apparently recognized the name. And then he came over, and he said, 'Oscar, what the hell have you been doing?'

"I said, 'What do you mean, I wasn't doing anything ...' I thought he was talking about this. He said, 'What did you do to the guy's car?' I said, 'Oh, that idiot! Where is he?' And I got mad all over! And he said, 'Never mind that. He made a complaint, he said some gorilla tore his car door handle off and threw it away.' I said, 'Where is he, why didn't he complain to my face?' He said, 'Why don't you just get back in your car? We'll handle it from here.' So next day, I got a call from the guy. Eric Smith got into it."

Oscar's old friend Eric was by now sales manager of a Toronto automobile dealership, Crosstown Buick. Feeling sheepish about the incident in the light of day, and finding out, furthermore, that the driver of the other car was about to leave on his honeymoon, Oscar arranged to have the car door repaired immediately by Eric's company.

Oscar moved the family from Chrysler Crescent to the suburb of North York. The new home overlooked one of the many wooded ravines that vein Toronto, making it one of the most beautiful cities in North America, particularly in the autumn. These were happy years.

Everyone who knew the family has trouble describing Lil. Yet she was universally liked, a tall woman, big-boned but by no means fat. "What a marvellous woman she was," Eric Smith says. "So quiet, so self-effacing. Good mother. Good cook. Good hostess. Always a pleasure to be with. You'd have a hard time scratching beneath that surface to know Lil. I don't think any of us ever saw any strife between them. She would go along with any kibitz. If

Oscar would start one of his famous put-ons, she'd side right with him, she knew how to do it.

"We had a lot of good parties during those years. She loved them, or at least she seemed to. Our friends included Stan Helleur, the newspaper columnist, and Frank Clair, who had come up from the States to be coach of the Toronto Argonauts. And of course Maurie and Daisy Kessler."

Maurice Kessler is a stockbroker and a vice-president of Standard Securities. "I remember at one of the parties," Eric said, "at my apartment on Bathurst, just above St. Clair, we had a thing called Husband of the Year. Ray Brown made a trophy for it, bought one somewhere and had it engraved. Each husband had two minutes to state his case. The wife could talk for a minute or so about why her husband should be voted for. Ray's wife, Cecille, was hardly able to speak for laughing. Lil spoke for Oscar. She said, 'He's so good, he brings back such lovely things from Europe for me and the children.' I had on my Air Force uniform, to try to get the patriotic vote. It didn't work. We'd rigged it so that Maurie Kessler would win. But that's the kind of party we used to have, and Lil was always a part of it, in her quiet and passive way. And we used to make eight-millimetre home movies, with very corny acting."

Maurie Kessler was close friends with the revered cornetist Bobby Hackett. One night Eric and Maurie took Hackett over to meet Oscar at Oscar's home. They had a few drinks and ate and listened to records until the early morning.

In the car, on the way back to Hackett's hotel, Bobby said, "You know, I wish I'd had the nerve to take my horn out of the car. I'd have loved to play with Oscar, but I didn't want to impose."

The next day, Oscar called Maurie and said, "I would have asked Bobby if he had his horn with him, but I didn't want to be presumptuous."

They never did get to play together.

Oscar, Ray Brown, and Ed Thigpen missed the stimulation of constant playing. Growing bored during a weekend, Oscar would telephone Ray and say, "You think you've got it today? Oh you do, do you? Well why don't you come on over, and we'll just see if you've got it. And pick up Thigpen on your way."

And they would play together by the hour. "Some of the best playing I've ever done," Oscar said to me almost wistfully at the time, "has been in the basement with Ed and Ray."

The glowing June Callwood article notwithstanding, the marriage was faced with problems. And students at the Advanced School of Contemporary Music found it difficult to sustain themselves financially during the five months of the school's teaching year – as did Peterson, Brown, and Thigpen, who were turning down concerts and night-club engagements during that period.

"To be frank about it," Oscar told Don DeMicheal in 1962, "the financial problems were so great that we considered closing it this year. As much as I believe in the school and what we're doing, you can't go to the point where you endanger the health and happiness of yourself and your family. And that goes for all of us. So we figured a one-month term was a better working period than a five-month one."

After the third year, the school term was shortened to two one-month segments, six months apart. Finally, in 1964, the Advanced School of Contemporary Music closed its doors permanently.

Of Oscar's marriage, Daisy said: "It was a childhood romance. You know, it's hard being married to musicians and artists and people who travel a lot. A man and a woman lose that contact with each other. Neither one really gets to know the other. Oscar and Lil decided that they were going to have certain hours when they could be together. Musicians might drop in after the gig at night. But this is the time you've been up with the children all day, and you're not ready to entertain. Yet you want to please your husband, naturally, and entertain his guests, but you have to get up early next morning with the children for school. Or you've been drained by them all day."

Oscar's view of it is in accord, as indeed is that of most people who knew the young couple. Oscar said:

"We were both probably too young. I didn't see that then. You can't tell youngsters that when they think they're in love. And, from a career standpoint, I see now where there's no way in the world where I should have been married. I was fighting for a certain niche in the musical world. All the travelling that was necessitated by the profession certainly didn't help. I missed an awful lot of the kids' growing up. Lil was just a soft woman, she was not an abrasive person in any way. She found it difficult to cope with some of these things, because she was easily embarrassed. She was very shy. Once she knew you, fine, but some of that was difficult for her. If a band was in town, or a group, inevitably they'd be by the house, or we'd go down to hear them, and they'd all come to the table, and I'm sure this was all overwhelming for her. And she couldn't do a lot of travelling at the time."

He used a curiously vivid expression to describe her reaction when he would tell her he was bringing someone famous or influential to the house. "Right away you'd see the panic behind the eyes," he said.

"And I was always a fireball person about learning things. Finding out. So I always had something going. If it wasn't photography, it was audio, if it wasn't audio, it was art, if it wasn't art, it was something else. Because, don't forget, I gave up some of my education early to get into music. I didn't even finish high school. I didn't have a phobia about it, but there were things I wanted to know. So I was into everything. Name it, I was into it. And it must have been very demanding, because I forced a lot of living into the time I was home. In those days I wasn't at home as much as I am now. Coming home for two weeks was like coming home now for three months. And I'd *pack* it. I tried to fulfil the commitments we had with friends, who were anxious to see us. Because Lil didn't go that many places. She was a secluded person.

"I'm sure it put quite a strain on Lil – plus being cooped up with the kids. And then my demands when I came home, the things that changed just because I *was* home. Then my time. I *did* get up many times with the kids just to see them. And she had to be up in the morning with them. I think what happened then is that I started growing in areas that she couldn't because she wasn't involved in those areas. And I became dissatisfied with wanting to do certain things that maybe she didn't feel like doing. Which I now understand, but I didn't understand then.

"I wasn't tolerant of it then. And you're not that way when you're young. I realize now that there is one tremendous pitfall, for lack of a better word, or cliff you can easily go over ...

"Public adulation creates a certain amount of skeptical thinking in one's mate. It's natural. Aside from the quote unquote 'other woman.' There is a thing about the fawning factor, if you will, that is involved in this profession. And I'm not saying this in a sarcastic way. People come to your table, and they don't just say, 'Mr. Peterson, I heard you and really enjoyed you.' They'll come over and say, 'Oh God, are you really something!' And they mean it, they're trying to express what they get out of this. But don't forget, the person that's with you sits through all of this. That's what I think psychiatrists ought to look into in these situations. What is the effect on the other person? What is the real effect? It's been touched on, but it's never really been explored and explained. I really would like to know what it is that takes place in the mate. I think there develops in the mate almost an aversion to this. I think this contributes to the dissolution of a partnership. It gives an inept feeling to the other person. 'What do I mean in all of this? Where do I fit? What am I?' With the result in many cases in show business I have heard of – and taken exception to, I might add – where girlfriends and wives say, 'He couldn't do this without me.' And I look at them and think, 'Don't give me that thing about I'm-out-there-with-him.' Yes, there is a certain pre-performance contribution to your comfort, your belief, your happiness, and all that, yes – but once you're out there ..."

To the absolute astonishment of Maurie and Daisy Kessler, Ray and Cecille Brown, Eric and Lucille Smith, and all their other friends, Oscar and Lil separated, then were divorced.

CHAPTER 12

TEARING DOWN OSCAR

Oscar Peterson won the *Down Beat* Reader's Poll for the first time in 1950 – only months after the September 1949 appearance at Carnegie Hall. Just that quickly did he climb in public esteem. The critics were slower to respond. He did not win the magazine's International Jazz Critics' Poll until 1952. By 1972, he had won the Reader's Poll fourteen times. But he would never again win the Critics' Poll. "By the time Ellis left," British critic Richard Palmer wrote, "Peterson was a hugely-established jazz star; but his critical reputation was, by and large, low."

Perhaps the earliest sign of critical disenchantment came in a piece by the late John Mehegan, jazz critic of the New York *Herald Tribune,* which appeared in the June 13, 1957, *Down Beat.* "Oscar Peterson is probably the finest jazz pianist in the world today," Mehegan's essay began. "In terms of concept, swinging, repertoire, in his handling of the three R's of music (rhythm, melody, and harmony) and above all in the high level of communication with an audience, Oscar is certainly the most mature."

But four paragraphs later, Mehegan begins making note of an uneasiness Oscar aroused in him: "The evolving of Oscar's career is a curious one, in that instead of following the classic design of ever increasing expression and control, we have here a reverse process of a gradual diminution of his expressive powers. Oscar is probably the most recorded pianist in the world today, and a study of his releases for the last eight years moves from a high point in 1949 (*Oscar Peterson at Carnegie*) to an unbelievable nadir around 1954 (*Plays Pretty and Sings*) and then moves up with the appearance of his composer series (Ellington, Kern, Rodgers,

Gershwin)." Mehegan is referring to the first composers' series recordings with Ellis; the second set, with Thigpen, had not yet been made.

"Oscar's consummate artistry dominates this trio on a plane that probably no other pianist in the world today could sustain. For all of this, one sometimes feels that Oscar has paid a musical price in becoming a stellar package to be shuttled about the world in the ubiquitous orbits of Norman Granz. To some, the answer lies in the simple fact that Oscar has become commercial."

Mehegan urges Peterson to "meet the ultimate challenge of any pianist, namely to play solo piano." Oscar had made a solo album on one of the early Granz labels, Clef. "In *Piano Interpretations*," Mehegan wrote, "there is an example of Oscar's solo playing that is vague, aimless, and completely lacking in any kind of architecture. To abandon the security of his sinecure with JATP and meet this challenge would indeed be a painful decision for Oscar, yet he stands today at the crossroads of this possible achievement."

As harsh reviews piled up over the years, Oscar would take to denouncing critics in interviews all over the world. Oscar has consistently dismissed their opinions on the grounds that they did not know what they were talking about. There is of course no other way to deal with the pain harsh criticism produces. But Mehegan was not so easily dismissed: he was himself a jazz pianist – though a somewhat rigid one – and teacher, and, later, author of a textbook on jazz piano that became widely used. He taught jazz at the University of Bridgeport, lectured at Yale University, and gave clinics not only in universities all over the United States but in Scandinavia as well.

Four years later, in London, critic Max Harrison – also a pianist by training, and known equally as a reviewer of classical music and jazz – wrote in the January 1960 *Jazz Journal*, "If Peterson's work is individual and always immediately recognizable that is because of its negative qualities. His technique, at least in digital dexterity, is formidable and he clearly has abundant vitality. Unfortunately these admirable qualities usually are employed to little purpose. Peterson's figurations derive, rather obviously, from Art Tatum but have none of that great musician's harmonic vision or skill in melodic variation. This is partly because they are so firmly based on commonplace scale and arpeggio formulae. Almost entirely unrelated to the themes, his improvisations often seem to be haphazard structures of more or less complexity imposed upon the material without much thought and not arising from any overall conceptions. Most of us have been bored by the monotony of Peterson's mechanical posturings but it is hard to convey their meaninglessness in words. Perhaps it is enough to say that he appears to be concerned mainly with playing the piano and only incidentally with making music. This monotony is accented by the lack of variation in dynamics and altogether the impression with which Peterson's work leaves us is one of insensitivity, of a man who has played so much piano he no longer bothers to listen. It is sometimes claimed, in extenuation, that Peterson swings so well and so consistently that much else should be forgiven him. Even this is debatable. Swing may be conveniently half-defined as getting the notes in the right place" – Harrison is referring to a well-known but banal definition of swing by the French critic André Hodeir – "in relation to the beat but essentially it arises from the rhythmic pace and structure of a performance and is a fluid, not static, phenomenon. Peterson's metre and accent are far too mechanical to mean anything very positive. While they sometimes convey a frantic, hypnotic impression of swing, that swing almost always seems to be something imposed from outside and not part of the music's essence. Usually one is forced to conclude that, for all its busyness, little of Peterson's vitality is rarely communicated through his music."

The discussion occurs in a review of *Oscar Peterson Plays "My Fair Lady,"* recorded during the brief period when Gene Gammage was the trio's drummer. It was shortly after that that Norman Granz decided to re-record the composers' series albums. In a ten-day period in Chicago, the trio recorded 117 tracks. Richard Palmer speculated that they were made "presumably with the partial aim of acquainting Thigpen thoroughly with the group's book." This is curious reasoning. The logical circumstance in which to learn a book is private rehearsal, not under pressure in a studio in the process of making records to be issued publicly. In any case, much of that material wasn't in the group's book: some of those performances amounted to first readings. The real reason was much simpler. The earlier composers' series records were monaural. Granz re-recorded the material in stereo to take commercial advantage of the new market, and had Ellis still been with the trio, he would have been the third member of the group. Even Palmer, Peterson's most ardent champion, was compelled to write, "In full-blown jazz terms, these 117 tracks are candidly second-rate stuff, consisting usually of theme-statement-plus-two-three attractive choruses of embellishment."

By 1962, Peterson was recording on a crushing schedule in many contexts for Verve. The albums that year included *Very Tall* with Milt Jackson, *West Side Story* with the trio, *Swinging Brass* and *Bursting Out*, in which the trio worked in a big-band context with arrangements by Russell Garcia in the first instance and Ernie Wilkins in the second, *Affinity* (in which Peterson recorded the Bill Evans composition *Waltz for Debby*), *The Oscar Peterson Trio Plays*, *Night Train*, and four "live" albums made at the London House: *Live from Chicago*, *The Sound of the Trio*, *Put on a Happy Face*, and *Something Warm*.

Oscar's own friends began to murmur that he was being over-recorded – that no one could be expected to maintain high creative standards on such a schedule of continuous outpouring. Even Richard Palmer, whose admiration of Norman Granz is second only to that he has for Peterson, said, "Granted, some of Oscar's 'Granzwagon' albums were at times somewhat tenuous in their jazz content or achievement; but many more were the real stuff ..." And Palmer makes a tacit if unwitting admission that the group and Peterson were being overworked when he praises their "triumphant survival" of this astonishing recording schedule which, it should be remembered, was being met in the stream of night-club, concert, and festival appearances.

Indeed, Peterson and the group's sheer animal stamina became a cause of wonder. It is doubtful that any group in jazz history ever

worked as hard or was recorded as much: Miles Davis, whose popularity was comparable to Oscar's, made approximately one well-
planned and prepared album a year; and many of his records –
Kinda Blue, for example – became influential milestones in jazz
history. But Davis was allowing the well to fill up again before
returning to it. Oscar, or so went the argument – not only of jazz
commentators but often, too, of Oscar's friends – was burning up a
magnificent talent by its overuse.

In one of the more balanced essays on Peterson written during
this period, the British critic Burnett James wrote in *Essays on Jazz*
(1961): "He is at once too easily dismissed and too easily
worshipped ... It is often impossible to tell to what precise artistic
ends all that technique and all that vitality are directed. His playing
has consistent force but not consistent swing. He is particularly
disconcerting because he can veer to extremes in the course of a
single improvised chorus. Sometimes his melodic sense appears
sensitive and distinguished; at other times he seems oblivious to
everything but exhibitionism and empty display. A man of parts but
not all of them obviously, even recognizably, related.

"Not long ago Peterson was being hailed as the greatest living
jazz pianist. Today that opinion would not be considered in serious
jazz circles ...

"The trouble with Peterson is not so much that he is frequently
mechanical or that he abuses his great technique by substituting
bravura virtuosity for genuine musical thinking. Ernest Borneman
dubbed Oscar a 'chameleon' before the critical fashion had turned
against him ...

"My own feeling is that underneath all the flowery fussiness
there is in Oscar's style a vein of simple purity and austere beauty
that could, if he would let it, make him into a musician of eloquence
and significance. If only he would absent himself from success
awhile, and decline to take the easy way out, he might yet develop
into one of the outstanding pianists of modern jazz. The ingredi-
ents are there if they only come to the surface intermittently. There
is no doubt of his talent, but it needs constant disciplining. Too
much of his work seems to lack artistic integrity. In some ways he

reminds me of the late Mario Lanza. He is opulently gifted but he is either too lazy or too flushed with popular acclaim to make the best of his endowments. He prefers to stun rather than to move, for it is so much easier to generate a superficial excitement than to sink personal flamboyance and egotism. Easier, but not more satisfying, either for the listener or the performer.

"Peterson's inherent quality is revealed in his best work. Despite the regrettable infrequency of it there is no mistaking its distinction."

A reviewer for the French magazine *Le Jazz Hot* wrote on September 4, 1969: "He has attained triumph, and he sells great quantities of discs. He is known throughout the world and each of his concerts draws thousands of ecstatic and overwhelmed fans. He has a sumptuous technique. His bassist, Sam Jones, and his drummer, Bobby Durham, are accomplished musicians. He has the most capable and the most powerful impresario [Granz].

"That being said, I swear that I was bored to death and that I was able to stay right to the end of his performance only by superhuman effort ...

"Oscar Peterson has all the requisites of one of the great jazz musicians – dazzling technique ... definite musicality, percussing sonority, a sense of nuance, independence of hands, richness of the harmonic system, it's true ... save the essential ... Save that *élan*, that poesy, that unexpected, that folly, that Dionysian temperament, that profound sense of the blues, all that is difficult to define but makes the grandeur of an Armstrong, a Tatum, a Bud Powell, a Parker, a Coltrane, or a Cecil Taylor."

The American critic Martin Williams wrote in 1962, "One might almost say that Peterson's melodic vocabulary is a stockpile of clichés, that he seems to know every stock riff and lick in the history of jazz. His improvisations frequently just string them together. One has the feeling that Peterson will eventually work every one of them into every piece he plays, regardless of tempo, mood or any other consideration; it will simply be a matter of his going on long enough to get them all in."

Whitney Balliett, jazz critic of the *New Yorker*, has been quoted as saying Oscar's playing had a "clogged, airless sound," but in fact he wrote that not of Peterson as an individual but of a rhythm section consisting of Peterson, Barney Kessel, Ray Brown, and drummer Alvin Stoller. Balliett did write in a 1966 piece, "Peterson's playing continues to be a pudding made from the leavings of Art Tatum, Nat Cole, and Teddy Wilson. That he stirs it so vigorously fools most of the people most of the time." After a 1970 Peterson appearance at the Plaza Hotel in New York, Balliett wrote, "Tatum was an original painted American Queen Anne chair with fine Spanish feet; Peterson is an Altman reproduction." There is, however, respect in the reviews, including this comment, written in 1977:

"Two superior pianists grew in Art Tatum's garden in the late forties. They were the Canadian Oscar Peterson and the Englishman George Shearing. Peterson developed a technique, which eventually became his very style, just as Buddy Rich's had become his. Peterson exploded into his solos from his opening melodic choruses. The 'virtuoso' sign flashed incessantly, and it hid the fact that the chief content of his solos was packed into their first eight or ten bars; what came after was largely ornamentation and hyperbole."

Nor were all the reviewers in his native country kind. In the Toronto *Globe and Mail* of September 23, 1964, Patrick Scott wrote, under the headline "Prisoner of the Assembly Line," "I keep going back to hear Oscar Peterson for the same naive reason I keep getting his records: a childlike hope that one night he will lose the key to his automatic piano and be forced to play it by hand again." Over the years Scott's reviews of the pianist were so unrelentingly lethal, and seemingly frequent, that one of Oscar's friends said, "Pat Scott would fly to Frozen Lung, Saskatchewan, to catch Oscar on a one-nighter just so he could give him a bad write-up."

In Paris a critic said Oscar's was "music for Pavlov's dogs." In the New York *Times*, John S. Wilson, reviewing a Carnegie Hall concert by Ella Fitzgerald, Roy Eldridge, and Oscar, referred to the trio's "monotonously driving beat."

Granz counselled Oscar to ignore the press, for which he himself had unflagging contempt. He manifested this disdain in the inscription "Muenster Dummel High Fidelity" on the jacket of his Clef and Verve albums.

"It was a complete put-on," Granz told John McDonough in his 1979 interview for *Down Beat*. "I've always been skeptical of a lot of stuff I read about sound production. Today it's utter nonsense. The entire back of a sleeve is full of credits. The kid who goes for the coffee even gets a credit line. Well, back in the '50s high fidelity was the big thing, but I considered it something of a con by the record companies, especially when they began putting 'high fidelity' stickers on LPs that had been in their catalogues for years. Moreover, there were all kinds of strange, technical sounding names for this system or that. They were all coined by advertising types, no doubt. So I decided to put everybody on. Muenster was my favorite cheese, and Ernie Dummel was one of my engineers. So we came up with Muenster Dummel Hi Fi. No one knew what it meant, but it sounded impressive. We really had the last laugh when some sound magazine wrote it up."

Granz was attacking the industry and the press on terrain not his own, that of sound. His albums were known, among musicians and the press alike, for poor sound: curious resonances, bizarre balances – the bass as loud as the piano, for example – and curious equalizations. A number of musicians who recorded for him said that he really was not all that aware in the studio. But his hostility to the press reinforced Oscar's own anger at "the so-called writers of jazz who don't know a damn thing about the realities of life," as Granz put it in one of his many letters to *Down Beat*. Oscar too began to strike out at critics in interviews around the world. They always said the same thing: that he'd listened to records with critics, and they didn't hear things that a musician would notice, and they therefore didn't know what they were talking about.

In Toronto he told critic and attorney Jack Batten, "I've sat and listened to records with critics, and I've seen things that are important jazzwise go right over their heads, whereas the musicians in the room were aware of this. That's why I don't think criticism is an honest thing. If I happen to make a record today and impress this critic who is popular at the moment, then I've got a valuable record. But five years from now, if this particular school of criticism has gone out of favor, we look up and suddenly this 'great record' is outmoded. Why?"

Again, the grounds on which Oscar's attack is being made are shaky. Many of the records that were at the time being praised by the critics – a long series of Miles Davis albums on Columbia, the early John Coltrane records on Impulse, the Bill Evans records on Riverside, those of Gil Evans – have become classics of a status with the early Louis Armstrong and Ellington recordings, and more often than not the critics have been justified by time and the general judgement of the jazz community, particularly musicians. On the whole, time has not, as Oscar suggested it would, discredited the jazz critics.

In 1973, Oscar said to François Postif, during an interview for *Le Jazz Hot* in Paris: "I'm a musician, and just as the critics are sometimes hard on me, I'm hard on the critics. I don't believe what the critics say, because often I sit down at a concert beside them and they *ask me* what the musicians on the stage are doing. And they're supposed to know that kind of thing, not me. Recently, in Los Angeles, I went to hear a group with two or three critics, although I won't name them. I wasn't there to review anything, I was there to hear what went on, but they were there to write their reviews. I didn't want to say what I thought because I didn't think that it would be honest, for the good reason that I'm just a listener, not a critic. At a certain moment, the music changed tempo, but very quickly came back to the original tempo, and the critics said to me that the rhythm section wasn't tight …

"Some time ago I did some albums that we called the composers' series – Gershwin, Irving Berlin, Cole Porter. The critics asked me why I'd recorded these pieces, saying that I didn't play in my usual way, and I told them that Norman Granz had asked me to play during these sessions in a simpler way, more understandable to the people these albums were aimed at, who weren't necessarily jazz fans. Maybe to draw more people into jazz. To be sure, the jazz critics, who hadn't understood the point of these recordings, put them aside." Oscar probably said "fluffed them off"; I'm retranslating this material back into English from French. "I don't think one of them is a bad recording, but they were made in a spirit totally different from the discs I usually recorded. In reality, when I hear an artist, I react differently because I know the life and the artist, I know that he's coming from a lousy hotel, that he has money problems, that he's having problems with his wife, and that all that goes into the disc should be judged with the ears of the heart, not with those of the critic."

That of course is doubtful reasoning, although Oscar is by no means the only jazz player to use the musician's private problems as justification for his public failings. Mozart's poverty and the bureaucracy that bothered Bach do not enter into evaluations of their work. The excuse of insufficient spring rain will not sweeten tasteless strawberries. If the suit you purchase is badly cut, it will not do to explain that the tailor is having problems with his wife, and Oscar Peterson, so demanding of perfection from the players in his own group, would be the first to reject that kind of excuse. The artist's problems are his own, not the public's.

Not all the excoriation came from critics. Organist Jimmy Smith told a critic for *Le Jazz Hot,* "The first time I heard a [Peterson] record, I said to myself, 'There, that's a white who has worked hard at the piano and thinks he sounds black.'" And Miles Davis made the brutal – and widely quoted – assessment, "Oscar makes me sick because he copies everybody. He even had to *learn* how to play the blues." (So did Miles, the son of an affluent horse-breeding East St. Louis dentist. And Miles once said to me, "I got it all from Dizzy.")

Yet, for the most part, with that total self-control that permitted him not to raise an eyebrow when Herb Ellis and Ray Brown dyed their hair, a control that Ellis, Brown, Thigpen, and all his colleagues have seen manifested in a thousand little incidents, Oscar affected indifference to the drum-beat of derogation from critics.

If, in observance of the principle taught him by his parents, Oscar would not take his anger out on his fellow man, on one occasion he at least took it out on the furniture. And if for once his iron control of his emotions cracked, it was in private, in his hotel room.

The incident occurred in London in 1962. "What bugged me most," he told me long afterwards, "is that we'd played for charity." And one of the critics vivisected him.

Thigpen says that the incident has to be considered in the context of the social atmosphere of the time. The first hysteria over the Beatles was flowering. These musically illiterate young songwriters were being acclaimed by some critics as equivalents of Beethoven, and they were making untold millions in all the currencies of the Western world. They altered the character of the music business for ever, turning it from an industry with at least a modicum of interest in music as art into a money-making machine of unprecedented and unrelenting avarice. Nor were they the only rock stars growing unimaginably rich.

"I think many of us," Thigpen mused in 1987, "felt that the financial rewards were unfairly lopsided when we compared the content of the two kinds of music. We also felt somewhat cheated when comparing the difference in the amount of time it took for study and practice on one's instrument in order to gain the knowledge and technical expertise needed to even be considered a professional musician in the swing or bebop styles, as opposed to the limited facility required to be acknowledged as a professional in the accepted rock style at that time.

"These facts, together with a deliberate downplaying of jazz and the musicians playing in the swing and bebop styles, particularly those musicians who carried themselves with respectful dignity, as opposed to the adoration shown to some rock musicians – and also some jazz musicians – who seemed to have blatant disdain for the audience, for instruments, and for music in general, may also have contributed to Oscar's blow-up.

"I don't remember what the charity was that we played for," Ed said, "but I do remember Oscar being quite affected by the review."

Yet, struggling to maintain his control, he said nothing about it. He went to his room and stayed there.

Late the next day, when he had not come down, Brown and

Thigpen grew concerned. Finally Ray got the manager to let him into Oscar's room with a pass key.

Oscar has never been a heavy drinker, but the previous evening he had purchased a bottle of liquor. He was still asleep, sprawled across the bed. The room was a mess. Oscar had torn a huge wooden armoire apart with his bare hands.

Oscar's recollection of the incident is at variance with this. He says that he was angry because one of the musicians on JATP had accused him of stealing a camera.

Leonard Feather, in an article for *Nugget* magazine entitled "Oscar Peterson: Gentleman Cat," mentioned the attacks Oscar had taken year after year from "some of the more notoriously reactionary British jazz critics." Feather wrote: "One night, in a rare moment of capitulation, after reading a particularly vicious review of this type, he broke down and cried." (Later in that article, Feather flatly proclaimed Oscar "the greatest living jazz pianist.")

I believe Feather was describing the same incident. And after setting my own recollections beside those of Ed Thigpen and others, I believe that, for once, Oscar is in error on a matter of memory, and that it was indeed a review that set him off. The camera incident may have occurred at another time or just prior to the review, leaving him more than normally vulnerable. In the *Nugget* article, Feather described Oscar as "high-strung, hypersensitive, as easily touched by kindness as he is hurt by malice."

Whatever the reason, his composure cracked that night. He said long afterwards that he had consumed half a bottle of liquor and then dismantled the armoire with his hands. Of course, he added immediately, he had apologized to the hotel management the next day and paid for it.

"Did you hurt your hands?" I asked.

"No," he said with a slight chuckle. "I didn't hurt my hands."

CHAPTER 13

MRS. GALLAGHER

In the early 1950s, the Toronto room Oscar played regularly was the Paddock, a basement club with a horsy decor. Another pianist who played there often was the late Calvin Jackson, an American who for a time took up residence in Canada. Calvin Jackson once said he could carve Oscar Peterson any time, any place. Oscar put out the word: two Steinways, back to back, any time, any place. But the duel never occurred.

By the mid-1950s, Sammy Berger had opened the Town Tavern on the north side of Queen Street just east of Yonge. "When Oscar was there," Eric Smith remembered, "they turned business away. Tatum played one of his last gigs there. When Oscar was there, the customers were lined up down Queen Street, he was always a sellout, and he played there two or three times a year. Sammy Berger, the owner of the Town Tavern, was the worry wart of the city. This must have been about 1957 or 1958. Sammy was thrilled, saying, 'Look at them tonight.'

"One Saturday night Oscar said, 'I'm not feeling well.' 'What's the matter?' Sammy said. Oscar said, 'I have a pain in my arm and my shoulder.' Sammy didn't want to let on he's worried about the show. Oscar said, 'I think I can make it.' Now it's getting closer to show time. Finally Oscar groaned and said, 'That did it.' Sammy said, 'I'll call the hospital.' St. Michael's Hospital was right around the corner. 'Let's get going,' Oscar said, 'I'd hate to think it's a heart attack.' The office was downstairs at the Town. Sammy ran downstairs to make the call. While he was on the phone to St. Michael's, he hears Oscar upstairs playing the introduction.

"Sammy was wise to Oscar, but he went for that one."

177

It was in the Town Tavern that Oscar's relationship with Sandra King began. Sandra was the daughter of Alex King, vice-president in charge of personnel of the Simpson-Sears department stores. Sandra was a career nurse, working at the Toronto General Hospital. Striking and handsome rather than conventionally pretty, tall, dark-haired, and strong-shouldered, Sandra – Sandy to everyone, actually – was a good-humoured, gregarious, intelligent woman with a love of jazz and a liking for the company of jazz musicians. She had all sorts of friends in the profession.

One evening when his marriage to Lil was ending, Oscar went on a tour of the Toronto clubs with Eric. "We were just doing the town. We went into a couple of jazz places," Eric said. "We went out to the Seaway Towers in Sunnyside. Gene Amaro, the tenor player, had a little group out there. We wound up at the Town Tavern. Sandy was in there, as she was many nights."

"She was just leaving," Oscar said. "I took her by the arm, which was not like me – I don't come on like that. I said, 'Where are you going?' She said, 'Home.' I said, 'No you're not, you're coming back in with us.' She said, 'No I'm not, I have to get up for work in the morning.'"

But she went back into the club with Oscar.

They became all but inseparable, and Sandy gave up her job to travel on the road with Oscar – Chicago, Los Angeles, the major cities of Europe. "I loved it," she said years later. "I loved the life and I loved the people. I loved the jokes and the friendships."

Relations with the King family were cordial, or seemed so. And then Oscar got a call from Sandy's father, who wanted to have a talk with him. Oscar went to it with trepidation, expecting – at last and alas – a racial confrontation. Alex King told him that he and Sandy's mother were uneasy about the relationship. He did not think it seemly for Sandy to be travelling with Oscar. If they intended to continue the relationship, he said, he and Mrs. King thought they should get married.

Oscar left the meeting almost in shock, and shortly after that he and Sandy were married.

The relationship was troubled from the beginning, though race was perhaps only peripheral to its problems. In Chicago, when Ed

and Lois Thigpen's marriage was looking unsteady to their friends
– they were later divorced – Oscar and I had had a number of conversations about "mixed" marriages. I argued that the real issue of
desegregation was not in the schoolroom but in the bedroom. I
believed then and believe now that racism is essentially sexual, and
imposed by the male, that its unstated underlying principle is: We
have the right to screw your women but you do not have the right to
screw ours.

Oscar seemed to argue against "mixed" relationships, saying
they required "a vast intellectual unselfishness." When he married
Sandy, I couldn't resist teasing him, recalling that earlier discussion. Drawing on that uncanny memory of his, he said, "I didn't say
I was against it. I just said it took a vast intellectual unselfishness."
But many years later, he told me that he and Sandy had had a bitter
dispute the night before their wedding.

And yet they were good years, remembered by everyone in
Oscar's circle of friends and acquaintances for laughter and good
times.

Oscar and Sandy took an apartment in Toronto, just west of
Sunnyside and looking out on Lake Ontario. Maurie Kessler put
Carmen McRae up to a prank. Eric Smith tells the story:

"For weeks after Oscar and Sandy moved in, somebody would
call up on his new number and ask for Mrs. Gallagher. Sandy kept
saying, 'No, you must have the wrong number. This is a new list-
ing.' The calls persisted, with various people calling for 'Mrs. Gallagher.' Oscar came in from the road and said to Sandy, 'This goes
on all the time? This has got to stop.' He was home for two or three
days. These calls kept coming in, and Sandy kept handling these
calls as patiently as she could. Finally one night he heard Sandy on
the phone, exasperated, saying, 'There is no Mrs. Gallagher here!'
He said, 'Give me that phone.' And Carmen did that old joke. She
said, 'This is Mrs. Gallagher. Are there any messages for me?'

"And he ripped into her. He said, 'You're Mrs. Gallagher?
We're sick and tired of fielding your phone calls. Can't you get your
new number right?'

"And she said, 'Oscar, this is Carmen!' And he was so mad it
was a few seconds before he realized who he was talking to."

One of Oscar's most ardent fans has been Frank Sinatra, who, at the end of an evening in Las Vegas, told the audience, "I don't know where you people are heading, but I know where I'm going. I'm going over to catch Oscar Peterson." And of course he jammed the club where Oscar was playing.

Eric remembered: "One time when Oscar was playing the Hong Kong bar in Los Angeles, Frank called and said that he had a party on Friday. He said, 'I have always wanted you to come up and play in my home. Would you do it?' Oscar said, 'I don't know how I can do it. I work till one.' Frank said, 'That's fine. Please do it.' Oscar said, 'All right, I'll make a deal with you. I'll play if you'll sing.' And Sinatra agreed. Oscar said, 'Come with me.' I said, 'No, that's going to be one of those parties with a hundred people. That's not for me.' But when the night came, I said I'd do it. He said, 'Great. Come down and catch the last set, and they'll come down and pick us up.'

"Sure enough, Jilly Rizzo was there with the station wagon. We drove up Coldwater Canyon, to the top. I think Bowman was the name of the street, and you went right up to the crest. Out the front door of his house you could see all of the San Fernando Valley, and out the back door, the patio, you could see Beverly Hills and Santa Monica and the ocean. Frank was waiting at the door. We went in, and it wasn't anything like I'd expected. There weren't a hundred people, there were twelve. I'll tell you who was there. Irving Lazar, the agent. Godfrey Cambridge, Mike Romanoff's widow, Fred Astaire, and Gene Kelly. And their wives. Frank was knocking himself out being nice. The house was beautiful, but not palatial. A beautiful ranch-style home.

"There were two sofas, with the piano at the end. I went behind the sofa and sat at the bar. I got talking to Mike Romanoff's widow before Oscar started to play, and she said, 'You can't believe how excited Frank has been about this. He has been like a schoolboy. He planned this evening, who he was going to invite and who he wasn't. He said that after dinner there was going to be a treat, but he wouldn't say what it was.'"

Oscar said, "When we made that album with Fred Astaire, Fred gave us all ID bracelets, Charlie Shavers, Flip Phillips, Barney Kessel, Ray Brown, and Alvin Stoller. Ray's was stolen, somebody else lost his. On it he had engraved 'With Thanks, Fred A.' I became a friend of Fred's.

"All these years later, when Sinatra invited us up to the house, and I walked in, I saw Fred and Gene Kelly standing together by a little bar. Fred said, 'How are you, Oscar, it's so good to see you.' And he introduced me to Gene Kelly. Then he grabbed my wrist, and said, 'You've *still* got it, you've still got it!' I said, 'Of course I do, I wear it all the time.' He said, 'I know, I've seen you on television, and I see it.' He was so enamoured that I wore it, and I said, 'Except now and then, when I'm fishing or something, I never take it off.' He was amazed that I always wore it. Fred Astaire."

"One time," Eric said, "Oscar bumped into Marlon Brando in London. He'd known Marlon from before. Brando came in to hear him and sent a bottle of champagne over to Oscar. Marlon said, 'I flew over here to do a film, *Superman*. I checked into the hotel, and as I walked into the room, the bellman switched on the TV. Your program, the thing you did with André Previn, was just starting. I sat down on the bed with my coat, my boots, and my scarf on, and an hour later I was still sitting there. It was one of the greatest hours I ever saw on television.'"

One of the most amusing stories of Oscar's encounters with the famous involved Charles Laughton, who did *not* know who Oscar was. Oscar was standing outside a London hotel, waiting for a taxi, when he noticed that the large portly man next to him, also waiting for a taxi, was Laughton. Knowing all too well from his own experiences that the famous can be made uncomfortable by praise, he nonetheless was unable to resist introducing himself and telling Laughton how much pleasure he had derived from his work over the years.

Laughton accepted the compliment with equanimity and said, "And what do you do, young man?"

"I'm a jazz musician," Oscar said.

"Hmmm," Laughton mused, "a jazz musician." And no doubt his eyes blinked in that slow owlish way. "Do you have any pot?"

The bassist Bill Crow, known for his work with Stan Getz, Gerry Mulligan, and other major jazz musicians, described in a letter to me what it was like to travel with and for Norman Granz in those days:

> I was critical of his Jazz at the Philharmonic format when I was young, feeling the music was being bent out of shape to appeal to a mass audience that didn't understand or appreciate the real thing. But I later came to realize how much employment Norman created for musicians he genuinely admired. He found a way to the mass audience that made him and his musicians a lot of money, and the popularity of the format led to opportunities for other musicians when the concert jam session became a standard type of gig.
>
> I ran across Norman only a few times, but I got a strong sense of his style. Jimmy Raney had brought me into Stan Getz's quintet in 1952, just after Stan left Royal Roost records, and we did a few dates under Granz's supervision. On the first ones Norman only concerned himself with the balance and accepted Stan's choice of tunes and takes. Later, with the new group built around Bob Brookmeyer, Norman got a little more involved in the material itself.
>
> Brookmeyer had written three originals and a treatment of *Have You Met Miss Jones.*
>
> After a take of a Brookmeyer original, Norman asked from the booth, "Has this tune got a name?"
>
> "I call it *A Rustic Dance,*" said Bob.
>
> "Great," said Norman. "We'll call it *Rustic Hop.*" Bob shrugged, and we went on to the next tune.
>
> "What's this one called?" Norman asked.
>
> "*Trolley Car,*" said Bob.
>
> "I really liked the mix we got on this one," Norman said. "Let's call it *Cool Mix.*"
>
> Brookmeyer shook his head and laughed. "Whatever you say, Norman." I forget Bob's title for the third one, but Norman came up with *Erudition,* and that's how the tunes were listed on the album.
>
> Those records were released on 78s on the Mercury label and as 33s and 45s on the Clef label, so you can see it was a time

when the record industry and Norman's record business were both undergoing changes.

My second trip to Europe with Gerry Mulligan was under Norman's auspices. I really dug the way he handled it. We went first class, the money was right, and we were presented well. Jimmy Giuffre's trio and Gene Krupa's quartet were also on the tour. As soon as we arrived, Norman met us and made a little speech.

"I want you to know that you're here as artists, and that's the way you're going to be treated. You're also adults, and I'm not going to take you by the hand. I'll tell you when the buses and the planes leave, where the concerts are, and what time you hit. If you miss the transportation I'm providing, get there on your own. You're responsible for yourself. And I'm paying everybody a good taste, so don't be staying in any fleabag hotels. I've built a reputation for American musicians over here, and I want you to live up to it. Don't screw it up for the next group that comes over."

Having said that, he relaxed and had a ball with us.

We flew into Berlin from Frankfurt during one of those times the Russians were harassing the air corridor with MIGs, and our plane was delayed so long that we missed the concert. But Norman was cool. After doing everything he could and still not getting the plane off the ground until too late, he accepted the situation without a word. We flew into Berlin, spent the night, and flew out again the next day.

Norman had to be in New York for an opening of Ella Fitzgerald, and planned to meet us in Italy in a day or two, but he needed someone to drive his Mercedes 300SL from Frankfurt, where he'd parked it, to Milan. Pete, his road manager, and I volunteered. Norman gave us the route through Switzerland and told us it should take a certain number of hours. We realized later that he was talking about the way *he* drove. It took us so long we arrived in Milan after the band had left by train for Bologna for the concert that night. We headed directly there and made the gig.

When we got back to Milan, where we stayed for run-outs to other cities in northern Italy, we called Norman to find out where he wanted the car delivered. "Oh, there's no hurry," he said. "I got back a day early and needed a car, so I bought a new Maserati."

On the second tour we did for him, opposite Horace Silver's quintet, I was able to bring my wife. After doing a tour of one-nighters through France, Denmark, Sweden, Finland, Germany, and Holland, we wanted to go back to Paris for a week before we went home. I discovered we were on a special-rate airline ticket that expired on the last day of the tour, and extending the return flight a week would result in our having to pay several hundred dollars in extra fare. Norman heard us talking about it, called someone he knew at the airline, and arranged things so we were able to visit Paris and fly home a week later at no additional cost. We really appreciated his thoughtfulness.

Everyone involved, or close to the situation, agrees that the relationship between Oscar and Sandy was a stormy one. Neither, in later years, was inclined to blame the other, saying merely that they were both strong-willed people who clashed, and each to an extent accepting a large share of the responsibility.

Oscar thinks a major factor was the emotional pressure that inevitably is put on the wife (or husband) of someone who is heavily in the public eye, with the vortex of attention around that person. Sandy thinks Oscar was suppressing a great deal of pain from his childhood, the psychological consequence of discrimination in a man who was now world-famous. Both of them may be right.

Eric Smith said, "This tells you what kind of person Sandy is. Oscar and I got into quite an argument about it, though I could see his point too. It was one of those parties where we were doing crazy things. It was at Maurie Kessler's house on Ridell. We were all trying to sing. Oscar was giving everybody his note. He'd say, 'Here's your note. Now don't forget it. Keep humming it to yourself.' Then he'd go to the next person. Then he'd say, 'Hit it.' We'd all sing our notes, and it would be a beautiful chord, although there'd be a few who'd be off. And he could spot it. He'd hear twelve voices and say, 'That's not the note I gave you.'

"Then he had us all singing solo. He's going to judge who's in tune. I did my song, *I Can't Give You Anything but Love.* Then it came to Sandy, and she's singing, 'In the evening by the moonlight, you can hear those darkies singing.' There are different kinds of non-prejudiced people. There are those who have trained themselves – and by the way they get full credit too. People whose backgrounds may be southern, and who have overcome it. But there are others who are just naturally that way. It doesn't occur to them, they don't know why there's any problem. And Sandy is one of those people. Sandy wouldn't know if you're short, tall, black, white, or purple. Such people just don't know."

But the incident caused a scene between Oscar and Sandy. "She's just that way," Oscar said. "Without prejudice, without a trace of it. But I told her she had to be aware of the sensitivity of many people about such things, including some of the people in Jazz at the Philharmonic."

"But with Sandy, that pure innocence came through," Eric said.

"There were some stormy times, but there were some very good times. They had a lot of fun together. I like Sandy," Eric concluded.

So did all of Oscar's friends, myself among them. I met her in Chicago, when he brought her to one of his London House engagements. That was probably in 1960.

CHAPTER 14

END OF AN ERA

In January 1961, Joseph R. Vogel, president of Metro-Goldwyn-Mayer Inc., announced that the MGM Records division had purchased Verve Records from Norman Granz. The purchase price was later disclosed to be $2,850,000. All the recording contracts of artists signed to Verve went with the deal, including those of Red Allen, Ray Brown, Blossom Dearie, Roy Eldridge, Herb Ellis, Ella Fitzgerald, Stan Getz, Terry Gibbs, Dizzy Gillespie, Jimmy Giuffre, Johnny Hodges, Gene Krupa, George Lewis, Gerry Mulligan, Anita O'Day, Kid Ory, Paul Smith, Sonny Stitt, and Mel Tormé. And Jim Davis was appointed as Oscar's record producer.

The first Peterson album Davis produced was *Affinity*. Then came a group of four albums recorded in 1962 at the London House and titled *Live from Chicago, The Sound of the Trio, Put on a Happy Face,* and *Something Warm.* I was present for at least one of these recording sessions and remember the tangle of black cables from the bandstand on the north wall of the club out past the bar to the cloak room, where the recording equipment had been set up. I remember wondering how much of the clink of glasses and cutlery would end up in the sound, and I was mystified that Oscar and Davis would continue to record with a piano that kept slipping out of tune. These infelicities are the most serious flaws in the recordings, which, however, contain tracks that many critics rank among the Peterson–Thigpen–Brown group's best and capture moments of the mood Oscar used to generate in that well-remembered room in the after-midnight sets.

Richard Palmer, in his eighty-page 1984 monograph titled *Oscar Peterson,* wrote: "I have the highest regard for Granz; and over the

35 years of his close association with Oscar, there is no doubt that he has been a wise and creative influence on the pianist. But I don't think it can be denied that nearly all the '50s studio dates fail to present Peterson and his groups at their absolute best. Oscar more or less admitted this when he remarked that many people felt that 'the delicate and communicative rapport that they sensed in our in-person appearances was usually lost in the mechanical and cold confines of the studio' and 'I am inclined to agree to the extent that our group performs much better ... [when] a live audience is present.'" And the London House recordings, despite the unfortunate piano, attest to this.

I have peculiarly vivid memories of that time.

During the London House engagements, Ed Thigpen and his first wife, Lois, would sometimes stay with my then-wife and me in our apartment on Bittersweet Street, on the north side of Chicago, near the lake.

My wife, Micheline, was French and did not have a clear idea how idolized major jazz musicians were by their fans. Being French, she had worked up a good connection with a neighbourhood butcher, who turned out to be a jazz fan. When she mentioned that Ed Thigpen and his wife were staying with us, he was overwhelmed. When she got home, she told us that he had asked if he might come by and meet Ed. I had misgivings, but Ed saw no reason why he shouldn't, and the next afternoon the man turned up. In a rapture bordering on mesmerism, he hung on Ed's every word. Ed was patient with him, even as the afternoon turned into evening and he showed no signs of leaving. Finally, we made it obvious that we had to get dressed to go to the London House, and, reluctantly, the man left. And we dressed.

As we were descending the front steps of the building, the man returned, carrying a large tray covered in aluminum foil. He said he had a present for Ed and Lois and removed the foil, like an artist unveiling a painting or a sculpture. And a sculpture indeed, or at least a sort of bas-relief, was what it was: a great red heart made out of ground beef, pierced by strips of steak or veal, the whole strange thing surrounded by smaller hearts shaped out of filet mignon. He had made it, he told Ed and Lois, "as a tribute to your great love." I never forgot the phrase – or the tribute. It was one of the most astonishing things I had ever seen.

And one could not laugh. I remember vividly the graciousness and sincerity with which Ed thanked the man, who almost glowed as he went home, no doubt to listen to his Ed Thigpen records. We took the tray into the house, set it in the refrigerator, and left. In the taxi, we began to laugh. I am not sure whether Ed laughed.

But at the club we all laughed. I told the story to Oscar, Ray Brown, and Eddie Higgins, who roared with laughter. (Later, I came to view the man's action, as Thigpen did, as a remarkably gentle and touching gesture. But it seemed terribly funny at the time.)

There was much to laugh at in those days. One night a group of us were having dinner in a Polynesian restaurant. The spare ribs were excellent, and I was having at them. My wife reached out and found them gone. She said, in her French accent, "What happened to the ribs?"

"Look at Gene's plate," Oscar said. "It looks like the place where the elephants go to die."

Oscar would periodically quit smoking, during which times his weight would increase enormously. But whether he was smoking or not, he always carried a Dunhill lighter to light the cigarettes of others. It seemed to be already alight when he whipped it out of the right-hand pocket of his jacket. Because of this practice Dizzy Gillespie nicknamed him "The Flame." It was impossible to put a cigarette in your mouth without Oscar having his lighter out before you could reach for your own.

The tables at the London House crowded up close to the bandstand. One night when the trio was burning through some up-tempo number, a woman at the front-most table put a cigarette to her lips, and Oscar's right hand came out of his pocket in a flash to light it for her – as he continued the solo in his left hand. Thigpen started laughing so hard that he couldn't play. Ray Brown gradually crumbled, and the music came to a chaotic impasse.

"Chicago was always a piano town," Oscar has said, and so has

Eddie Higgins. Norman Simmons said, "The society of Chicago musicians was always warm, close, and sociable."

"It was endowed with any number of excellent resident jazz pianists, including Ahmad Jamal, and for reasons unknown it had audiences who appreciated them," Oscar said. "One of these pianists, still better known as a singer, is Audrey Morris.

"Chicago was always a very special town for us. Audrey and her husband, Stu Genovese, are very dear friends of mine." (Genovese is a bassist and a teacher of music.) "There was a very personal thing going with me and them. I used to live at their house. There were a lot of incredible moments. Yeah. I learned a lot from Audrey Morris. Audrey Morris, along with a couple of other people, taught me a lot about reading a lyric into my playing. I do various tunes she even taught me. The reason she is such a great vocalist is that what she does stays with you. I became so beguiled with the way she could read a lyric that on playing these tunes over I found myself trying to read them the way she read them. Also, she made me very cognizant of verses, and the impact that they can have on tunes. The other person responsible for that was Norman, when we did the Astaire album. Norman used to get after me about, 'Why don't you play the verse to that tune, is the verse not part of the song? That's a pretty verse.'"

The influence of Audrey Morris on Oscar Peterson has gone unremarked by critics.

André Previn, in those days known primarily as a virtuoso pianist and film composer but now the conductor of the Los Angeles Philarmonic, was playing in jazz clubs and concerts with his own trio, which included the great bassist Red Mitchell and drummer Frank Capp. One night the three of them dropped into the London House to hear Peterson, Brown, and Thigpen. Seeing them, Peterson turned up the gas, as is his wont when friends walk in. When the set was over, Previn said to his colleagues, "Can I fire all three of us?"

Oscar had a Mercedes Benz 300SL. Once he drove it from New

York to Chicago in eleven hours, in time to make one of the London House openings. On another occasion he was picked up for speeding by a black police officer as he cruised up one of the broad South Side parkways on his way to the London House. The cop had no idea who he was and took him to a precinct house where almost all the other officers were also black. In those days there were no black movie or television stars (Nat Cole's TV series having been swiftly dropped) and for the most part black celebrities were athletes or jazz musicians or singers, and such magazines as *Ebony* paid considerable attention to them. And the cops at the precinct house wanted to know how the officer could possibly *not* recognize Oscar Peterson. Oscar was immediately released and went on to work.

And I remember all of us – Oscar, Sandy, Ray, Ed – after the gig one night leaving the London House, which was at Wacker Drive and Michigan Avenue, looking out on that striking view: the bridge that was always being shown in winter weather shots on television to illustrate the bitterness of the Chicago cold, the frivolous wedding-cake architecture of the Wrigley Building, and the curious false-Gothic façade of the Chicago *Tribune* tower. That wind was coming in off Lake Michigan, cutting your face like flying razor blades. Ray, who was pushing his bass along on its little wheel, said, "I'm getting too old to play this damn thing and almost too old to carry it." He was all of thirty-five at the time. And he was talking now and then of leaving the trio. No one took him seriously. He and Oscar had been travelling together for twelve years, and he had been on the road with Dizzy Gillespie and other groups before that.

Oscar had had an abrasive confrontation or two with Charles Mingus, as many musicians had. One morning Mingus called me from New York, angry at something I had written in *Down Beat*. After about a minute's conversation, he lost all control and screamed, "You're a dirty white motherfucker!" and hung up. Five minutes later he called back and apologized for what he had said, but within a minute he had lost his control again and screamed the same thing. This happened three or four times. Finally he said he was going to fly out to Chicago "and throw you the length of your office and then run and catch you so you don't break your puny back!"

It was a remarkably vivid threat, and I described it to the late Don DeMicheal, my assistant editor. Don put our switchboard operator up to a practical joke. I was out of the office for a time that afternoon, and when I returned, just before five o'clock, she said a Mr. Mingus had called from the airport and was on his way in to see me. I was, needless to say, disturbed. Mingus had a reputation for violence. He had punched trombonist Jimmy Knepper in the mouth, for which Knepper sued him. One slim and slight alto saxophonist who worked for him was so afraid of Mingus that he carred a .32 automatic in his back pocket when he went on the bandstand with him.

That night I went with photographer Ted Williams to hear Oscar. Half believing Mingus was in town, I kept talking with Ted about my problem, probably to the point of boredom. "You had a run-in with him in New York, didn't you?" I asked Oscar.

Oscar chuckled. "Ray and I went to hear Phineas Newborn. He was playing somewhere in the Village. I remember Phineas came over and was sitting with us, and he was saying something – he's a very mild-mannered person – and then I was aware of somebody standing over me. And I heard Ray say, 'Hey, Charles.' Mingus said, 'Hey, how y'doin'?' And he was looking down at me. He said, 'Oscar Peterson.' And I said, 'That's right.' And he said, 'What're you doin' out here?' I said, 'I came to hear Phineas.'

"I believe Phineas really thought Mingus was going to hit me, or something like that. And I was sitting there hoping he would. Because I'd heard all these stories about he was great at hitting piano players, and I figured it was time a piano player evened up the score. I really was going to try to take him down the pipe. He stood there and tried to outmenace me. I just ignored him, turned my back on him, he ended up standing there by himself, I wasn't going to ask him to sit down.

"Afterwards Ray said, 'He sure was staring down at you. What would you have done if he'd reached out for you?' I said, 'You know what, if he'd reached for me, death, pure death. That's all, somebody would have died, and it would have been Mingus, not me, I wasn't going to go.' I was really prepared for that.

"And the next time I saw Charlie Mingus was in France, at Nice, I think, and he was up there on the stage playing piano. And he finished playing piano, if you can call it that, and I remember I went on shortly after that, and when I came off, he was sitting in the wings, he had pulled up a chair and was sitting in the wings, he was suffering with that swelling disease, oedema, I don't know what he had. He was sitting there and he said to me, 'You sure can play the piano, man.' I said, 'That's one of the things I do.' I was being sarcastic, and then I suddenly realized he was trying to be nice, and I tempered it."

"'That's fine for you,' I said. "You know karate, and I don't, and Mingus is big."

And at that point Ted Williams said, "You know, I don't know why you're so upset about it. I don't think anybody takes this seriously except you and Mingus."

Never have I seen Oscar Peterson laugh as hard. He kept repeating what Ted had said, or trying to, put his head down in his arms on the table, his big body shaking helplessly, and laughed till, when he raised his head, you could see tears on his face.

But a time in all our lives was ending. Ray Brown was quite serious about retiring from the road life. Thags – Ray's nickname for Ed Thigpen; Ray had nicknames for everybody – was thinking about leaving too. As racial tension at last gave rise to flames and violence in Newark, Los Angeles, and other cities, Ted Williams moved away to Mexico, his mother's homeland, even as many black jazz musicians, the superb trumpet and fluegelhorn player Art Farmer among them, took residence in Europe.

I moved to New York and never saw the London House again. When I went back to Chicago years later, I made a little pilgrimage to the location of this great restaurant and jazz club, remembered with such curious affection by both customers and musicians. George and Oscar Marienthal, the brothers who owned it, and who had treated musicians with dignity, were long since dead, and the place was one of the outlets of a fast food chain. It was a Burger King now.

Art Farmer made the same pilgrimage. He looked at it and got tears in his eyes.

According to the terms of the 1961 sale of Verve, Norman Granz was to stay on as an adviser. But he had less and less to do with the company, and Creed Taylor was hired by MGM as the label's new executive director. Richard Palmer, in his monograph on Oscar, says that Taylor "at once embarked on a policy very different from Granz's. It was, in a word, commercial: he had been hired to make money with jazz artists, and Granz's original ideals were forgotten. Taylor's first major decision was to fire all Verve's contract artists except Johnny Hodges, [Stan] Getz, [Ella] Fitzgerald, and Peterson."

That's not exactly the way it happened. Taylor did not forget Granz's original ideals; he shared at least two of them: to get jazz to the largest possible audience and to make money so that the music could survive. Granz is on record a number of times in stating that view. Taylor felt that the label was overloaded with artists, none of whom could be given the individual attention necessary to his or her commercial and aesthetic development. But he also disliked the Verve image that Granz had built – everything about it, including the cover designs, liner notes, sound mixes, and that assembly-line quality that Richard Palmer almost deplores. Taylor felt so strongly about it that he suspended all releasing by Verve for six months, stopped the flow of product to market, in an attempt to erase the old Verve image as much as possible from the public mind.

Verve became an immensely successful label under Taylor's management. He signed Bill Evans, and for a brief time the two pianists many people (particularly pianists) considered the greatest in jazz were under contract to the same company.

Ed Thigpen left the trio in 1965. Like Herb Ellis, he had spent six years with the group. He settled for a time in Toronto. Then he and Lois were divorced and he moved to Denmark, married a Danish girl, fathered two children, and became a fixture of the European jazz world.

Shortly after that Ray announced that he too was leaving. He had been with Oscar fifteen years. "That's longer," he said later, "than most guys stay with their wives."

"Mr. Brown Goes to Hollywood," a headline read in the New York *Post*. The date was November 14, 1965. "The role played by partnerships in jazz is without parallel in any other form of music," Leonard Feather wrote beneath it. "Very shortly the most effective musical collaboration of the 1950s will come to an end. Ray Brown, winner of wall-to-wall trophies as the foremost bassist in jazz, will leave the trio of Oscar Peterson, whose achievements as a pianist are comparably distinguished, and will settle in Hollywood.

"Since 1951, the Pittsburgh-born bassist has played Castor to Peterson's Pollux, helping to generate some of the most exciting combo music of our generation – first as a duo, then with guitar added, and from 1958 with drums replacing guitar.

"So keen has been the Peterson–Brown empathy that Brown admits the artistic peak of his career may have passed.

"'Regardless of who liked our music and who doesn't, I think we have worked up the kind of feeling that can only come with years of co-operation, and I like to believe we've done it better than anyone else.'

"Brown's departure will take place without any element of B-movie Tommy Dorsey-quits-Jimmy-in-a-huff melodrama. He and Peterson, still close friends, understand that there comes a time in every jazzman's life when suitcases, hotel rooms, and long-distance calls home no longer are a substitute for living.

"'It wasn't just the fifteen years with Oscar,' Brown said. 'It was twenty years on the road, counting Dizzy Gillespie and other bands I was with, and all those tours with Jazz at the Philharmonic. So it's about time to sit down.

"'I can't predict how much jazz I'll continue to play; I do know that I expect to get a lot of commercial studio work.'"

Legend has it that within forty-eight hours of his arrival in California Ray was working. The legend is correct.

Two years later, in Los Angeles, Leonard Feather did another interview with Ray, one that indicated just how weary he had become of the schedule with the trio. "I generally thought that with more money, you could afford not to work as hard, but we were still going to Europe – well, we had a stretch in 1965 of forty-seven one-nighters without one day off. Frankly, at that pace I don't need that kind of money, because it only can be used in the hospital sooner or later.

"I guess the best job I had all that year was with Sinatra. Sinatra would only work three days one week or two days the next. He's big enough to do that.

"I had one very close friend out here, Herb Ellis, whom everybody knows I worked and roomed with for eight years. I had told him that I was coming out – I had intimated for a couple of years that I was coming – but I finally caught him one night and told him that I was coming out around the first of the year, around February or March.

"Two good things have happened.

"That summer, around August, '65, Henry Mancini came into Chicago to do something at McCormick Place, and he came down to the London House a couple of nights to have dinner and hear the trio. One night he asked me to come over, and he introduced himself and said, 'I hear you're going to move to California.'

"I said, 'Yeah, around the first of the year.'

"He said, 'Let me know when you get out there, and I'll call you to do some things.'

"I thought that was very nice of him, but generally you can't count on something like that, you know. Somebody says, 'Call me when you get to the Coast,' and six months from now anything could be happening …

"I had gotten back from Tokyo around the 23rd of January and I was lying across my bed. My phone rang, and it was Hank Mancini. He asked me if I was still coming out, and when I said yes, he said he had a couple of dates for me. This was really heartening. It made me feel good."

Oscar replaced Thigpen with Louis Hayes, who had previously

been with the Cannonball Adderley Quintet. When Ray left, Oscar hired bassist Sam Jones, who had been Hayes' team-mate with the Adderley group.

This fascinated me. During one of the countless Chicago conversations, Oscar had cited the failure of critics, in their praise of the Adderley group, to notice that Sam Jones played out of tune. It was too good to pass up, and when I ran into Oscar in New York, I grinned and pointed a finger at him and said, "I thought you said Sam Jones plays out of tune!"

And Oscar, not retreating an inch, said, "He does!"

CHAPTER 15

BLACK FOREST SOLO

Peterson's contract with Verve ran out in 1964 and he left the company. He signed with Limelight, a new subsidiary of Mercury that would prove to be desultory and ineffectual and eventually was closed down. The Limelight albums are not rated among his best, although one is notable as his first substantial venture as a composer. This was the *Canadiana Suite*. Oscar sent me a test pressing in New York and asked me to write the liner notes, which I did.

For some time Oscar had been playing a series of private parties for a German millionaire. They would eventuate in some of the most acclaimed albums of his career – indeed, Richard Palmer would write, "some of the most remarkable recordings in jazz history." These included his first important solo albums.

Hans Georg Brunner-Schwer's grandfather was a small businessman named Hermann Schwer, who manufactured bicycle bells in the Black Forest – Schwarzwald, in German – in the late nineteenth century. During the pioneering days of radio broadcasting, he began manufacturing receivers. The business grew.

Schwer had no sons to whom he could leave his business. He had only a daughter, Gretl, and she disappointed him when she married. She chose a musician, a symphony conductor named Brunner, who had been a classmate and friend of Herbert von Karajan. Brunner lived just long enough to father two sons, Hans Georg, born a little less than two years after Oscar Peterson, on July 21, 1927, and Herman, who arrived two years later. His widow married a career army officer named Ernst Scherb.

Schwer's company was SABA, the acronym of a much longer name. Its factories were in the lovely little Schwarzwald city of

Villingen, not far from the Swiss border. The surrounding folded hills are covered with steep-sloping farms and deep pine forests. In the 1930s, SABA patented an automatic tuning device that locks a radio to a frequency, eliminating drift. It is still in use, though the patent has long since expired. SABA grew to be a major manufacturer of radio receivers. When World War Two arrived, the company was impressed into military manufacturing and prospered – until the Allied air forces put the small industries of Villingen, SABA among them, on their target list. They destroyed the SABA facilities.

With the defeat of Germany in 1945, Villingen fell into the French zone of occupation. The French commandant appropriated the finest home in the community for himself – the Brunner-Schwer house built by the grandfather and standing next to the ruined SABA works. The teen-aged boys, Hans Georg and Herman, and Gretl, their mother, were moved into the chauffeur's cottage. By then the grandfather was dead, and they, along with their mother, had inherited the estate, its lands, and what was left of SABA.

Stepfather Ernst Scherb, who had been captured on the eastern front, was at last released by the Russians, returned, and took over the reorganization of SABA, which he carried out with military discipline and clarity. In the meantime the French returned the home to its owners. Scherb decided the two boys should be trained to direct the company. Herman was a brilliant student who was chosen to run the business side of SABA. He obtained an MBA degree. Hans Georg was an indifferent student – in the formal sense at least – with a brilliant flair for those technical fields that interested him. He was elected to run the engineering and manufacturing side of the company.

Hans Georg had inherited from his father more than the love of music. Like the father – and like Oscar Peterson – he had the odd gift of absolute pitch. Again like Oscar, he was big, and he liked big things. He began collecting and restoring classic automobiles made by the now-dismantled Maybach company; some of his restorations are worth as much as half a million dollars. And Hans Georg built up, of all strange things, the world's largest collection of air-raid sirens, indicative of his intense interest in sound.

Hans Georg had learned to play accordion, then piano. Herman Brunner-Schwer, an enthusiastic soccer player, liked to associate with athletes; Hans Georg preferred the company of musicians and sound engineers. He knew the owner of the Berlin company that manufactured the excellent Neumann microphones, and people at Telefunken, as well as the manufacturers of the most sophisticated loudspeakers and recording equipment. He designed and installed on the third floor of his home at Villingen one of the most advanced recording studios in the world. An associate put it this way: "Hans Georg loved sounds that matched his personality, full and deep, going down if possible to ten cycles and up to twenty thousand cycles. Commercially, these things were not available, but he was striving to achieve them." The human ear cannot hear frequencies as low as ten cycles, but the body can feel them. And whereas the ear cannot hear higher than about fifteen thousand cycles – and many people can't hear even that far up the sound spectrum – the upper partials, as they are called, of sounds, which are in the very high frequencies, determine the timbres, the characteristic colours, of instruments.

Brunner-Schwer experimented with his advanced studio by recording German folk musicians from the Schwarzwald. But his deepest musical passion was for American bands of the swing era. Despite Hitler's formal proscription of jazz as "decadent Negroid Jewish music" – many musicians were sent off to concentration camps and eventually gas chambers for playing it – thousands of Germans nursed a secret love for the music and listened to caches of pre-war records or to the BBC from London, on whose signal they could hear Glenn Miller's air force band. Brunner-Schwer was one of these listeners.

In 1962, the Brunner-Schwer brothers began an association with a business consultant named Baldhard G. Falk, who had emigrated to the United States after gaining his doctorate in economics from the Free University in Berlin in 1951 and lived in San Francisco. Falk says the name Baldhard, drawn from Norse mythology and then misspelled on his birth certificate, is almost as odd in German as it is to the ear of the English-speaking, and even his American wife calls him BF. Falk cleared up a business problem in the United States for SABA and the Brunner-Schwer family, after which he became their American business agent. A tall, fair-haired, humorous Prussian of considerable personal charm, Falk got along well with Hans Georg. For one thing, he too was a jazz fan. Once during the war, he was almost arrested for playing *The Lambeth Walk* outdoors on a wind-up gramophone. "And that," he said with a chuckle, "wasn't even jazz."

One of Hans Georg's early musical assignments for Falk was to find the American jazz accordionist Art Van Damme, whom Brunner-Schwer, an accordionist, considered one of the greatest players of the instrument in the world, and have him go to Villingen to record.

In the last days of the Ray Brown–Ed Thigpen edition of the trio, Oscar was invited to perform in a paid engagement for a small group of Brunner-Schwer's friends. From that point on, he would go to Villingen at least once a year to play under exquisite circumstances for Brunner-Schwer. The audiences were small, no more than twenty or twenty-five persons, and raptly attentive. "They were really only props," Falk said with a smile. "I don't think Hans Georg cared whether they were there or not."

These parties were reminiscent of the nineteenth-century salon gatherings at which Chopin and Liszt were heard to advantage. The Brunner-Schwer house is in the midst of two and a half acres of groomed gardens. Musicians stayed as guests of the family in the home, which has a huge entrance foyer, a sweeping curved stairway, and wooden detailing hand-carved in the last century by Schwarzwald craftsmen. The parties were superbly catered by the staff of the Schwarzwald-Hotel Königsfeld.

Brunner-Schwer was never present except at the start of these recitals. He would first set his microphones, then go up to his recording equipment in a studio under the mansard roof, watching the performance on a television monitor. More perfect circumstances in which to make music would be difficult to imagine, and every musician who ever performed for Brunner-Schwer came away vaguely dazed by the pleasure of the experience. Sometimes there was no party at all: Oscar would sit at the piano in shirt sleeves, as at home, and muse pensively on the instrument while Hans Georg, unseen and for the instant forgotten, captured these reflections on tape.

A friendship developed between Brunner-Schwer and Oscar Peterson, despite the fact that Hans Georg spoke almost no English, although such was the perfection of his ear that the few words he did command were pronounced so well that one was deceived into assuming he spoke it fluently. But Baldhard Falk, when he flew in from San Francisco, or Brunner-Schwer's wife, Marlies, would translate for them. Both Oscar and Hans Georg, Falk points out, were physically big men, and they shared several passions – for jazz, for the piano, for advanced technology, and for sound.

Oscar was fascinated by everything about Brunner-Schwer's equipment and use of it, including the radical (for the time) way he miked a piano. He used, at least in the early days, two microphones, usually Neumanns, placed inside the instrument and so close to the strings that they were almost touching; a much more distant mike placement was usual at the time. Some of the microphones, in fact, were prototypes Brunner-Schwer had borrowed from their inventors before they were even marketed commercially. And the piano itself was superb, a full nine-foot concert grand, a German Steinway. The German-made Steinways were rated much more highly by pianists than the American-made instruments. Because of the power of his technique, Oscar dislikes pianos with light actions, and the action of Brunner-Schwer's Steinway was crisp and strong. After the salon recitals, when the guests were gone, Oscar and Brunner-Schwer would listen to the tapes, and Oscar would shake his head and tell his wife Sandy and anyone else who was there that no one had ever captured his sound the way Hans Georg did. And it seemed that these tapes were destined to languish unheard by the world, like Gerry Macdonald's tapes of the trio with Herb Ellis.

SABA was by now marketing high-fidelity equipment with capacities that exceeded the quality of available commercial recordings.

Hans Georg had gone into the recording business in a limited way, setting up the SABA label, on which he issued his Art Van Damme and other recordings, a total of forty albums sold through equipment dealers in Germany. The Oscar Peterson tapes could not be issued because Oscar was under contract to Limelight, and there was no plan to issue them, although they were far superior to the Limelight albums.

SABA continued to grow throughout the 1960s, finally reaching the point where it had to be refinanced or sold. The Brunner-Schwer family decided to sell and considered offers from several companies. Falk – after long and complex negotiations – finally made a deal with the American company General Telephone and Electronics. GTE acquired SABA but Hans Georg retained the music division, including the inventory of tapes. At this point Hans Georg decided to go fully into the record business, marketing his material through his MPS label – Musik Produktion Schwarzwald. He thought that nothing could announce his entry into the business with as much éclat as the Peterson material. And Oscar's Mercury contract had elapsed.

Falk flew in for Brunner-Schwer's 1968 Oscar Peterson house party. Oscar and Hans Georg listened to hours of the tapes they had accumulated, selecting not the best of the material but the best that was not covered by the Mercury contract. Recording contracts specify that the artist cannot re-record material for a certain period, usually five years. None of the tunes recorded for Limelight could be issued in an MPS version. Oscar called Norman Granz to discuss possible release of the material by MPS. Falk, whose fluent English was one of his important business assets to Brunner-Schwer, spoke to Granz, who named a price to which Hans Georg agreed, and, that being done, Granz sent them a contract.

"It was the shortest contract I have ever seen," Falk said. "Only a page and a half long. It was a world-wide contract for release of four albums by Oscar, for a lump sum and royalties. So MPS started with that, those four albums. Hans Georg got his money from GTE for SABA and started investing heavily in music and hiring salesmen. It was at that time that we met you in New York."

So it was. Oscar returned from West Germany in 1968 with test pressings of the first albums. Falk and Hans Georg flew to New York. Oscar called me. Given his developed skill at hiding his emotions, I was surprised at the enthusiasm in his voice.

Oscar had told me on several occasions that his best playing had been done in private. I had heard him play with a wonderful muted pensiveness, and nothing on record – even the London House records themselves – equalled what I used to hear in the late-night sets at the London House.

So when Oscar told me that he believed these German recordings were the best he had ever made, my eyebrows rose. He said he wanted me to write liner notes for at least two of the albums, both containing only solo performances. For now, he wanted me to meet the company's owner and his consultant in the United States. "The owner," he said, "is Hans Georg Brunner-Schwer, and his associate is – you're not gonna believe this name – Baldhard G. Falk." In the argot of jazz, Baldhard is slightly salacious.

I met Oscar, Brunner-Schwer, and Falk for lunch at the Carlisle Hotel, after which Hans Georg and BF, as I was learning to call him, repaired to my apartment to listen to the pressings. I remember being astonished by the recordings. I told Oscar, "This is the way you really play," and one of the albums was titled *The Way I Really Play*. In the days after that, I played the albums for various jazz musicians, who agreed that these were the best Peterson recordings they had heard. By then Oscar had left New York to tell interviewers in various places that he thought the MPS recordings were his best.

And critics were soon agreeing with him, including some who had been among his skeptical listeners. In *The Times* of London, May 11, 1970, Max Harrison wrote that, after the Carnegie Hall concert of 1949, "in terms of fame and fortune he never looked back: he toured the world and made far too many LPs. Indeed, musically he seemed never to look forward. He traded in the dullest sort of virtuosity – keyboard mobility as an end in itself, the effect frantic but uncommitted. That was sufficient to enthral an international audience, yet gradually the *cognoscenti* gave Peterson up, and I recall describing him, in *Jazz Monthly* a decade ago, as 'the biggest bore in jazz.' Always there were a few people, chiefly jazz pianists, who stubbornly maintained that in private he played in a manner which flatly contradicted his public image, but evidence was lacking and we never believed them.

"Peterson's apparent satisfaction with his easy successes confirmed such incredulity, yet between 1963 and 1968, when pausing from his travels, he was recording, almost secretly, at Hans Georg Brunner-Schwer's Villingen studio in the Black Forest. As never before, Peterson had sole charge of repertoire, tape-editing, etc., and many performances accumulated over those years were rejected. The survivors amount to about 170 minutes' jazz, however, and show him in so new a light as to compel reassessment. Earlier, irrespective of his material's character, Peterson strung together quite mechanical pianistic devices, the detritus, it sounded, of a thousand half-hearted improvisations, but here, as, say, the compact exploration of *Perdido* shows, spontaneity is balanced with the fruits of long consideration. These 26 treatments last from two minutes to over a quarter of an hour and always the length feels exactly appropriate. They are, in fact, substantially different one from another, and as the contrast between *Little Girl Blue*'s velvety quiet and the bouncing gaiety encapsulated in *Lulu's Back in Town* proves, the range of expression is wider than on all Peterson's other discs together....

"To hear Peterson's *I'm in the Mood for Love* pass from sombre opening chords through increasing but always cogent elaboration to its churning double-tempo climax is like watching the speeded-up growth of a natural organism, and the transmutation process whereby so much is drawn from so bad a tune is inexplicable....

"[Oscar Peterson] is, indeed, a conservative, a rare type in this music, but he has learnt one of Tatum's main lessons well, for, as the lithe, bounding phrases of *Foggy Day* or *Sandy's Blues* show, in his best moments decoration assumes a functional role and so is no longer decoration, ornament becomes integral to the processes of development."

Two years later, when *My Favorite Instrument* – one of the two solo albums for which I had written the notes – came out in England, Harrison wrote in *Jazz Monthly,* "It is a luxury to be able to indulge in a categorical statement for once, and to assert that this is the best record Peterson ever made. Of course, the sleeve note gets too excited and says he is better than Tatum" – the barb's aimed at me – "although even an offhand comparison between this version of *Someone to Watch over Me,* described as a tribute to the older man, with the master's own performance of this piece reveals a considerable difference in executive refinement, and further listening uncovers the more concise yet more subtle structure of Tatum's reading. Such claims on Peterson's behalf are futile, but it is important to define just what his musical and pianistic achievements are.

"He is not original. Unlike, say, a James P. Johnson or a Cecil Taylor, there is very little in his music that can be isolated as being his alone. Peterson's strongest suit is his knowledge. He has learnt every procedure that has occurred in piano jazz up to his time and uses them in his own way. Put something in a new context and it can take on a fresh meaning: what is personal in [these] performances is not the musical and pianistic elements of which they consist but the particular way these are put together. Peterson's other point, obviously, is a technique which, unlike the techniques of most jazz pianists, has been systematically developed in all areas. This accounts not only for the feeling of completeness which all these improvisations convey despite their diversity of musical character, but also for his powers as a soloist: what Peterson *does* share with Tatum is that, contrary to popular superstition, he has no need of bassist or drummer. This is confirmed by the above program's freedom from that mechanical aspect which makes so many of his trio performances infuriating, and this in turn is underlined by such factors as that each track seems exactly the right length – two minutes is just right for *Lulu,* as are six for *Little Girl Blue.* And from none of the editions of his trio have we often encountered, say, the mood of wistfulness that sounds through *Bye Bye, Blackbird* or the lyricism of *I Should Care.*

"That Peterson's stance is essentially retrospective is shown by such things as the music's rhythmic vocabulary, as on *Perdido*. But notice that he displays a far better sense of dynamics here than we should ever suspect from his trio recordings, and that he makes a use of the bottom register superior to that of almost any other jazz pianist. The integration of bravura into the overall shape of *Body and Soul* is fine, too, even if it lacks the continuity which (no matter how often he is accused of not having it) is one of Tatum's most conspicuous qualities. Hear also the internal balance of the chords in *Who?*, the depth and warmth of tone – all taken for granted by non-pianistic listeners but none of them easy to achieve. Perhaps *Little Girl Blue* is Peterson's best recorded performance: its velvety quiet follows most tellingly on *Lulu's* brief yet bouncing gaiety, and while nobody would claim for him the depth of Powell or Yancey, this music is more than merely pensive.

"Here, I am sure, is the one Peterson LP that should be in every collection."

The first four MPS albums were not only a critical success, they sold well in Europe, particularly West Germany.

Brunner-Schwer made two more albums with Oscar and then suggested a more formal and planned contractual arrangement. In view of the expansion of MPS, Norman Granz negotiated a contract calling for higher fees. And he suggested that for the first album, Oscar be recorded with a large orchestra, including strings. Oscar had made only one other album of that kind, a somewhat abortive and forgotten Verve recording with Nelson Riddle. Granz suggested that the arranger be Claus Ogerman, and Hans Georg immediately agreed. Ogerman – like Falk a Prussian by birth – was a far different arranger from Riddle. A former jazz pianist himself, he had revealed, in albums made for Creed Taylor at Verve after Granz sold it, deep sensitivity for soloists in albums with Bill Evans and Antonio Carlos Jobim. Ogerman had a distinctive gift for writing string arrangements of a curiously austere lyricism that somehow enhanced but did not interfere with the featured player. Granz suggested that the album be made in New York, and since Ogerman then lived there, it was a sensible arrangement, to which Brunner-Schwer agreed.

The session was set for the A&R recording studio, one of the best and best-known in New York. Oscar at that time was a contracted Baldwin artist. In exchange for the endorsement of their instruments by major artists, which they are able to use in their advertising, piano companies provide instruments on command for the engagements of their contracted artists in various locations. Steinway was noted for its indifference to endorsements; Baldwin sought them sedulously. And when Oscar arrived in a city, he had only to pick out a Baldwin he liked and the company would send him the instrument.

But the concert grand Baldwin he chose for the album with Ogerman for some reason could not be used, and Oscar confronted a studio piano he found inadequate – "I don't like the box," as he put it. He declined to record on it. Brunner-Schwer faced a dilemma. He had committed substantial funds to this recording, including Ogerman's arranging and conducting fees, the cost of the A&R studio, and the salaries of the musicians who sat there waiting, and would be paid whether they played or not. He made a decision: to record the orchestra now and to overdub Oscar's part in Villingen on the piano Oscar liked. Oscar instantly agreed, the session proceeded, and he completed the album later in Villingen. The album, *Motions and Emotions*, is a lovely piece of work. It would be described by some jazz critics as a pop album, but the definition is irrelevant. Oscar plays an extended embellishment of Jobim's *Wave* that is breath-taking.

Oscar made in all fifteen albums for MPS. The concepts for them were planned and prepared, often in conversations with Brunner-Schwer. One of them was a quartet album with Bob Durham on drums and Sam Jones on bass – and guitarist Herb Ellis. It was called *Hello, Herbie,* the first words Oscar said when his old friend arrived from California for the sessions. Another was an album called *In Tune,* with the brilliant vocal group known as The Singers Unlimited, which Oscar had brought to the attention of Brunner-Schwer. Led by Gene Puerling, the group's arranger, and with the young Chicago studio singer Bonnie Herman as the lead voice, the group made elaborate orchestrational albums by complex overdubbing of the four voices. Bonnie Herman vividly remembers the sessions. By then Brunner-Schwer had built a new studio on the property, installing therein a Boesendorfer Imperial concert grand piano. It was there, in fact, that Oscar became familiar with the Boesendorfer, which instrument he would embrace. "You could look out the window when you were recording," Bonnie said. "You'd see all the gardeners working, and the paths leading from the main house, lined with roses. And every morning there was the smell of fresh-ground coffee. Marlies, Hans Georg's wife, would make us fresh-ground coffee."

The last recording for Brunner-Schwer, a trio album with Niels-Henning Ørsted Pedersen on bass, was made in the spring of 1972. Norman Granz had returned actively to the record business, with the Pablo label – named for Picasso – in Beverly Hills. Oscar became a contracted Pablo artist, doing all his recording from then until 1986 for that company.

Oscar told the French writer François Postif in an interview published in *Le Jazz Hot* in April 1973, "I've never counted the number of albums that have come out under my name or under that of my trio, but I think it has to be about 60 now. And I made lots of albums with other artists, like Dizzy and Roy. But I think the best album I've ever recorded was the first solo album for MPS." He was referring to *My Favorite Instrument.* "Perhaps it was because it was the first album where I was completely free, and in which I did what I felt like. I chose the tempos, the keys I wanted to play in, if I wanted to change keys in the middle of a tune, there was no problem, because I was alone at the piano, alone with no one to give me problems."

It is a wistful statement. "Wistful" is the word his nemesis, Max Harrison, used to describe his performance of *Bye-Bye Blackbird* in the Villingen recordings. Harrison said of the first Schwarzwald albums: "It would be ridiculous to sound a valedictory note on a man of 45, yet it is through such music that Peterson will be remembered."

The great improvisers of the past, Chopin and Liszt among them, had only one way to leave their music for posterity: to write it down on paper. But the jazz improviser can leave his actual performances, and his recordings are his legacy. It is not coincidence that jazz evolved coeval with the development of recording technology.

Those MPS recordings, the sound quality of which was the state of the art at the time, are so important a part of the Peterson body of work that one is forced to ask, what happened there in the Schwarzwald?

For one thing, the man who once made ten albums in a week in Chicago recorded only fifteen albums in Villingen in eleven years, and mostly under ideal conditions.

Oscar Peterson is quite possibly the bravest man I have ever known. Challenge him, and he will respond. If it's a drunk in the London House or the Hong Kong bar who is distracting him, he will simply put on the pressure until he has conquered both the distraction and the distractor. If bravura display is all that will reach the back of a huge concert hall, that will be what he does. He simply will not surrender.

But at Villingen, with the roses in the garden and the smell of coffee in the morning, he had no need to command or demand respect: he already had it, had indeed the adoration of the people around him.

Jack Batten described one of Oscar's appearances in Toronto. "Peterson," he wrote in *Maclean's* (April 17, 1965), "was introduced to the Massey Hall audience with a lavish encomium by a local disc jockey, and the crowd – the house had been sold out two days earlier – hailed him long and vigorously as he walked onstage, a huge coffee-colored man of bearish contour, resplendent in a modish jet tuxedo and laceless patent-leather shoes. His hands and wrists dazzled with gold – gold cufflinks, gold wristwatch band, gold identification bracelet, and large beveled gold wedding band on his left hand."

The identification bracelet was the one Fred Astaire had given him.

What happened at Villingen?

Nothing had to be conquered. The gold, as it were, came off, the patent-leather shoes were slipped aside. There in the Black Forest the shy and sensitive boy from Montreal High School sat down at a Steinway and played *Bye-Bye Blackbird.*

CHAPTER 16

RUSSIAN JAM

The success of the Beatles and other rock groups during the 1960s caused considerable hardship in the jazz world, not to mention major social changes and the commencement of the drugged society. Minor labels grew into major labels, and major labels began to be absorbed into conglomerates. The companies were no longer interested in high-quality music with a long shelf life, they wanted high-turnover material that would sell hugely in a short time and be replaced by more of the same. Those jazz performers who retained contracts were being required to record current pop music that had neither the musical nor the lyrical content requisite to serious interpretation.

Norman Granz accurately assessed the situation in a 1971 statement to Leonard Feather: "It's a disgrace what the jazz artists of today are being forced to do, recording material that is all wrong for them. It's criminal, too, that someone like Sarah Vaughan was allowed to go without making a single record for five years. And it's an outrage that of the 27 albums I produced with Art Tatum, not a single one is available....

"The record companies have changed. Executives today are only concerned with the fact that they can gross $9 million with the Rolling Stones. They forget that a profit is still a profit, that you're still making money if you only net $9 thousand. I keep telling people that, and they think I'm crazy."

Finally, disgusted by the industry's ignoring of such people as Count Basie, Granz announced the formation of his Pablo label. One of its first releases was *The Oscar Peterson Trio: Live in Tokyo*, recorded in June 1964. He followed up with a two-volume package called *History of an Artist,* recorded in December 1972 and February 1973. In these recordings Oscar was reunited with various players with whom he had been associated in the past, including Irving Ashby, Barney Kessel, and Herb Ellis. It was in this period that he began working with the young Danish bass virtuoso Niels-Henning Ørsted Pedersen and, sometimes, guitarist Joe Pass. This trio was recorded at the London House in May 1973.

An afternoon in the spring of 1974 found Oscar in a Vancouver television studio, taping a re-creation of Jazz at the Philharmonic for TV. The set was decorated with plastic plants and plaster Greek urns. The group he led included trumpeter Dizzy Gillespie, tenor saxophonist Zoot Sims, trombonist Al Grey, bassist Niels-Henning Ørsted Pedersen, and drummer Louis Bellson. Nearby at all times was Norman Granz, and, taking notes for an article that would appear June 22 in the Saturday newspaper supplement *The Canadian,* reporter Paul Grescoe.

They ran through some of the music, then took a break. Oscar chatted with Grescoe. Oscar was then forty-eight and talking of retirement. Grescoe could not know that he had been doing this for years. He used to tell me in Chicago that he was thinking of giving it all up, that he had never played in public as well as he played at home.

Now Oscar confided to Grescoe: "I'm at a tremendous crossroads. I still love to play, but I'm really undecided how much longer I want to keep it up. There are certain things I want to do that I haven't done. Photography: I've reached the darkroom stage." That statement is extremely puzzling. He had been an expert in the darkroom for years, processing colour in his own lab at least as far back as 1960. In his 1962 *Nugget* article, Leonard Feather noted that at last count Oscar owned a Leica, a Hasselblad, a Bolex, a 3-D, a Lenhof, a Gami, and several more. Lil had given him a colour enlarger for his birthday two years before that. "Several photos have been published," Feather wrote, "and he could make an excellent living as a photographer."

"Astronomy," Oscar said to Grescoe. "I was into it for a while, but I just didn't have the time...

"I wouldn't retire really – just because I stopped playing publicly

... I'm looking forward to that day. There are too many other players around for me to hog the stage. Even if I were to give up playing
entirely – and I'm thinking about it – I can write, I can listen.

"I wouldn't solve it just by taking a year's sabbatical. I detest airports, for one thing, and I've had enough of hotel lobbies. I'm
almost fifty years of age." The most unpleasant hotel lobby experience of his life in fact lay a few months in his future.

"I must say that for the last five years I've been home for two and
three months a year and sort of feel normal. I'm not a road person.
This is not my idea of existing." He said he had already cancelled
some concerts because of the arthritis in his hands. And he said of
the Canadian attitude to the country's talent, "We're very rough on
our own in Canada. I'm so happy to see Anne Murray come along. I
don't think it should be as it was in my day, that to make it, you had
to go to the States." He had apparently forgotten Murray's statement that the Canadians ignored her until the Americans recognized her.

Still another detail about how Granz first came to discover
Peterson came up at this TV session, possibly because being in
Vancouver jogged Granz's memory. Granz told Grescoe that he
first heard the Peterson boogie-woogie records on the juke-box of
a delicatessen in Vancouver back in 1945. And that makes sense. It
will be remembered that he took his earliest Jazz at the Philharmonic tour up the North American West Coast and went broke in
Victoria. "I didn't like him at all," Granz said. "He just didn't
impress me. Probably it was a built-in arrogance I had because my
show was the biggest thing around."

Granz said he had first been impressed by Peterson during a
1949 trip to Montreal to book a concert.

Neither Oscar nor Norman Granz mentioned to Grescoe that they
were about to tour the Soviet Union for the Canadian Department
of External Affairs. "We didn't mention it because we didn't know
until the last minute that we were really going," Granz recalled in
April 1987. "The negotiations had been going on at the government level for two years. The kind of money the Russians were
offering was ludicrous. We couldn't afford to go for it. It began

inching up, but it still wasn't what we were accustomed to. And the Canadians didn't have the vaguest idea where Oscar was going to play or where we were going to stay. I was uneasy about the tour from the very beginning."

It was not the first tour of the U.S.S.R. by foreign jazz artists. The first *unofficial* appearance by foreign jazz performers occurred in mid-1959, when the Americans Dwike Mitchell and Willie Ruff went to Russia in the guise of members of the Yale University Russian chorus. Pianist Mitchell and bassist Ruff soon showed their true musical colours, playing at Moscow's Tchaikovsky Conservatory – the first jazz concert by Americans in Soviet history. Then, in 1962, Benny Goodman took a big band on the first *official* jazz tour of Russia, causing one sensation among the jazz fans there, another in the U.S. press because of reports of friction between Goodman and his musicians.

For two decades the American broadcaster and jazz authority Willis Conover's *Music USA* programs had been beamed into the Soviet Union and indeed all over the world by the Voice of America. Soviet authorities had given up efforts to jam his broadcast, and, in the age before cassette recordings, Russian jazz lovers had been making illicit engravings of his broadcasts on used X-ray plates, which then circulated in the Soviet underground. Granz says there was a fascination with anything from the West. "I could have taken Johnny Cash there, and he would have sold out," he said.

Authoritarian governments have always manifested a paranoia towards jazz, from Hitler's Third Reich to modern Czechoslovakia, which in September 1986 imprisoned seven members of the jazz section of the Czech musicians' union for purported illicit business activities. The music's call – indeed, demand – for idiosyncratic and very free personal expression within a democratic musical format has obvious political symbolism.

During the czarist domination of Finland, performance of Sibelius's stirring *Finlandia* was forbidden. Russian authorities, then, have shown a nervous sensitivity about the political effects of music since before the revolution of 1917. And Soviet authorities have further revealed a penchant for tit-for-tat retaliation for slights, real or merely perceived.

In October and November 1974, two Ukrainian singers, baritone Dmytro Hnatiuk and coloratura soprano Yvhenia Miroshnichenko, visited Canada. Canada has a large Ukrainian population, much of which remains unreconciled to the Soviet domination of the land of their forefathers, and Hnatiuk and Miroshnichenko were picketed during their Canadian tour. Some observers suggested that this might have had something to do with events that unfolded when Peterson arrived in Russia with drummer Jake Hanna, bassist Niels Pedersen, Norman Granz, Oscar's wife, Sandy, and Granz's Danish wife, Grete.

Arrangements for the tour, including travel and hotel accommodations, had been made by the Soviet concert booking agency, Gosconcert. Peterson and Granz were advised on their arrival that the four engagements in Moscow were sold out, as were the eight scheduled for Tbilisi, the capital of Georgia, and Yerevan, the capital of Soviet Armenia. Three concerts set for Tallinn, the Estonian capital, had been sold out for more than a month.

A professional freelance photographer who worked for Gosconcert at that time was Naum Khazdam, then head of the Leningrad Jazz Club. Khazdam had photographed some of the Mitchell – Ruff Duo performances and recalls a jam session in which they participated in a Leningrad apartment. With characteristic ironic Russian wit, Khazdam said, "They were questioned by musicians, jazz fans. KGB." Khazdam, who later emigrated and joined the photography staff of the New York *Times,* said, "In 1974, I was connected with jazz musicians and jazz activities in Soviet Union, and this was third trip of big great American musicians." (The Russian language does not contain definite or indefinite articles, which structural characteristic is carried over into the way Russians speak other languages.) "First was Benny Goodman, then Duke Ellington, and third is Oscar Peterson. As I found out later, Oscar Peterson came not from United States but from Canada.

"Whole story of Oscar Peterson was complex of troubles. One, for example, is not-tuned piano, which they gave him in Ural Hotel in Moscow. He was very angry. And general treatment of foreigners make Norman Granz angry. And I think he think troubles part of racism, too. I don't have proof of this, but I think it is. There is very big racism in Soviet Union. Different kind as here. And black people feel very uncomfortable." Khazdam turned out to be right: Granz notes pointedly that African students in Moscow suffer severely from discrimination.

"And Ural in Moscow is second-rate hotel," Khazdam said. "It's very bad hotel, it's not even an Intourist hotel. Intourist hotels mostly built by foreigners, service is much better, equipment better, food better." And with a wry smile: "More microphones."

Granz was puzzled that no concert was scheduled for Leningrad, the beautiful city on the Neva delta designed and built by architects and artisans from all over the world for Peter the Great as his "window on Europe." Granz and Peterson simply wanted to see it, in particular the collection of modern art in the Hermitage. "I told Oscar," Granz said, "the Hermitage has some fantastic Picassos. Also Matisses. I knew the Hermitage Picassos very well from reproductions."

So he arranged for the group to visit Leningrad as tourists, before the start of the concert tour. They arrived on a November evening to be picked up in what Granz described as a broken-down old bus. "I told the Russians," Norman recalled, "if Herbert von Karajan or Leonard Bernstein was arriving, you wouldn't meet them like this. There was no point in my asking if this was racism, because they wouldn't answer." They visited the Hermitage only to be disappointed by the Picasso collection. The best of the paintings, Granz said, weren't even on display.

They stayed one night in Leningrad. Next day they were to make a one-hour flight to Tallinn, but they were told they would have to travel by train. The twelve-hour trip was made overnight. They stayed three days in Tallinn, playing concerts and some jam sessions with Russian musicians. Granz arranged for a Russian technician to record one concert as a memento of the trip. The sound quality was sufficiently good that he was later able to issue the material on Pablo; the record is one of Peterson's better-known albums. (The liner notes carry the credit: "Produced by Norman Granzinsky.")

Then they travelled by plane to Moscow. "And that," Granz said, "is where things really started to jump off."

They arrived at one of the smaller airports, where their Intourist guide left them, though there was no one there to meet them, no one else to translate for them. "You can't be without an interpreter in Russia, where you need a paper for everything, to get in anywhere," Oscar said. "We waited for three hours at the airport, the six of us."

"Finally," Norman said, "someone came from the Canadian embassy and provided, with the Russians, another bus. When we got to the hotel, about five in the afternoon, I could see that it wasn't very good."

"It was bad news," Oscar said. "At that time the Russiya was the only hotel to stay in. They told us the Russiya was full. Someone told me that the Ural was the hotel where the farmers stayed when they brought their produce to Moscow."

Granz said, "I told the Canadian attaché, 'We're not staying here. No way.' We went to the Canadian embassy in the bus, and I told the attaché, 'Look, the way you're going to have to deal with these people is to tell them that if we're not put up in the best hotel, we're cancelling.' So he called the Gosconcert people, and they said that Oscar and his wife could stay at the Russiya, and the rest of us at the Ural. Oscar and I said, 'No. We're all going to the Russiya or we cancel the tour.'

"Finally they agreed and we went to the Russiya."

Everywhere they had stayed, "they had the famous ladies on each floor," Oscar said, referring to the women who monitor the movements of hotel guests. Goods had been disappearing from their luggage, stolen by government agents or by the maids – they never knew which. Grete Granz lost sweaters, cosmetics, and stockings. Musicians who took part in the Benny Goodman tour of 1962 encountered actress Shirley MacLaine in Moscow. She told them her purse, containing among other things her passport, had been lifted, by a thief or by government agents harassing her in retaliation for her meetings with students.

Oscar said, "It looked as if the Russians were doing the same thing to us they did with the Canadian hockey team. Whether all this was because they were trying to make us play badly, or fatigue us to the point where we couldn't play, so they could say afterwards, 'This is the kind of crap that comes from Canada,' I don't know. We weren't about to play badly, as you know about my group. But things began to happen – like the problem of getting meals."

It was late evening by the time they got their rooms at the Russiya. "And we couldn't get into the restaurant," Granz said. "It was booked. And we had no one to help us. We went down to a canteen and got something to eat. By now it was midnight. Oscar and I discussed the situation for two hours. I said, 'Look, if you're thinking what I'm thinking, let's cancel the tour.' He agreed. The next morning we went to the Canadian embassy."

Canada's ambassador to the Soviet Union at that time was Robert A.D. Ford, whom Oscar described as "a very tall, elegant man." Oscar recalled, "He was very sympathetic to our cause, and he said, 'I agree with you totally. They just finished doing this to our hockey team. I think it's unfair.'"

Granz said, "The ambassador told us that when the Canadian team played in Moscow, he was given an ordinary seat among the people, not among the officials – the representative of the country whose team was playing."

Ambassador Ford takes up the story at this point. Retired and living in France, he said in March 1987, "I don't think Soviet distrust of the Ukrainian-Canadian [situation] had anything to do with Peterson's treatment. It came partly from a combination of sheer incompetence and lack of organization, plus a distinct vein of racism. I was eight years dean of the diplomatic corps in Moscow, and I spent a lot of time trying to smooth the ruffled feathers of my African colleagues, who were treated with supreme indifference by the Soviet authorities.

"But the Soviets quickly realized that they had made a bad mistake with Peterson."

The ambassador called Gosconcert and advised it the tour was cancelled. "Then," he said, "when they saw he was earnest about cancelling, they did something unprecedented in my experience. A very senior member of Gosconcert together with an assistant deputy minister of culture called on me in my embassy to beg me to persuade Peterson to reverse his decision. I told them that it was up to them to do so, and the decision was his."

"There were three of them," Granz said. "There were always three of them, and one of them was usually a woman. She was the one who spoke English, but I always got the feeling the others did too. They pleaded with us. They said, 'You've got a contract with us.' I said, 'No we don't. We've got a contract with the Canadian government.'"

Oscar said, "I told them, 'When Ashkenazy or Igor Oistrakh comes to Canada, to my country, we put out the red carpet for them.'" Oistrakh was to visit Canada shortly after the Peterson visit to Russia. "I told them, 'We have pride in what we're doing in the jazz medium, and we're respected all over the world for it, and I'm not going to lose it here.'"

Oscar returned to the Russiya Hotel. Granz had a meeting at Melodiya, the Russian record label, which wanted to contract for the Russian release of one of the Peterson albums.

And Oscar got some visitors in his room. "It got very touchy," he said. "They sent some gentleman to see me."

The gentleman in question was Gennedy Pleshkev, who told Oscar that he represented the Soviet minister of culture. Oscar believed then and still does that Pleshkev was a KGB agent. Whatever Pleshkev's position, he harangued Oscar for more than an hour. He shouted that under no circumstances would they cancel the tour.

Pleshkev began pushing and shoving Oscar. "I finally told him if he put his hands on me again we were really going to have an incident. We ended up in the lobby, still arguing."

And at this point Granz returned. He saw Oscar in heated

conversation with Pleshkev and the same woman who had been at the Canadian embassy. And then, Granz recalled, a strange thing happened. The woman burst into tears. "She said, 'You've got to stay, we love Oscar Peterson!' I told her we were not staying. And she said, 'You're probably with the CIA.' I said, 'No, I'm just the manager.'"

Oscar said that Ambassador Ford stiffly told the Russians, "I want to know at the diplomatic level, are you preventing these people from going? Are you saying they cannot leave? Is that what you're saying? You have to tell me." The Russians became somewhat subdued, on this threshold of an international diplomatic incident, and denied that they were trying to detain the Peterson group. The ambassador said, "Fine. I want you to know they're going to the airport in our cars."

"He was wonderful," Oscar said.

Granz told the ambassador, "We want a plane out of here, the first plane, going anywhere. I don't care. Tokyo."

The convoy of Canadian cars made its way to the airport, where Granz found that the first flight out was to Copenhagen via Helsinki. The group took it and checked into the Plaza Hotel in Copenhagen. This was Tuesday, November 19. Two days later, on November 21, after word of the tour's cancellation had spread throughout the world, *Toronto Star* reporter Frank Rasky telephoned Oscar in Copenhagen. Oscar was critical of the Gosconcert people but had nothing but praise for the Soviet audiences. "The Russian people are fantastic jazz fans," Oscar, now feeling rested, told Rasky. "They're terrific. They gave us a fantastic reception."

Meanwhile, Jacques Asselin, chief press officer for the Department of External Affairs in Ottawa, had told the newspaper that his department was "seriously concerned" about the maltreatment of the Peterson group in Russia. And from the Canadian embassy in Moscow, a spokesman issued a statement that "an unfortunate series of errors had been committed and Gosconcert has apologized for the terrible foul-up."

Ambassador Ford said, "The public interest was immense. I

had organized a big luncheon for the day after the Moscow concert with Nikita Bogoslovsky, a well-known composer and secret jazz fan, and many Soviet critics. I had the luncheon [anyway], and the Russians were furious – not at Peterson, but at their government for fouling things up. They were sure it had been done deliberately to play down the importance of the concerts, but they did not anticipate Peterson's reaction or that of the Soviet public. And, of course, in spite of the censorship, everyone knew what had happened."

The official Gosconcert apology did nothing for jazz lovers who had flown from as far away as Siberia for the trio's appearance at Moscow's Variety Theatre. Some of them had spent half a year's income on the trip and tickets, and there were reports that many of them were in tears at the cancellation.

In the ranks of the disappointed was Naum Khazdam. He had photographed both the Goodman and Ellington tours and was preparing to photograph the Peterson tour when he learned that it had been cancelled. Not a word appeared in the Russian newspapers. "In Soviet Union, if something wrong, they never publish it," he said.

Oscar flew from Copenhagen to Canada. He went to Ottawa, where he was debriefed on the events of the tour by the Department of External Affairs. From Ottawa he flew to Toronto, where he had time only for a newspaper interview during a stopover, and then on to Los Angeles for a recording session with Granz.

In Moscow, Ambassador Ford said he had never known an artist to be treated as badly in Russia.

Oscar said that he had no hard feelings about the aborted tour and that he hoped to return to Russia some day.

But he has never done so.

The tour had done nothing to improve the relationship between Sandy and Oscar. Indeed, the strains appeared to have worsened it.

"I would finish playing and we would argue and fight in the hotel all night, until plane time the next morning. Then we'd get on the plane, scowling, and get off the plane and start all over again, and go to the gig bleary-eyed. Norman said, 'When are you going to come in looking like you've had four hours' sleep?'

"She joined the golf club here. That's not my speed. I'd have to pay dues. You know, 'Hey, Oscar, come on and play the piano for us, it's Saturday night.' She thought we were passing up a lot of friendships, and I said, 'I don't even have time for the friends I have.'

"After the Russian tour, I sent her home, that was it. She didn't think I was serious, I had done it once before."

Eric said, "I remember being awakened at home about three or four o'clock in the morning. It was Sandy, in tears, saying Oscar was angry at her, and she didn't know where he was. Then she called again a couple of hours later, and I tried to get her to calm down. Then Oscar called, and I said, 'I want to talk to you.' We met later, and I said, 'It's unfair, the way you're acting.' Then just before they broke up, and she was trying to save it, she called me. By then I was living in Los Angeles. I moved here in 1966. Oscar called me from San Francisco, and I flew up to try to be of some help."

Seventeen months after the Russian tour, Frank Rasky asked Oscar how he felt about at last being given something approaching appropriate recognition by his fellow Canadians. Oscar told Rasky, "I don't resent it. I can understand it. It's as though Muhammad Ali were to become my next-door neighbor. At first I'd revere him. After that I'd accept him as part of my environment.

"Don't get me wrong. I enjoy the way Canadians have shown their appreciation of me within the last ten years. I'm an ardent nationalist, and it's a great ego trip to be awarded the Order of Canada and to represent our country's culture on a jazz tour to Russia."

He told Rasky, using a term he'd employed two years earlier with Paul Grescoe in Vancouver, "Sure, I'm at a crisis crossroads in my career, and I've been living through a period of turmoil and upheaval. But man, I tell you I've never felt more at peace with myself. Never felt so blessedly lucky. Despite all my hit-and-miss bruises, I'm happy to count my blessings."

The interview was published in the *Toronto Star* the afternoon of July 10, 1976. Oscar and Sandy had been divorced one week.

"She's said to me since," Oscar said, "'Oh, I was such an idiot,' and that makes me feel funny, because it isn't that she was an idiot, we were both idiots. If I were not into what I am into, which is so demanding ... She was a great person, and I loved her deeply. I think she felt belittled."

CHAPTER 17

SERVICE TO CANADA

Jiro (Butch) Watanabe was born June 7, 1924, in New Westminster, British Columbia. New Westminster is a suburb of Vancouver, a pleasant community at the mouth of the Fraser River. Vancouver and its surrounding communities occupy one of the handsomest sites on earth, surrounded by snow-covered peaks of the Coast Range of the Canadian Rockies and on one of the major harbours of North America's West Coast.

There were innumerable Japanese communities to be found along the Pacific coast, all the way south to San Diego, made up of small merchants, fishermen, and farmers. They were apparently aware that war was coming. Butch attended a Japanese school where he was imbued with the virtues of the Japanese and taught to take pride in their military tradition. He remembers that his boyhood ambition was to go south to work in the Boeing aircraft plant in Seattle, become a great aeronautical engineer, and go home to the Japan he had never seen to design great bombers that would fly to the United States and Canada and kill occidentals. This ambition was seriously compromised by the acquisition of a trombone, on which he had five lessons before going on to teach himself music, and by a taste for the music called jazz.

After the Japanese attack on Pearl Harbor on December 7, 1941, the Americans rounded up all the Japanese population along their West Coast and herded them into concentration camps, although they did not use that term. Canadians, as usual, did what the Americans did and, as usual, more moderately. "There was no barbed wire," Butch said. But his parents and other families were transported to small towns in the valleys of central British Columbia, where they would be unable to do such things as spy on Canadian shipping or the American formations of B-17s. The bombers flew north during 1942 to begin pounding installations the Japanese had established in the Aleutian Islands.

"I was in my last year of high school when the war started," Butch recalled. "I got all kinds of pressure from my classmates after Pearl Harbor. They started moving the younger Japanese lads out of the coast regions in the spring of '42. I didn't want to go to a ghost town in the interior of British Columbia, which is where they sent most of the older folks and the kids.

"So I lied about my age. I was seventeen. I said I was eighteen and volunteered for a road gang. I was sent to a road camp in northern Ontario for several months, and then to southern Ontario, and worked on the sugar beet farms down there. By that time my sisters had moved to Montreal, where they were working as domestics. They called me up and asked me if I wanted to come to Montreal and go back to school. I went to Montreal and worked as a houseboy for a year and then went to Montreal High School and graduated. Trombone was just a hobby then. I wasn't trying to make any statement or anything."

It would be his profession. Butch came to know the whole Peterson family, and he was after 1946 a fixture of the jazz scene, playing at such places as the Club St. Michel, often with Oscar. He was something of an anomaly, with his Japanese face, blowing hot trombone with musicians most of whom were black.

Butch eventually moved to Toronto, where he became one of the first-call studio trombonists, and when Oscar moved to Toronto, they continued their association. Now and then Butch would travel with Oscar, just for the pleasure of the companionship. And it was Butch who found the piece of land on which Oscar would build his summer home.

Indeed Butch owned the property first, a lot overlooking a lake in the Haliburton region, 135 miles or so northeast of Toronto. Oscar fell in love with the place the moment he saw it, and Butch offered to sell it to him.

"Butch offered to *give* it to me," Oscar corrected. "I couldn't let him do that. So I bought it from him, and he bought another lot nearby."

During the summer of 1964, Butch and some friends from Toronto worked with Oscar on the construction of a small house. "The roads were terrible, all mud and gravel," Butch said. "We used to go up there weekends, and stay in tents. The house is built of British Columbia cedar logs, with interlocking sides. It took us a week or two at most to put the shell up."

The house stands on a sloping bluff above the lake, which is filled with lake trout, rainbow trout, and bass. "It was originally three small bedrooms, and a living-dining room," Oscar said. "Another bedroom and a music room have been added. The music room looks out on the lake, and I can work there and compose. It's placid. It's a total removal from the working world."

Often, when no one can find him, that's where he is.

As the 1960s progressed, so did Oscar's mother's arthritis, which finally confined her to her bed, and by circumstance the responsibility of caring for her fell on the youngest of her children, May. She was afflicted also with diabetes, which often involves the circulation in the limbs. Oscar was touring in Japan when Daisy telephoned him to say that the doctors had amputated one of their mother's legs. She died in 1970 at the age of eighty.

One evening early in the 1980s, home from the road, Oscar was watching television, growing increasingly annoyed at the commercials.

All the American networks are received across Canada, along with many of the independent stations. Acquiescing to the demands of black activists in the 1960s and '70s, American TV commercials had long reflected the ethnic diversity of the United States, but those of Canada remained all-white.

I was interviewing Oscar for an article for *Toronto Life* magazine. He said that there was something he would like to talk about publicly – discrimination in Canadian television commercials. "If," he added, "they'll print it."

"If I write it, I'm sure they'll print it," I told him. It was at that point that he urged me to watch Canadian TV commercials for the utter absence of black or Indian or oriental faces. And he talked about the smugness of Canadians towards American racial attitudes and periodic confrontations.

"It's only now," he said, "that we suddenly look and find that we're all human beings, and we've got the same kind of bigotry and greed as the rest of the world. We can't point the finger any more. We find that we have the same isms that many people in the world suffer with. We were too bloody complacent before. We'd sit around and say, 'Do you *believe* what's going on *there*? It couldn't happen here.' It could and it did.

"The world has changed. There are no more borders. You can't run home and be safe from the bomb, from the terrorists, from anything. We're all open to anything – certainly to the viruses we're sharing. If we're going to share the ills, I think we should share the good things."

I wrote the article for *Toronto Life,* including his comments on racism in television commercials. It was published in the issue of September 1981.

Much later, elaborating on the subject, Oscar said, "I really got annoyed – first, at the beer companies. I have a thing on for them anyway. There are so many of their ads on the air. I think Canada's national ailment is maybe beer drinking. It's such hypocrisy. On the one hand they're telling people not to drink and drive, and on the other hand it seems like every minute and a half you get a beer commercial.

"What really incensed me was that all of them projected the good life – the people out surfing, a bunch of guys at the cottage fishing, a bunch of guys playing rugby, a bunch of guys and girls having a party, having a good time – and never once did I see a black, or a Chinese, or a Japanese. It was a blatant affront to all the races that make up the fabric of Canada. They totally ignored them.

"I called a friend of mine at one of the newspapers. He recommended that I get in touch with an ethnic affairs group, a protective group. I told him, 'Look, I'm not a group person. I don't want to get into one of these things where we're going to be attending meetings and have social evenings. There's a problem here, and we've got to attack it.' But I went to see the group.

"There was a Chinese lady who came to my house with another lady who was a broadcaster, to interview me.

"The newspapers started picking it up. They called and said, 'You sound like you're displeased with something. You very seldom say anything,' and I said, 'Well I've got a lot to say now.'

"Then the television started. I called a press conference at the Toronto Men's Press Club. And then I got a communication from the office of Roy McMurtry, Ontario's attorney general. He said that he would like to meet with me. I'd cited certain things, examples of racism in Canada."

The Chinese woman who visited Oscar was Susan Eng, a volunteer worker with the Urban Alliance on Race Relations. As a result of their conversation, Oscar gave a speech on the morning of Saturday, December 3, 1983, to a meeting on "Minorities in Media: Advocacy Strategy." Approximately a hundred persons, including people from advertising industry professional associations, attended the gathering, held at the Ontario Institute for Studies in Education, on Bloor Street in Toronto. No copy of the speech seems to have survived, but one of the women present said he dwelt particularly on the effects on the children of minority groups of seeing only white faces in advertising. "I remember it well," she said. "It was a very moving speech."

Oscar described an incident to me:

"When I was preparing to build my cottage, looking at Butch's lot, I met the neighbours, George Christie and his wife. They were American, from Pennsylvania. And they were very nice to us. That day we ended up getting stuck in his driveway, which had a lot of mud in it. I told him I was thinking of buying the lot.

"The next time I came up, I said 'Hello' to him. He said to me, 'The lady in charge of these lot sales was up here the other night after you left. And she wanted to know if I had any aversion to a black living next door to me.' I told her, 'I don't care who lives next door to me, as long as they're decent neighbours.' My retort to him was that it was very strange that she didn't come and ask me if I had anything against someone white living next door to me. I think I have the same kind of rights.'

"I cited things like this as being denigrating to the various ethnic community members. I said, 'People like GM, Ford, Nissan, and other companies, never seem to admit in Canada that any blacks drive their cars or brush our teeth.'

"I met with Roy McMurtry, and he said, 'Let's think about this. There is legislation that says this should happen and that should happen. We can toughen it up. But sometimes when you go at people from the law, it just makes enemies of them. Let's try to talk to them. What if we invite them to lunch?' He wanted to get some company presidents together, some marketing people, some ad agencies. McDonald's and General Foods and some others. Well, the people from the ad agencies started scampering and skating about, and saying, 'Well, we don't have any blacks who apply for work in ads,' which was a lie.

"Meanwhile, a lady I knew who worked for a casting agency told me – and this is the amazing thing – that one of the black airlines from the Caribbean was coming up to do a commercial and requesting some children. And, she told me, they requested that the children not be too dark. So that shows you that that sickness is rampant in all races, even in one race against itself."

McMurtry contacted, among other people, John Foss, president of the Association of Canadian Advertisers. McMurtry had several meetings with the association and then set up a series of luncheons in Toronto – one at the University Club and most of the rest at the Albany Club. He and Oscar were able to express their concern about discrimination in advertising directly to the heads of major corporations and their ad agencies.

Suzanne Keeler, director of the advisory division of the Canadian Advertising Foundation, said, "The whole approach, by Oscar Peterson and Roy McMurtry, was very low-key. Many people at these meetings recognized that there was validity to what they were saying. Others of course did not see it."

Oscar's memory of the meetings is similar: "Some of the people at those luncheons were non-committal, some were very co-operative, and some said nothing. The day before one of these luncheons, one of the marketing managers from one of the beer companies made a remark in one of the papers that they were not going to change their policy just to suit me. He came on very harsh about it all. One of his bosses was at that meeting the next day. We called him on that. Roy's secretary or aide had the clipping with him. We asked, 'Is this the kind of co-operation you're planning to give us?' Of course he was so mad he didn't know what to say. He jumped up from the table and went to the phone. I don't know what happened.

"We met all kinds of reactions, some good, some bad, some indifferent."

In April 1988 in London, McMurtry, then high commissioner to the United Kingdom, told Michael Hanlon, the *Toronto Star*'s bureau chief there, that race relations had been one of his major interests as Ontario's attorney general. After becoming aware of Oscar's concern over discrimination in TV commercials, he got in touch with Oscar. "We co-hosted several luncheons, trying to get to the major ad firms, to express our concerns," McMurtry said. "We were trying to get them on our side. The response was very positive: most of them admitted they'd never thought about the issue. We were trying to raise their consciousness level.

"Oscar played a very major role. He was the big attraction, being such a well-known, distinguished Canadian. They were interested in getting to meet the great Oscar Peterson.

"Oscar is somebody I'm very proud to know. He brought a very passionate message and he was very concerned."

Because of Oscar's presence, it was possible for McMurtry to stay more or less in the background. McMurtry said he wanted to co-opt people rather than have them think the government was putting pressure on them. "You know how people can react to politicians," he said.

The luncheons continued over a period of six or eight months, in 1983 and '84. "I think it was a very important initiative,"

McMurtry said. "The response was gratifying. We did see, over a period of a few months, many more black faces in print ads. We weren't happy at first with some TV advertising, but we knew it would take time."

John Foss said, "It's impossible to say exactly how much influence Oscar Peterson had. But after those meetings, the industry largely corrected what was a terrible imbalance. I think today there is a much better reflection of the changing community, and Oscar Peterson played an important part."

Oscar said in April 1988, "I kept an eye on it, as best I could, but that's not easy when you're travelling around the world. But when I did come home I did start to see some changes. Once in a while you saw a black in a beer commercial. But you know where it goes from that. Tokenism. One! Have none or have three. Not one. There's always one. I call it one TTS, one Token Television Spook. We met the rule, folks. It's ludicrous. Here's Bill Cosby in your face every day for Jello. Telling you to buy Kodak film. Other than Bill Cosby, I have yet to see a black doing something for Kodak.

"I'm surprised at the Japanese car makers for nurturing this. When in Rome do as the Romans do, but you don't go to Rome to become part of the Mafia. If you're going to come to Canada with your product, and do nothing but spread more bigotry, when the people are bigoted about you, you're in the middle of a dilemma. Butch experienced discrimination.

"I look what's happening today and I'm still not pleased. I see a lot of American companies like Coors and Budweiser that have come up to Canada and completely skirted the issue.

"I haven't decided whether to speak out again or not.

"A very strange battle has gone on within me. I do not like to see people with exalted names directing traffic politically or interfering in whatever issues. On the other hand, people will argue, 'Well, Jesus, if you believe in an issue, why can't you say something about it? You can't help who you are.' Over the years I've been fighting that battle with myself. But finally it came down to issues that were obviously and visibly wrong, as in South Africa, and here in Canada with TV, where you couldn't really see an ethnic on our commer-

cials. It's the old subtle thing, except that I knew what the under-
current was in the ad agencies. They were getting away with it in
Canada. They thought they just didn't have to use ethnics in commercials in Canada. So there was a certain amount of shock value
when I spoke out on the subject, because I think I have a fairly
creditable record as a human being, and as a Canadian.

"I know I haven't been high profile, trying to swing my weight
around. I think I've used some kind of discretion. Whatever I said,
it did benefit some people. There are black actors and Chinese
actors that are *working*.

"All these years I've had that battle going in myself. I'm not
looking to be a raving radical. You can't stand away from these
issues, but I have always questioned, 'Where is the line?' And I still
do."

In the early 1970s, the country he so loved began to reveal that the
love was not unrequited. In 1973, Carleton University awarded
him a doctor of laws degree. This was followed by similar degrees
from Queen's University (1976), Concordia University (1979), a
doctor of music degree from Sackville University (1980), a doctor
of laws from McMaster University (1981), another from the University of Victoria that same year, a doctor of letters from York University (1982), another doctor of laws from the University of
Toronto (1985), and a doctor of music from Laval University
(1985) – as well as a doctor of fine arts degree in 1983 from North-
western University in Evanston, Illinois. He has ten doctorates in
all.

In addition, he has won the *Down Beat* Reader's Poll as best jazz
pianist fourteen times, the *Playboy* poll twelve times, and the *Contemporary Keyboard* poll five times. He has been awarded the Carnegie Hall Anniversary Medal, the Charlie Parker Bronze Medal,
the Ville de Salon de Provence Medal, and the Mexico City Award
of Thanks. He has been nominated for the Grammy award nine
times, winning four of those times.

On June 23, 1972, he became an officer of the Order of Canada.
There are three stages in the order: member, officer, and compan-

ion. In the spring ceremony of June 25, 1984, he was invested as companion, along with singer Anne Murray.

The criteria for appointment to companion are "outstanding achievement and merit of the highest degree, especially service to Canada or to humanity at large." The citation, which is on the wall of his studio in Mississauga, reads: "With his classical bent and passion for perfection, Oscar Peterson is probably today's finest jazz pianist. By virtue of his many world tours, he has become Canada's musical ambassador. He is a staunch champion of the equality of our ethnic minorities."

In 1973, the City of Toronto gave Oscar its Award of Merit, First Mention. Further honours followed: the Diplome d'Honneur of the Canadian Conference of the Arts (1975), the Olympic Key to Montreal (1976), the Queen's Medal (1977), the Canadian Band Festival Award (1982), the City of Toronto Award of Merit, Second Mention (1983), the Volunteer Award, Roy Thomson Hall, Toronto, for Musical Merit (1987), and the Canadian Club Arts and Letters Award, New York City (1987).

In 1982, he was named honorary lifetime member by the Montreal Musicians' Association. On April 17, 1951, he had been called before a board meeting of that union local (406 of the American Federation of Musicians) for a breach of its rules. The union record reads: "Member Oscar Peterson appears in connection with 'sitting in' at Ciro's. He admits the infraction but argues that he didn't want to defy our rules; he played on the insistence of our own members who wanted to hear him; in view of the circumstances a fine of $100 is imposed; however, the fine will be under suspended sentence."

Despite all this recognition, on February 2, 1980, the *Toronto Star* carried a story by Peter Goddard headlined "Oscar Peterson's familiarity crisis" and subheaded "Recognition, please, for Canada's great jazzman."

The story reports that a series of television commercials Oscar had made for the Royal Bank of Canada were about to hit the air. Meanwhile, at the RCA studio on Mutual Street in Toronto, he was recording an album of Canadian material with a Canadian band and arrangements by Rick Wilkins. Present at the session were Norman Granz, disc jockeys Ted O'Reilly and Phil McKeller, and an orchestra that included guitarist Ed Bickert and trombonist Rob McConnell.

A photographer asked Oscar, "Where are you going to stand when you play your trumpet, Mr. Peterson?"

CHAPTER 18

A RICH TRADITION

Jazz was in its formative years a music of wind instruments, those used in the marching bands of New Orleans, and so it has remained. Despite the proto-jazz work of Scott Joplin, and later the music of Jelly Roll Morton, its innovators and seminal influences have been horn players – Louis Armstrong, Sidney Bechet, Bix Beiderbecke, John Coltrane, Roy Eldridge, Dizzy Gillespie, Coleman Hawkins, Charlie Parker, Jack Teagarden, Frank Trumbauer, and Lester Young.

The piano has had an almost separate history within jazz, and its history has also stood outside the main development of European concert music, paralleling its evolution in European concert music. This is inherent in the nature of the keyboard instruments, particularly the piano, which is in its basic character a non-linear percussion instrument. It has hammers that strike taut strings. It is normally not used at all in symphonic music except, somewhat, for coloristic effects in twentieth-century works such as Stravinsky's *Symphony in Three Movements*. In such instances it is, significantly, classified in the percussion section.

Since the time of Bach, who in the court of Frederick the Great tried out an early prototype of the instrument and made suggestions for its improvement, and then Mozart, one of its first master players, composers have written for it as a separate instrument.

Like all keyboard instruments since the time of Bach, the piano is a tempered instrument. The relationships between the tones in a scale are fixed by mathematical principles inherent in acoustics. On modern keyboard instruments, certain notes have been adjusted artificially. On a piano A-sharp and B-flat are the "same" note. In nature they are not. It was perceived in Bach's time that since A-sharp is only a shade lower in pitch than B-flat, keyboard instruments could be made much more flexible if they were adjusted to be the same tone – if, that is, the note was considered to be a slightly raised A-sharp and a slightly lowered B-flat. This was done, and became standard in tuning keyboard instruments, producing what is called tempered pitch. This made it possible for keyboard instruments to be played in all the keys. It was to illustrate this principle and its advantages that Bach wrote *The Well-Tempered Clavier.*

But this practice renders the piano something of a rogue instrument. It is implicitly, subtly, inherently out of tune. It is incapable of playing true pitch. This is so of none of the instruments we could call "pitch-making" – the string family, the horns, the woodwinds. To be sure, the instruments with valves or keys are a little less flexible than the trombone or the strings, but the better players can and do lip them into tune. In other words, the other instruments can play true untempered pitch. The moment a piano is introduced into an ensemble, the other instruments are forced to play to its tempered pitch.

The keyboard instruments, furthermore, are capable of playing simultaneous tones. The only others that can do so are those fretted instruments descended from the rebek and the vihuela – the guitar and similar instruments, including the lute. To be sure, the unfretted string family can be forced into such duty through what are called double or triple stops, but they rarely play more than two notes at a time, and even double stops are uncharacteristic of the violin, viola, and cello. All the pitched instruments except the keyboard and guitar families, then, are essentially single-note, single-line instruments.

It is for this reason that composers so rarely have written solo pieces for them – the outstanding exceptions being some violin pieces by Bach. Composers throughout history have treated the piano and other keyboard instruments, and the guitar, as what they essentially are: self-sustaining, free-standing, self-accompanying solo instruments.

When the piano has been used with orchestra, other than for coloristic purposes, it has been perceived as a *solo* instrument in front of and accompanied by the orchestra. Most of the works in this form are concertos.

Beethoven's writing for piano is largely for solo instrument (the thirty-two sonatas and some works in other forms) or for piano *with* orchestra (the five concertos). One of the instrument's most perceptive composers and important explorers was Chopin, who wrote very little orchestral music at all. Almost the entire body of his work is for solo piano. Liszt, its next major virtuoso explorer, similarly treated it as an instrument apart. Thus too Brahms, Grieg, Debussy, Ravel, Rachmaninoff, Bartók – and Scott Joplin. In the nineteenth century composers gradually discovered the vast emotional and technical range of the instrument, developing that great bravura Romantic tradition that is embodied, as Paul de Marky foresaw and as Lalo Schifrin, among others, later confirmed, in Oscar Peterson. To see him as a derivation of Art Tatum is to display an ignorance of the history of the instrument and of a literature of which Tatum too is an extension. But jazz criticism has tended to a simplistic explanation of the music's history: Miles Davis came out of Dizzy Gillespie, who came out of Roy Eldridge, who came out of Louis Armstrong, and so forth. It is much more complex than that, particularly in the instance of the piano.

It is necessary at this point to consider afresh exactly what jazz is and what a jazz musician does – although a difficulty arises from the habit of critics and some musicians of shifting the lines of its borders to justify their own subjective responses and attitudes to it. This is a sort of aesthetic gerrymandering in which the frontier is enlarged or contracted by the whim of the definer, so that he may dismiss anything he does not like by saying, "That's not jazz." As a matter of fact, the word itself presents certain difficulties and has been deplored for its limitations by, among others, Duke Ellington, Miles Davis, and Artie Shaw.

In its essentials jazz is an idiomatic music, developed by black

Americans, with a strong rhythmic pulse that produces a characteristic "swing" that gives it a powerful and, at its best, enthralling propulsion. Its rhythmic roots are African, its melodic and harmonic roots European. From its earliest days it put a strong emphasis on instrumental improvisation, a tradition that had faded away in European concert music, although it lived on in the music of Hungarian gypsy fiddlers, Spanish flamenco guitarists, and French musette accordionists.

Jazz is essentially a theme-and-variations music in which the individual or group performs what jazz musicians call the "head" – a melody that may be drawn from the thirty-two–bar popular song literature, from the twelve-bar traditional form called "the blues," or for that matter from opera or any other source – following which the players embark on improvised variations based on the melody and, particularly important, the harmony. It is indicative of the domination of horn players in jazz that this process of spontaneous invention is not referred to as "improvising." It is called "blowing" even when done by a pianist.

Every song has a characteristic harmonic pattern, a sequence of chords that determines its nature and colour as strongly as the melody. A jazz musician must know hundreds or even thousands of songs, including their harmonies – which they call the chord changes, or more commonly, simply "the changes" – and know them in all the common keys. These "changes" become the lingua franca of the jazz musician, enabling him to walk onto the bandstand with total strangers and improvise coherently with them on a given tune. Sometimes the changes become abstracted completely from the original song. The *I Got Rhythm* changes are almost as common in jazz as those of the blues. And sometimes entirely new tunes are written on the changes of other tunes. Charlie Parker's *Donna Lee*, for example, is erected on those of *Back Home Again in Indiana*.

The bass player has two functions in a jazz group. He carries the basic pulse of the music, a duty he shares with the drummer. And he puts out the "bass line," the bottom of the music, the sequence of tones that in part determines its harmonic character. Indeed, the harmonic content of the music can be conveyed entirely by a bass player and a horn soloist, because they touch on notes within each chord. Gerry Mulligan for a time had a quartet without a pianist.

But when a group does have a pianist, he has a critically important harmonic function. He "feeds" the chords to the soloist in his comping. "Comping" is one of those terms, like "time," that is peculiar to jazz. It derives from "accompanying," but it doesn't mean exactly that. It connotes a punching accentuation of the rhythmic pulse and a flowing statement of the harmonic character of the tune being played. If a pianist doesn't do it well, he can impede and embarrass the soloist. Comping is one of those things Oscar Peterson does superbly. In lectures to college students, Artie Shaw cites Louis Armstrong's performance of *You Go to My Head,* accompanied by Oscar, as "the epitome of jazz."

The function of the piano has been restricted in jazz. The great stride players, such as Fats Waller and James P. Johnson, stood apart from the mainstream of jazz. They were *pianists,* and the piano is, for reasons already noted, another thing.

Because of what the horn players who dominated jazz demanded of pianists comping for them, an unpianistic style of playing developed in which the emphasis was put on right-hand melodic improvisation imitating "horn lines," accompanied by laconic chording by the left hand. Some wonderful jazz piano was played in this manner, which is ascribed to Earl Hines. But Hines deliberately restricted a formidable technique that is manifest in his early recordings, as Basie did when he played in his own band.

Oscar Peterson, though he was influenced strongly by Nat Cole, who in turn was influenced by Hines, never embraced this approach.

In his landmark study of the work of William Blake, *Fearful Symmetry,* Northrop Frye enunciated a principle which, if widely implemented, would raise the level of critical discussion of all the arts: "The identity of content and form is the axiom of all sound criticism."

A more broadly understood principle of criticism, though it is honoured more in the breach than the observance, is that a work of art should be judged according to its intentions. A work should not be derogated for failing to do what its creator never intended it to do, even if the critic wishes to see or read or hear something else.

"You've got to realize, critics think in blocks," Oscar said. "They think in blocks of technique, what they call sensitivity, and acceptance. Those three blocks. And they gauge their reviews on them. They think they understand technique. They don't *really* understand technique. I'm not negating their opinions. They have every right to an opinion, to say I don't like this or I don't like that or I like that, but don't come at me with that cerebral bullshit. You know, I wouldn't take it on myself to be a critic of jazz piano records. I would sooner be a critic of classical records.

"But jazz is such a personal creative thing that I wouldn't take it on myself to judge. I know what I think about certain things by the standards *I* use, but not about someone else. They hear somebody make a run that they think is fast, they say, 'My God, he's copped Tatum.' Or 'He's copped Peterson.' That would make one hell of an interesting project for you. Interview critics."

In fact the question is simpler than Peterson thinks it is: good criticism tells you about the art; bad criticism tells you about the critic. The only real function of criticism is the exegetical, that which explains the art. But too much of it consists in a writer telling what he likes and dislikes and why. He assumes his subjective responses to art to be facts about the art, when they are facts about him. To say that something is "too" this or "too" that tells you only about the standards of the critic. He is making some inner comparison which may or may not coincide with the recipient's – or the artist's. For him to say that Peterson plays "too many" notes tells you only that there is some certain though unspecified number of notes that he wants to hear.

Much criticism of jazz piano has foundered on a failure of some critics – and some musicians, too, including a few pianists – to understand the separate nature of the piano itself: its separate history, literature, character, and problems. Carl Engel took note of the problem in a 1922 *Atlantic* essay. It is worth re-examining his observation: "Franz Liszt could give a suggestion of gypsy music on the keyboard. He had a way of playing the piano orchestrally. There are few figures who can play jazz on the piano. Jazz, as much as the gypsy dances, depends on the many and contrasting voices of a band, united in a single and spontaneous rhythmic, harmonic, and contrapuntal will." It is worth remarking Paul de Marky's comment that Liszt would have been proud of Oscar, Oscar's own comment that the piano could be made to sound like the Basie band, and Don Cameron's recollection that Oscar played a Harry James band piece note for note during their early years. Liszt transcribed Beethoven's Fifth Symphony so that he could play it on piano.

Because jazz was developed as a music of horns, the standards of horns have been applied to the piano – and they do not fit, since the piano is for all the reasons mentioned a separate musical entity. The horns in turn were influenced by black American vocal music from a period before instrumental jazz was born. The horns imitated voices even as, later, scat singers imitated horns: Jon Hendricks standing before the microphone and fingering an imaginary saxophone. Jazz has a vocabulary of vocal effects, including portamento, both rising and falling; the burry distorted trumpet sound that is referred to as a growl; constricted half-valve effects that Dizzy Gillespie, like Rex Stewart before him, uses to telling effect; and even the articulation of notes through the use of a rubber plunger, called a "wah-wah" effect. Clark Terry has carried vocal effects on trumpet probably further than any player in jazz history, and sometimes you can understand the words his horn is saying, profane, specific, and funny. Significantly, jazz musicians working out a routine on instruments will be heard saying not "play" but "say": "First you say, and then I say, and then you say ..."

The piano is incapable of these effects, although Oscar, in his control of the instrument, sometimes creates the illusion of some of them. For example, when he violates his perfect execution by delaying the release of one note until a fraction of a second after he plays the tone above it, he creates an effect like the one-note upward bend, characteristic of trumpet players, that jazz players call a "doit." (There is a marking for it in jazz orchestration.) Nonetheless, the piano cannot do what horns can do, as horns cannot do what the piano can do.

But for the reasons already examined, a whole body of opinion holds that this is exactly what jazz piano should do. Oscar Peterson has never accepted this aesthetic canon. He has said repeatedly and consistently throughout his career that he loves the instrument, loves all its resources, and set out from the beginning to master and use them. Like no pianist in jazz history, he has succeeded.

Because jazz developed as an art within the lifetime of persons now living, and because some persons, Oscar among them, have met if not worked with almost every major figure in its history, there has been a tendency, a strong one, to judge it entirely in terms of originality – who did what first. That has been the chief criterion, and sometimes the only one, of its value. European musical history from the time of Carl Philipp Emanuel Bach onwards has been to a large extent the constantly more complex exploration of harmony, at a cost of rhythm and spontaneity.

Those critics who had a modicum of knowledge of classical music tended to judge jazz by that standard. But by the end of the nineteenth century, the harmonic system was considered to have become impossibly ponderous, leading to the dubious conclusion that the vocabulary of Western music as we knew it had become exhausted. The application of this standard to jazz required not that the musician use the vocabulary of the music to good effect but that he invent his own language. It was thought that Charlie Parker had done this, but seen in a longer context of musical history it is clear now that Parker and Dizzy Gillespie were not departures but extensions – and inevitable ones – of the music's vocabulary. There is indeed no deeper traditionalist than Gillespie. And Parker's work was full of quotations from old songs and even exercise books for the saxophone, although only a few saxophone players detected the latter source.

Critics have repeatedly charged that Oscar is eclectic, as if that term somehow had an odour to it, and that he is an "unoriginal" musician who uses the material of the past. He is, they say, a conservative, although the curse of an obvious bias is removed in the latter case if you substitute "conservationist" or "preservationist." He has strong feelings about the preservation of the tradition in the music.

Peterson is seen as a summational artist. So he is. So was Mozart. So was Bach. Bach and Mozart were both dealing with known vocabularies and an accepted body of aesthetic principles. Bach did not start baroque practices; he finished them. He was the ultimate eclectic, using materials from various other sources, including Vivaldi, just as Oscar uses a curious spinning figure that he got from Dizzy Gillespie. Perhaps Dizzy played it and Oscar immediately imitated it, making Dizzy laugh hugely, after which it became part of Oscar's own vocabulary. The history of music does not seem to award the highest marks to whoever did it first but to whoever did it best, which is why some of Bach's precursors are forgotten and Vivaldi, from whom Bach stole, is rated as a minor, though pleasing, musician beside the colossus of Bach.

Billy Taylor tends to minimize the significance of improvisation when he defines jazz. "That's deliberate," he said. "I think too much emphasis is placed on the spontaneous creativity that we call improvisation. Louis Armstrong played things which were set solos. Art Tatum too did things which were set solos. You can't say that it wasn't jazz and that it wasn't swinging. I heard Louis Armstrong play ..." Taylor sang a Louis Armstrong lick. "I've heard him do that a million times, and those quarter notes swung every time."

Dave Brubeck, who has also suffered at the hands of critics and has gradually become inured to their attentions, made a point about them to writer Doug Ramsey, who quotes it in his book *Jazz Matters: Reflections on the Music and Some of Its Makers.* "The word bombastic keeps coming up," Brubeck said, "as if it were some trap I keep falling into. Damn it, when I'm bombastic, I have my reasons. I want to be bombastic. Take it or leave it."

247

Similarly, critics keep suggesting that when Oscar plays his simplest, he has overcome his shortcomings and has, as it were, found his way home. But he has repeatedly stated that he *intends* to play, to the extent that he can, the full range of the instrument's possibilities. He can reasonably ask to be evaluated in terms of whether he has succeeded.

It has also been the practice of Oscar's detractors to point out that he repeats phrases, as if all jazz musicians didn't use what they call "licks," phrases of vocabulary used in different ways, such as the scales and arpeggios appropriate to various chords, certain preferred chord voicings and voice-leadings. Ray Brown said to me once, "They think we just roll out of bed and play the D-major scale," meaning that there is an assumption that the jazz musician does these things by natural talent, that he hasn't practised as diligently as any classical musician to master the vocabulary of his craft. There is a further assumption that a jazz musician improvises each note, when in fact he uses whole groupings of notes, either vertically or horizontally, in his expression. You do not think "go ... to ... the ... store," to invent a simplistic analogy. You think "gotothestore," as a group of words.

The phenomenon known as persistence of vision makes the motion picture possible. The eye briefly retains a still photo as another replaces it, and a sequence of photos projected rapidly onto a screen creates the illusion of moving images. It's like what happens when a child waves a sparkler in the night: the sparkler leaves a tracery of line in the vision. When a musician can produce a stream of notes with the rapidity that Oscar Peterson commands, the sensitive ear hears not the succession of notes but the line they leave behind. We might call it persistence of hearing. Oscar Peterson's musical method at rapid tempos entails a vocabulary not of notes but of entire fluent groups of them.

When the nature of the audience and the ambiance require him to do so, Oscar has no reluctance to dazzle. But often he uses his command not simply to dazzle but for striking aesthetic effect.

The great guitarist Andres Segovia, according to a story which may be apocryphal, was asked after a concert why he had played a certain piece so fast.

"Because I can," he replied.

There is in all music an element of the athletic, and part of a listener's enjoyment lies in seeing how far a man can excel, how far he can exceed the normal mortal limitations. This is particularly so in jazz, where the fierce competition of the "cutting contest" has been part of the tradition since its beginning. It is strange that this value is suddenly suspended by some critics in their case against Oscar Peterson.

A discussion of the criticism of Oscar Peterson – and it should be remembered that most of it has not been negative, as witness the enthusiasm over the years of Leonard Feather, Bill Simon, Richard Palmer, Len Lyons, and many others – must make serious examination of the statement of organist Jimmy Smith that the first time he heard an Oscar Peterson record, he said to himself, "There, that's a white who has worked hard at the piano and thinks he sounds black."

This remark is racist at two levels. It assumes that high technical accomplishment and the capacity for hard work are inherently white characteristics – and implicitly are not black. Thus Smith lends credence to the racist white image of blacks as shuffling, no-account incompetents. It gives weight to the argument of those racists who would bar blacks from careers in such exacting tasks as those of the heart surgeon, airline mechanic, astronaut, and computer programmer. It sets up a standard that would justify keeping blacks out of symphony orchestras, and it lends justification to segregation and a tiered structure of society according to race.

If at this level it manifests an unconscious self-hatred, illustrating an anti-black condescension that Smith has by osmosis absorbed from white racists, it also assumes in exquisitely pained balance that whites are inferior to blacks and must "try" to emulate them and cannot succeed. Like so much criticism, it tells us more about the critic than the subject. It is implicitly segregationist, as was Gerald Wilson's perhaps unwittingly patronizing remark that someone's was "one of the better non-white bands."

The comment is particularly ironic coming from Smith. Once at Sarah Vaughan's home in California I heard someone playing piano in an adjacent room. He was doing a fairly good imitation of Art Tatum. It was competent, though not inspiring, and highly derivative playing. I went in search of its author. I found Jimmy Smith playing a spinet. I had never heard him play piano before.

Oscar's friend for many years, clarinetist, arranger, and composer Phil Nimmons, said of him, "The piano is like an extension of his own creativity. I am not talking about mere technical capabilities, although his are awesome. I'm speaking of the times when you find him under optimum conditions of creativity. His mind can move as quickly as his fingers and that is what is so astounding. It's all going by so fast that it's almost too much to absorb, which may be why some critics have had trouble with it."

"He is not only a virtuoso pianist," said Billy Taylor. "He's a remarkable musician. The thing I admire about him is that he is always growing. His phenomenal facility sometimes gets in the way of people's listening, but he has a big heart and he plays beautiful things."

Film composer Lalo Schifrin, one of the most thoroughly schooled of modern musicians, trained at the Paris Conservatory by Charles Koechlin and Olivier Messiaen, and once Dizzy Gillespie's pianist and arranger, said, "Oscar represents a tradition lost in this century – the virtuoso piano improviser, like Chopin, the tradition of bravura playing that started with Beethoven and reached its apotheosis with Franz Liszt. After that, the pianists began playing what was written. Oscar is a true Romantic in the nineteenth-century sense, with the addition of the twentieth-century Afro-American tradition. He is a top-class virtuoso."

One of the most interesting perspectives on Peterson comes from Mike Longo, one of Schifrin's successors in the piano chair with the Dizzy Gillespie Quintet and Gillespie's music director from 1968 through 1973. After taking a bachelor of music degree at Western Kentucky University, Longo went to Toronto in 1961 to study with Oscar at the Advanced School of Contemporary Music. Longo said:

"I think Oscar's training was in the mechanics of the instrument, the same things everyone who has studied classical music learns. I think Oscar should be given credit for the innovative part of his work in jazz piano. His main training, over the classical studies, was probably the digestion and incorporation of techniques from Art Tatum, Nat Cole, and others. He digested his peers. It is supposed to be that way. I think all the great musicians go through the three phases of imitation, realization, and maturity. Stravinsky said in one of six lectures he gave at Harvard – they're in a book called *The Poetics of Music* – that no new music has ever come from anything but the tradition. Meaning that all great musicians digested what went before them and then went further with it. There have been a lot of ignorant critics in jazz, not only ignorant in terms of jazz but in terms of music. And I think Oscar has suffered from the jealousy of others – the Mozart syndrome – particularly the critics."

"We were very conscious of the reviews Oscar got," Herb Ellis said years later. "They all said the same thing, in essence. It's cold, it's mechanical. Granted he's a technician of the piano, they said, but he's got no definitive style. First of all, they're really not hearing him. They're not hearing the depth of it. They're only hearing the surface. They're only hearing a lot of notes. Because sometimes he does play a lot of notes. Of course I'm not saying that's bad. I think they arrive at the conclusion that if you have a tendency to play a lot of notes, it's got to be cold. They miss the point. They just miss the whole point. I've played with a lot of people, and a lot of piano players. I've never played with anybody who had more depth and more emotion and feeling in his playing. He can play so hot and so deep and earthy that it just *shakes* you when you're playing with him. Ray and I have come off the stand just shook up. I mean, he is *heavy*. If you're not up to hearing it, well that's your loss. I won't even discuss it with anybody, because there's nothing to discuss. If that's the depth of their hearing, then we don't have anything to talk about. You can listen to the first two or three choruses of some of his solos. Sometimes he plays very sparingly. And it's *grooving*, it's about as hot as you can get. Then later on he may play faster and double it up to give it some build and some flavour. You see, most piano players end where he starts.

"And his ballad playing is absolutely lovely. Harmonically, it's quite involved. He's got a love for playing the melody. And the sound that he gets out of a piano is so lyrical. If you have to name the world's best piano player, I can't see that there is much competition. There might be somebody that someone might like better, personally. But as far as playing the piano, and I'm not just talking about chops, I'm talking about all of it, the feeling, the emotion, he's the man.

"Art Tatum didn't have the deep hard swing that Oscar has. I'm not taking away from him. Oscar has that earthy, deep commitment of swing."

In a 1981 essay Richard Palmer wrote: "Peterson is a much more direct player than Tatum, too. There's an earthy simplicity in the way he begins a tune or an improvisation that contrasts vividly with Tatum's wonderful but decidedly floral approach. Moreover, he is, to these ears, one of the greatest blues players in the history of jazz; and not even the most passionate devotee could make that claim for Tatum. And, most importantly, Peterson is a superbly adaptable and unselfish accompanist."

Shortly after he became conductor of the Los Angeles Philharmonic, I was talking on the telephone to André Previn about Oscar. André said, "He is the *best*." I said that I didn't hear much Tatum in his work. André said, pointedly, "I don't hear *any*."

Palmer says in that same essay: "Peterson's [style] is unique, and in all major respects it always has been. He has, for all the awe in which he's held by fellow musicians, never been a prime or even a substantial influence upon the genesis of jazz piano. A Petersonian aura is evident in certain players – Ross Tompkins, Phineas Newborn, at times Hampton Hawes, and, most obviously, Monty Alexander; but it would be inaccurate to speak of a Peterson 'school' in the way one rightly refers to the effect of Monk, Bill Evans and Bud Powell."

Palmer is quite right about this. There is, however, a very considerable *hidden* influence of Oscar Peterson in the work (by his own statement to me) of Bill Evans, who in turn was influential on Herbie Hancock, the brilliant New Zealand pianist Alan Broadbent, and many more. Roger Kellaway does not sound remotely like Oscar Peterson, but the influence is there, again by his own statement. The better pianists have *internalized* the influence of Oscar Peterson and gone on to develop their own voices. If, as an arresting axiom has it, an institution is the lengthened shadow of one man, Oscar Peterson must be considered more than an influence. He has become an institution.

And his influence extends far beyond the piano. Ed Thigpen says that the standards Oscar set altered and improved his playing forever. Everybody who has been through the various Peterson trios reports a similar experience.

Ray Brown said: "It lasts you all your life when you work for a motherfucker like that. Anybody on this earth has some good stuff and some bad stuff. And Oscar has some bad stuff, just like all the rest of us. But I'm telling you, his good stuff was good enough to keep the rest of your life. He laid some things on me that I will retain, and I will use."

CHAPTER 19

SECOND OPINIONS

Oscar Peterson's relations with the press have on the whole been excellent. British-born Leonard Feather, probably the most influential of American jazz critics and certainly the dean of them, has written ardently of his work over the years. In a 1987 radio interview, Feather was asked who, if he could be reincarnated as another musician, he would want to be. Without hesitation he said, "Oscar Peterson." This ardour arouses the ire of Oscar's detractors, who feel impelled to respond to it, which increases the energy of their assaults on him. There can be little question that he would not have been so vindictively damned had he not been so lavishly praised.

Jazz criticism has been marred from its earliest days by intemperate partisanship. Critics and fans alike seem to treasure an illusion of it as an undiscovered music the liking for which is their credential of uncommon taste. For all the lamentations that it has not had a mass following, they do not truly want it to be widely accepted, since this would deprive them of especial status. This is true of many admirers of all the arts, but particularly jazz fans and critics.

Among fans and critics alike, this takes the form of "my favourite tenor player is better than your favourite tenor player." It has been called the hipper-than-thou syndrome. Grover Sales, author of *Jazz: America's Classical Music,* who teaches jazz history at San Francisco State College, has wrily observed, "The average jazz critic would rather catch another jazz critic in an error than bring Bix back from the dead."

And having made up their minds, the followers of jazz are unlikely to change them.

Yet, in Oscar Peterson's case, a number of writers have put themselves on record as having done just that, sometimes with the fervour that one associates with religious conversion. In a column titled "Second Opinion" in the July 19, 1969, issue of Britain's *Melody Maker*, Alan Stevens wrote:

I want to start this Second Opinion right away by apologising to Oscar Peterson for my first opinion of him. The first time I heard him I was very unimpressed. During the early 1950s, disc-jockey Sam Costa invariably played a Peterson recording ... and he would always rave about this new pianist.

I just couldn't share Costa's enthusiasm for this young Canadian. Maybe my unfailing devotion to Hines, Tatum and Teddy Wilson blinded me to the virtues that Costa declared Peterson possessed.

Nor was I impressed when I saw him in the flesh for the first time. This was on the occasion of his first British appearance in March, 1953, when the Jazz at the Phil package played at the Gaumont State in Kilburn to raise money for the National Flood and Tempest Distress Fund.

Either I had left my critical faculties at home or I was so knocked out at hearing such favourites of mine as Lester Young, Charlie Shavers, Willie Smith and Gene Krupa, my idols since I first became interested in jazz way back in 1939, that I dismissed Oscar out of hand.

I heard him again two years later at a concert in Belle Vue, Manchester. There was only one other artist, namely Ella Fitzgerald, on the show, so Peterson had plenty of time in which to stretch out and display the talents Costa had hinted at.

I was rather disappointed with his performance, although I'm bound to admit that most of the audience thought differently.

Jazz at the Phil came to Manchester in May, 1958, and once again Peterson wowed the audience. Me? Well, I just didn't enjoy his playing. I even identified myself with the critic (I believe it was Bob Dawson) who described Peterson as the man who had brought automation to jazz.

In a review of this concert which I wrote for a local paper I referred to Oscar as "the Charlie Kunz of jazz." No disrespect was intended toward Kunz, or to Peterson, but I was trying to make the point that the Canadian was no more than a pleasant stylist who could be relied on to always sound the same.

By this time (1958), though, he was rated by many critics and fans as the world's greatest jazz pianist. Under the aegis of Norman Granz ... he'd become one of the biggest box office attractions of the postwar years. But popularity is not, I think, a valid guide to greatness.

To my mind, Peterson was lacking in originality, the creative ability wasn't there all the time. Think of such fine pianists as Earl Hines, Art Tatum, Teddy Wilson and Billy Kyle, and you will find that if you analyzed Peterson's style you would discover an amalgam of these four.

I'd never considered him as a jazz giant and I didn't suppose then that I ever would. Jazz giants such as Armstrong, Hawkins and Parker were originators who have made a pioneering contribution to jazz. Listening to them you never know what to expect, their creative ability was such that there was always a surprise round the musical corner.

With Peterson you knew what was coming next: he was so repetitive, so predictable – just like Charlie Kunz.

After that 1958 visit, Peterson came to Manchester on several other occasions, and I gradually became more and more enchanted with him. Then, in April, 1966, he came again, and I decided that I would give him a miss. But the *Melody Maker*, obviously not knowing my feelings about Peterson, asked me to do a review, so off I went to the Free Trade Hall. And, brother, was I glad I went!

That marked the beginning of my second opinion. Of course, his greatest attribute (and one which, I suppose, I had too long kidded myself he didn't possess), the ability to swing like mad, was well in evidence, but his whole performance was a revelation.

I can't do better than quote from my review:

"No longer the predictable Oscar, the pianist of the sterile cliches, the automaton lacking creative ability and emotional depth, this was a rejuvenated Peterson, brimming with new ideas, using his technique not just for technique's sake, showing more art than artifice, full of musical surprises, scintillating with sinuous arabesques, and producing a more prodigious swing than ever before."

I remarked to my friends that this was a new Peterson. They said he'd always been like this. But I'd never noticed it, and I'd held an intractable and somewhat denigrating first opinion for over 13 years ever since I'd first heard him.

The reason why I changed my opinion is perhaps best explained by the theory I advanced in that review. It was probably Oscar's new rhythm team of Sam Jones and Louis Hayes who had provided a stimulus. They hadn't really adapted their style from that of their days with the Cannonball Adderley group when their function was to stimulate, inspire, excite, push, drive, goad and, sometimes, coax their colleagues. I felt that Peterson's favourable reaction to the promptings of the new bassist and drummer was good for him, for jazz, and for audiences. And above all, for me!

Up until that moment, I hadn't any Peterson discs in my collection. Now, I have several and I must say that they have proved conclusively to me that he is the most accomplished and finest all-round pianist in jazz today. To say that I'd misjudged him is putting it mildly, for some of these recordings had been made during the period of my first opinion.

Alright, so he isn't an originator and there's still a certain predictability about his playing, but he has no peer as a rhythmic pianist. And notice that he doesn't just play his way through a tune – he builds it up with power and tension to a staggering climax.

His harmonic conceptions? His gift of melody? Superb. His sense of dynamics, too, is quite fantastic. And if it's excitement you want, then he's your man. Don't just take my word for it, go and listen to *Bursting Out with the Big Band* (Verve).

As an accompanist, he stands supreme, as witness his tasteful and imaginative work on *Oscar Peterson with the Jazz Giants* (Verve).

But the sheer brilliance of the man comes through best of all when he's just with the trio. As I write I'm listening to *Alice in Wonderland* from *The Way I Really Play* (Polydor) [originally MPS] which is as perfect a piece of piano playing as I've ever heard.

There's no gainsaying Oscar Peterson's marvelous virtuosity. His wonderful two-handed piano playing has become to me a great joy. But, my God, what a dickens of a time it took me to really appreciate him; when I think back to that first opinion, how could I have been so adversely critical, so stupid?

Oscar, I really do most sincerely apologize.

Given that sort of response, and the wide support of probably a majority of critics and certainly most musicians, you would think that Oscar would be far above comment on critics and criticism. But he has criticized them in interviews over the years, saying essentially the same thing in one city after another. *They don't know what they're talking about.* (Some do, some don't.) *If they can't do it, they shouldn't criticize it.* The latter is an untenable thesis. We hire experts in our lives precisely because they can do what we cannot do as well or do at all, whether it is making beef Wellington, a suit, a sofa, a symphony, a movie, an abdominal incision, or a safe landing at Orly. We have every right to discuss this work and make recommendations for or against it, and each such discussion is an act of criticism.

Further, there is no basis for a belief that musicians are necessarily good critics, since their very own aesthetic commitments render them reflexively biased. American jurisprudence takes the view – sensibly, I believe – that politicians and entertainers cannot sue for libel in matters of comment and opinion, since the one group is soliciting votes and the other soliciting money from the public, and they are therefore open to comment, criticism, and analysis. For all its abuses, for all the ignorance of some of its writers, for all the biases, criticism is something we have to put up with in an open society. And in the arts, criticism is, as Virgil Thomson put it, "the only antidote we have to paid publicity."

Norman Granz too has kept up an enfilade on critics, criticism, and the press in general. The thick file of newspaper and magazine clippings on Granz at the Institute of Jazz Studies at Rutgers University consists to a surprising extent of his excoriations of this critic or that and even a criticism of Dave Brubeck – letters to the editor of *Down Beat*, a full-page ad in variety, interviews. The press never hesitated to print these assaults on itself which, in their collective tone of imperious contempt, leave an unmistakable impression of his belief that no one knows anything or has any right to an opinion about jazz but Norman Granz. Given four decades of his assaults on them, the members of the press have been painstakingly fair to Norman Granz, no matter what Oscar believes.

And he is fierce in Granz's defence.

"I think Norman Granz is probably the most misunderstood human being I know," Oscar says. "The predominant factor has been his honesty. I think he decided a long time ago to say what he had to say and do what he had to do and be the kind of person he had to be, and he's managed to do it.

"Nobody that I know of, but nobody, with all due respect to George Wein and John Hammond, has done as much for jazz as Norman. In a Grammy awards acceptance statement several years ago, I said – I remember what I said, because I intended to say it – 'I accept this not for myself but on behalf of Norman Granz, the man who continues to believe and believe and believe and believe …'

"And I walked away. And I meant that. You know, I've heard him bad-mouthed so much, but right now I can pick fifteen names of people you can go to and I would defy you to get a bad word about Norman Granz from them. I can name fifteen without stumbling. Why has this annihilation program taken place? Why has Norman been overlooked with all the awards? When has he ever gotten a Grammy?" Oscar's eyebrows lifted. "Norman has never received a single award that I know of. And how can you make that many recordings with that many important jazz names and win no awards? Are you going to tell me Coleman Hawkins wasn't important? Ben Webster wasn't important? Roy Eldridge? Bird? Billie Holiday? That huge collection Norman put out on Art Tatum? Dizzy? Ray Brown? Barney Kessel? Ellington? Basie? Zoot? How can you make all these records by people of that stature and never get an award? It's past the point of being ludicrous.

"And Norman Granz is the best manager that I know of, bar none. Forget about as a friend. Any level you want to argue on. You want to argue intelligence? I'll put him up against anyone you want to name. Name them, it doesn't have to be in jazz. There isn't any one that I've seen, and I've met quite a few of the impresarios in the classical world, who has the intuitive creative sense about what an artist should be doing to further their creative importance. I think that's the way you have to put it. Not just to sell records, not just to make more money. No no no no no. Norman has sat down and said to me, 'You know, there's an important area I think you have totally overlooked.'

"As much as they may say what they say about him, I know what he did for Bird. I know what he did musically, creatively, and personally. I know what he did for Billie. I know what he has done and still is doing for Ella Fitzgerald. I know what he did for Sarah Vaughan. I know what he did for Basie, and he wasn't even, really, Basie's manager. I know the calls that went back and forth from Basie to him. I know what he did for Ellington, even through the period when he and Duke didn't talk. There was a period where he and Duke didn't talk.

"I know what he did for Ben Webster. Roy Eldridge. The list goes on and on. It's crazy. Roy was always one of Norman's favourites, and still is. Norman admired him so much. Norman's totally crazy about Roy. He thinks Roy's maybe the all-time jazz great.

"Yes, I said Norman is shy. Totally. You wouldn't know it. He would probably never come on that way to you. With a lot of other people he is. I'm one of the few people who know how to embarrass him. The humility that he has in front of the artist that he reveres. It doesn't just have to be in music. He looks at Roy and shakes his head. Benny Carter too.

"He reads everything. Everything. He's one of the most dedicated readers I know. To talk politics with him is unbelievable – the depth of his understanding of the political scene in the world, whether now or ten years earlier, or fifteen years earlier, or twenty years earlier. We'll get to London and he'll say, 'I've got to go down and do my book shopping.' And he isn't kidding. He'll come out with ten, fifteen, twenty, books. I mean, they have to deliver them. And he'll buy me books. He's responsible for a lot of my understanding in certain cultural areas – art. When he took on his interest in art, and really got involved in it, he insisted that I had to go with him. I went through the galleries. The same thing when he got involved in food. He'd say, 'We have to play this gig here, because they've got a restaurant we've got to go and eat in.' And he's like that about his music. Don't fool with him about early Ellington or anything like that. He knows all that, he's dedicated to all that. He's probably the most rounded person I know. He's a hell of a tennis player, hell of an athlete. He was a good basketball player. He's got a mind that is lightning quick to this day."

Whose approval has Oscar Peterson been seeking?

"There's the hand-me-down of all time," Ray Brown said. "The taskmaster. Oscar got it honestly. From his father."

One wonders if Oscar, as so many of us do, has spent a lifetime seeking the approval of a parent who always – by Oscar's own and Daisy's testimony – withheld it.

His feelings about his father, as expressed over the years in interviews, have been conflicting. Sometimes he would portray him as a firm but almost kindly man. At another time he could refer to "the hassle with Dad." Those feelings seem to have been resolved.

"My father had great objectives and aims for us," Oscar said. "He was a man who was trying to forge a beginning for all of us, so we wouldn't end up being porters on the railways and maids in homes. And anything he could throw at us that would cause us to think, he would throw. He threw some horrible mathematical problems at all of us, some of which I couldn't solve to this day. He threw all kinds of reading material at us, because he admired a well-read person, although he was very quiet about it. I guess he had a lot of faults, as we all do, but that's one thing you can't fault him for, he wanted his kids to be able to cope with the world that he saw out there."

There was also, it would appear, a larger approval that Oscar sought, perhaps without being aware of it. When saxophonist Jerome Richardson – who is, which is relevant to this discussion, black – asked me to try to explain Oscar Peterson, who, he said, had always puzzled him, I said, "Well, first of all, he's a Canadian."

"Say no more," Jerome said. "That says it all." Well, yes and no.

Oscar is, by his own definition, a Canadian nationalist, for all that he is an international musical figure. But he was born, as we have already noted, into layers of cultural separation, a little like the structure of an onion, unique to Canada and perhaps to Montreal alone, a member of a minority within a minority: part of an English-speaking black Canadian community surrounded by a French-speaking culture which was walled around in turn by a dominating English-speaking element that excluded both groups.

Oscar told me something that touched me far more than I let him know; he is not the only one who can wear a mask. He said:

"Sandy and I had a terrible fight one day – over the Order of Canada, as a matter of fact. She used to make fun of the various awards. Who asks for these things? I didn't ask for them. I can't remember the remark. She started to make fun of that and one of the doctorates.

"I said, 'I don't think that's too funny.'

"She said, 'Don't be impressed with yourself.'

"I said, 'Hey, that means a lot to me. It may not mean a lot to you, but it means a lot to me. I should be able to tell you. I can think back to when I was a kid, I never *dreamed* my *country* would honour me!"

CHAPTER 20

NEW DISCOVERIES

Contrary to what most people think, electronic music has been around for some time. The first electronic instrument was developed late in the nineteenth century by a native of Iowa named Thaddeus Cahill. Called the telharmonium, it was designed to distribute music over telephone lines, but it did not prove particularly useful: the monstrosity comprised thirty carloads of steel and copper machinery and weighed many tons.

Not until the development of the vacuum tube did electronic music become practical. In the film *Spellbound* (1945) Miklos Rozsa's musical score used an instrument called the theremin, which studio publicists palmed off as something new. In fact the instrument, named after the Russian scientist who developed it, was perfected in 1924. Then came the ondes martenot, the Hammond organ, the Novachord, and other electronic instruments, each of which was in some way severely limited.

Synthesizers came into prominent use in the late 1960s, the first important one being the instrument invented by Robert Moog (who pronounces it Moag). The Moog synthesizer shot to fame almost overnight with the album *Switched-on Bach*, sales of which took it to the top of the pop-music charts. The music was performed by Walter (later Wendy) Carlos and produced by Rachel Elkind.

The first Moog synthesizer was not polyphonic. It could play only one note at a time, and Walter Carlos recorded that album one line after another by overdubbing. But polyphonic synthesizers were soon developed, and today all sorts of complex, sophisticated, and sometimes very expensive synthesizers are in use. Just before *Switched-on Bach* was released, Rachel Elkind and Walter Carlos brought a test pressing of the album to my apartment in New York and asked what I thought.

"I think," I said, "that in a hundred years, some little boy is going to say, 'What was an orchestra, Daddy?' and Daddy is going to reply, 'An early form of synthesizer that took a hundred men to play.'"

The prediction was off by eighty years: we have just about reached that point now. The use of electronic music for film scores and pop albums is so widespread that it has produced a serious recession among musicians in Los Angeles and other major recording centres. The drum machine is so common in the studios that some young engineers have never had occasion to record real drums. Musicians who have returned to full-time jazz playing after years in the studios as either composers (J.J. Johnson and Benny Golson) or players (Herb Ellis, Ray Brown, and Bud Shank) were wise to get out when they did.

The fact that so much of the electronic music with which we are being flooded is bad has set up a false dichotomy, the assumption by many people that good music and electronic music are mutually exclusive. But electronic music, like any other kind of music, is as good as the musician who makes it, and some excellent musicians have ventured into the field. Oscar Peterson is one of them.

A story in the *Melody Maker* on October 24, 1981, said, "Find him away from his Boesendorfer grand and slotted behind a rack of synthesizers, sequencers and special effects and it could be like spotting a 1925 claret on the booze shelf at Sainsbury's.

"That's the simile many of his jazz fans would apply, since modern electronic keyboards and synths are generally spurned as upstart toys by jazz pianists."

Not really. Les McCann had been recording with synthesizers for some time. Dave Grusin, Don Grusin, Clare Fischer, Roger Kellaway, Ralph Grierson, and many other pianists had either recorded with them or begun to use them in private. Studio pianists indeed are expected to be adept with synthesizers. Given the ubiquity of this evolving musical technology and Oscar Peterson's insatiable curiosity about gadgets, it was inevitable that he would take up synthesizers. He went about it in his usual thorough fashion, getting experts to explain the workings of the various new instruments. The basement studio at the house in Mississauga began to fill up with new equipment.

"I'm an impatient arranger," Oscar told the *Melody Maker*'s interviewer. "I don't like writing something on the piano, then having to wait for an orchestra to learn the parts before I can hear how it sounds. With the keyboards today I can play the brass or string parts immediately."

In due course he enlarged the basement of his house to accommodate his library, his business files, the recording studio, and the synthesizers. Sitting at the keyboard of one of them, surrounded by electronic gear, he looked not unlike the captain of a spaceship in some sci-fi film as he and Oscar Jr. taped complex electronic compositions.

In 1977 Oscar met Charlotte Huber, a native of Zurich, on a Swissair flight during a concert tour of Europe. She was one of the stewardesses. He promptly named her Charlie. Charlie was much younger than he, but they married in spite of that, in a quiet ceremony at the house in Mississauga. Fifty or so friends and relatives were present, including Maurie Kessler, Butch Watanabe, and Oscar's sister May. On January 9, 1978, in Mississauga General Hospital, Charlie gave birth to a son, Oscar's sixth child, whom they named Joel. Count Basie and Eric Smith became his godfathers.

Few of Oscar's friends seem to have known Charlie well. Without exception, they were all fond of the shy and gentle Lil and the warm and outgoing Sandy. Charlie seemed somehow aloof. The marriage eventually ended. Charlie remained in Toronto. Joel lives with her, although Oscar sees him often.

By now Oscar was playing more solo recitals, at the same time reducing his travel schedule and spending more and more time composing, producing not only melodies of distinctive charm and sometimes deep poignancy but larger works as well, including an *Easter Suite* that received its première performance on London Weekend Television on Good Friday, April 20, 1984.

The family scourge, arthritis, had made Oscar's mother an

invalid in her final days, and more and more it tormented Oscar and his sister Daisy. He walked with difficulty at times and occasionally cancelled a performance because of the pain in his hands. Daisy was bent with the malady. She tried a folk remedy: cod liver oil. It seemed to diminish the arthritis and soon she was walking upright. She told Oscar about it and he too found it effective, and now would not travel without it. Though the treatment is controversial, there is some clinical evidence that it is valuable.

One by one Oscar's friends and heroes were dying off. Tatum was long gone, so too Nat Cole and Bud Powell, then Lester Young, Billie Holiday, Coleman Hawkins, Duke Ellington, Jo Jones, Ben Webster, Erroll Garner, Count Basie. Even his own generation began to go. Eddie (Lockjaw) Davis was gone. Sonny Stitt and Al Cohn died. Some years earlier Oscar had told an interviewer that he thought jazz had only about ten years left. With the death of Bill Evans, three years his junior, he told a newspaper reporter in Victoria, British Columbia, that the giants were disappearing. Zoot Sims, with whom he had so often and so joyously recorded, died. So did Sam Jones. Oscar has never handled death well – that inevitable negation of everything and everyone. This man who conquered the piano and created a life far above the Montreal ghetto of his birth by sheer will, who dominated his various trios to the verge of alienating its members, cannot do a thing about death.

William Count Basie, aged eighty, died in April 1984, a few days after Oscar played that concert in Milan. On December 4, 1984, New York *Newsday* carried this item:

Only 2 Make Bids For Memories At Basie Items Sale

by Stuart Troup

The last traces of material affection that were exchanged between Count Basie and his wife, or given them by friends and admirers, were sold at auction yesterday at the William Doyle Galleries in Manhattan.

The Basie jewelry brought more than $120,000, but apparently only two bidders were concerned with the joys, tears and memories the pieces may have represented for the bandleader, who died in April, and his wife, Catherine, who died a year earlier.

Seated among the 100 or so jewelry dealers were two Basie friends with a mission. One of them successfully bid $650 for a 14-karat yellow-gold wristwatch engraved on its back with the message: "To our most famous newsboy, Red Bank Register, 3-9-61." The Count was born William Basie in Red Bank, N.J., in 1904. The watch purchaser, Jean Bach, said afterward that she wanted something of Basie's that carried a personal inscription.

Bach had earlier bid on an 18-karat yellow-gold wristwatch, which carried the inscription, "To the Count, from Norman." But she had little chance. Norman Granz, who had given Basie that watch about 30 years ago, outbid her at $1,500.

Ten minutes later, Granz outbid everyone at $1,500 for a 14-karat yellow-gold identification bracelet engraved on the front with "The Chief" and on back with "Love, Ella." It had been a present from Ella Fitzgerald after a recording session that they did together – one of about 50 Basie albums that Granz recorded.

"I can't remember exactly when I gave Bill the watch," Granz said afterward. "It must have been in the '50s when I was touring Europe with him. I think I bought it in Zurich."

Granz, who lives in Geneva, said he heard about the auction from a friend in Paris, who had read about it in a trade paper last week.

Granz, who first met Basie in 1940 and began recording and promoting him after the war, has recorded and promoted Ella Fitzgerald, Oscar Peterson, and others for about 35 years.

There were two other items among the 123 that carried personal inscriptions, but apparently none were purchased for their sentimental value. The highest bid in the sale commissioned by the estate's executor was $44,000, made by a New York jewelry dealer for Catherine Basie's 10-karat diamond engagement ring.

The chances of the Granz purchases falling into unsentimental hands again are slim. "I'm going to give Ella the bracelet," he said. "And I'll give the watch to Oscar. He's the logical one to give it to. Basie loved him."

"I got the watch back here and put it on one day and it stopped," Oscar said in January 1988. "I sent it to a dealer here, and when it came back, it wasn't fixed. And the bill was bigger than the price of the watch. I sent it back, and they sent it to Switzerland, and I didn't hear about it for nearly a year. I called up one day with blood in my eye, and they said it was back, and they didn't charge me a cent. They redid the face and everything. I treasure the watch. I feel very close to Bill when I wear it, although with my big hamhocks, it's a little smaller than a watch I would wear. Having Basie's watch means a lot to me."

Their relationship dated back at least to 1944, when Basie praised Oscar to a *Down Beat* reporter. Stories persisted that Basie, like Lunceford, asked him to join his band, which seems unlikely in that Basie was himself a pianist, indeed the band pianist par excellence. "Oh, I think Bill just wanted to take me to the States," Oscar said. "Obviously I wasn't going to play in the band – at least I don't think that was the idea. I think he was just that enthralled with whatever I was doing, and it was a great compliment. I loved Bill Basie."

Oscar was still suffering from another loss when Basie died: on October 3, 1983, Lil Peterson, his first wife, who had never remarried and with whom he had continued a cordial and affectionate relationship, died suddenly of a heart attack.

And Oscar's brother Chuck was in Royal Victoria Hospital in Montreal, on the slope of Mount Royal at Peel Street and University Avenue. At one time you could see from the hospital down into St. Antoine, which for so long was home to all the Petersons and their friends, but now that neighbourhood was disappearing, and in any event tall glass office buildings and hotels blocked the view. Chuck Peterson suffered at the end from emphysema, high blood pressure – a problem that ran in the family – and kidney failure.

For nearly a year he was on dialysis. Daisy said the hospital was short-staffed, because of budget cuts, and he did not receive the treatment she thought he deserved. On Christmas morning, 1983, Daisy went to visit him with her daughter, Sylvia Sweeney, a news- and sportscaster for the Canadian Broadcasting Corporation. In the chilly room he shared with two other men, they found Chuck asleep on a bed without sheets. "Let's take him home," Sylvia said. They doubted that the hospital would allow it, but, surprisingly, the authorities granted permission and Chuck Peterson spent his last Christmas at Daisy's home in the west Montreal district of Notre Dame de Grâce. He returned to the hospital at nine o'clock that night.

He did not want visitors. Perhaps the only person other than immediate family to see him was Oliver Jones, who adored him. Oliver visited him faithfully. Sometimes Oliver would hold Chuck's one hand. "I think he said his last words to me," Oliver said. "All the years I knew Chuck, he never talked about the loss of his hand. And that day he started talking about his youth, which was very unlike him. He said, 'I'm sick, I can't do anything any more, and I lost my arm.' He talked about it as if it had happened last week. And he said, 'I never had any luck.' That was the last time I saw him."

Sandra King Peterson did not return to nursing after she and Oscar were divorced. She went to work at Sears, becoming a direc- tor of the personnel department that had once been headed by her father. She and Oscar settled into a friendship more comfortable than anything they had known when they were married and now and then would have dinner together. Her speech reflected the life that late she led: scattered with the hip and sometimes impenetra- ble slang of the jazz world. She said she had met an English gentle- man she liked a great deal. In 1987, they were married and she left Toronto.

Ed Thigpen's Danish wife died, leaving him with two beautiful light-brown and bilingual children to raise. Though they had never been to the United States, they would ask Ed when he was going to take them home. He continued to live in Copenhagen, returning frequently to the United States and becoming prominent in jazz education.

Herb Ellis and Ray Brown were like veterans of a war, army buddies who cannot get past the experience. Both of them earned considerable amounts of money in the recording studios and played golf together regularly, but for all the sweet lures of California life, they longed for the stimulation of the old days and finally did something about it. They left the studios. They had resigned from the road in their forties on the grounds that they were too old for it; in their sixties they decided they were not too old for it and formed a new trio with Ray as leader – Lawyer Brown, as Lester Young called him – on the model of the old trio, using the closest approximation of Oscar Peterson in the world, one of Oscar's protégés, the brilliant Jamaican pianist twenty years their junior, Monty Alexander.

In early 1986, I went to a night-club in Los Angeles called Loa's, of which Ray Brown is music director and one of the owners. Ray was playing that night with pianist Gene Harris and drummer Mickey Roker. At the end of their first set, I said to him, "C'mere, I've got something I want you to hear." We went back to the club's office and sat down facing each other. I handed Ray my little Walkman stereo tape player, told him to put on the earphones, pushed the button, and let him hear some of the Gerry Macdonald tapes. He shut his eyes and tilted his head back. His foot began to tap. Then his eyes flicked open.

"When?" he said, looking almost alarmed.

"Nineteen fifty-four," I said. He closed his eyes again. Then they opened.

"Where?"

"Zardi's."

And once more he closed his eyes, listening in a kind of transport.

"How?" he said at last, and pulled off the headset. I told him of Gerry's experiments with prototype stereo equipment.

"Has Herb heard any of this stuff?" Ray said.

"No, not yet, although I've told him about it."

"He's coming in tonight. You'd better play it for him. Why hasn't this stuff been issued?"

"I don't know. Ask Oscar. He knows the tapes exist. Ask Norman Granz. I guess because the piano's out of tune." It had slipped my mind for the moment that it was also out of tune on the London House recordings. But the Macdonald tapes were the only existing stereo recordings of the trio with Herb Ellis.

"The piano's out of tune?" Ray said. "Who gives a shit! Play these for Herb."

We went back out into the night-club, and with perfect timing Herb walked in with his wife, Patti. Herb always has a ruddy glow of health about him. He had long since won his battle with alcohol, and Patti is a certified medical counsellor in drug and alcohol abuse. "We know why I got interested," she said once with a chuckle. "Don't we?"

"I want you to hear something," I told Herb. "These are the tapes I told you about." We were standing by the bar in a crowd of people. Herb put on the headphones, started to listen, and, like Ray, went into a kind of transport. He walked away to be alone. When he returned, perhaps ten minutes later, he was in slight shock. "You're right," he said. "This is the best we ever sounded on record!"

Ray went back to the bandstand, and we listened to him and Gene Harris and Mickey Roker. Three weeks later, Herb, Ray, and Monty Alexander left on a month's tour of Europe.

Surprisingly, there was a period when Oscar and Ray Brown were estranged. "I wrote him a letter," Oscar said, "that was very caustic. But I was hurting. I always had that unbreakable unquestionable thing with Ray. At that point it became questionable, let's put it that way. And I wrote him a letter and we had a very sensitive and emotional meeting in Europe after that. We met in a bar in Montreux, Switzerland, and he said, 'You can punch me in the mouth when you see me, or whatever you have to do to me, but don't ever write me another letter like that. Because it really upset me.' I wasn't pleased to hear that it had upset him. But I was kind of busted up myself because he hadn't been communicating. You know, you don't have to communicate with people if things are right. But if there's anything wrong, you can feel it, and maybe that's when you should communicate and get it straightened out. I can't think of what was wrong. I don't remember now.

"I have had that kind of relationship with the guys – any one of those guys. Same thing goes with Niels. I only see Niels so many times within a year, and we just pick up where we left off. He'll fly over here to do something with me or I'll go to Europe. We hug and we're into our thing. He and I hang out afterwards, have a drink at the bar, talk about foolishness, politics, that sort of thing. Herbie's the same way. To be close musically, you have to be that close personally. No matter how great each one plays individually, you have to dig each other to be able to get into the innards, each other's vitals.

"Of course, when I meet Ray and Herb and Ed and the others today, I can't really approach them on the same basis that I used to. They have had to make adjustments in their musical lives, and I've made adjustments too. Ray comes in for a festival as Ray Brown with a group. He's become a separate entity within himself. So has Herbie. So has Barney. Consequently it's not the same as me coming in as the leader of the trio. Not that we ever really operated that way. Well, yes we did to a certain extent. Yeah, they'd look to me for certain things. But it wasn't a thing that pervaded everything we did. The times that I had to be a leader, I don't think I enjoyed it too much, I'll put it that way. Today I can't approach them the same way. I've been a separate entity on my own too. So they look on me in, I'm sure, a different light. Whenever I play with Ray, on a record or a concert or anywhere, we have to do this, I have to forget (a) that I am a solo pianist at times during the year, and (b) that Ray Brown is a separate entity at different times during the year, and to say, 'We're playing together again.'"

On March 5, 1988, Oscar played a concert at El Camino Community College in Torrance, a suburb of Los Angeles. I attended it with Artie Shaw, long since retired from music but at seventy-seven unflaggingly attentive to and aware of it. Oscar's first American engagement after the 1949 Carnegie Hall concert was at Bop City in New York. He played opposite Shaw, who was appearing with what amounted to a small symphony orchestra.

After the El Camino concert, in Oscar's dressing room, he and Shaw embraced, laughed, told musicians' jokes, reminisced. They talked about a time when young jazz musicians learned to play the great solos of the masters, absorbing their content into their own work, a time that seems to be gone. They remembered that when Shaw came off the bandstand that first night at Bop City and Oscar readied himself to go on, Artie said, "Go out and kill 'em, kid."

The El Camino concert was fascinating. Oscar played the first half solo, the second half with bassist David Young, who had come out from Toronto with him.

Oscar's playing had reached a new level. It had become deeper and very abstract. I heard things in it I had never heard before; and things that I had heard before had disappeared. The figures he plays with such astonishing facility had become like brush-slashes of colour on a canvas, no longer devices but great blocks of material used with abandon. Sometimes he would barely hint at the tune on which the improvisation was based, leaving it to the listener to deduce it from the chord changes. The phenomenon was comparable to what happens to painters, such as Lawren Harris, A.Y. Jackson, Rembrandt, and Turner, as they grow older and become bored with what they have been doing: the subject matter ceases to be the point of the exercise, the design and the materials themselves become the meaning. You don't look at a Turner painting to learn what the sea looks like. It is assumed that you know what it looks like. You look at the painting to find out what Turner thinks and feels about the sea. You don't listen to Oscar Peterson play *Old Folks* for the melody; you listen to what thoughts and feelings its materials arouse in the artist. If jazz is largely a theme-and-variations form, Oscar at times now abandons the theme.

Others have noticed the change in his playing. If there is one, he says, it may have to do with the fact that he is spending more and more time composing, and the process is affecting his playing.

Many years ago the Chilean composer Juan Orrego-Salas and I talked about the influence of terrain on a composer. He said that the sharp angularity of his compositions almost certainly derived from his growing up in constant sight of the Andes. He thought that way. We discussed the music of Sibelius, and its evocations of the landscape of Finland, which looks strikingly like much of that of Canada, particularly northern Ontario and Quebec, the lakes and the woods and the great outcroppings of Pre-Cambrian rock so magnificently abstracted by Tom Thomson, A.Y. Jackson, and Lawren Harris. Sibelius seems always to have been more popular with Canadian audiences than with Americans. Perhaps we feel what his music is about more acutely than Americans do.

For all its late start in most of the arts, Canada has long excelled in one: painting. And it is particularly transcendent in landscape painting, which its great figures have abstracted. A Scandinavian influence may or may not have been involved, but even if it was, Jackson, Thomson, Harris, and their colleagues carved up all the competition in sight. I am not in the least hesitant to say that the greatest body of landscape painting in the twentieth century is Canadian.

Glenn Gould used to talk about "the idea of North" as it affects Canadians. I think Glenn was right about this. It pervades Canadian thinking. It's a tough land, and we get good at what we do, because the emptiness at our backs and the concomitant dark winter threats are never far from our thoughts. Butch Watanabe has frequently been offered the moon and all to move to Japan, which he has visited several times with Oscar. He won't go. He finds it too crowded, too claustrophobic. He needs the space, he perversely loves the cold of Canada, he needs it for his cross-country skiing. He is Canadian.

It is almost certainly not an accident that Oscar's first extended work, the *Canadiana Suite,* is a kind of landscape painting in sound.

None of this is to suggest that you have to be Canadian to enjoy the work of Oscar Peterson. A large world-wide audience proves otherwise. But I suspect that there is something in his work that Canadians alone can perceive, as there is perhaps something in the work of Orrego-Salas that Chileans alone can feel. Good art is always particular, achieving generality through its particularity. But it will always have more meaning to those who share to some extent the experience and culture of the artist.

Oscar Peterson is a deeply Canadian artist. He uses sound the way A.Y. Jackson used paint. I think that puzzles some people.

Perhaps the change in his playing is simply a matter of his own emotional evolution. No, it's more complicated than that. But that undoubtedly has something to do with it. "Do you ever cry?" I asked him on impulse.

"When I've been hurt. And I won't come on that I've been hurt. I'll live under a cover, a subterfuge, water running off the marble, until such time as I can sit in a corner by myself and hurt. I cry quite often. More so in the last ten years than I've ever cried in my life. I cry, strangely enough, when something moves me very deeply. I never used to do that. I used to cry when I'd get angry and hurt. I'm in a funny part of my life. It isn't that I don't give a damn. I have given the best years of my life to producing the absolute best that I have in me musically. There isn't another group that played as well as our groups did consecutively. I know there were people who walked in when we had a different guitarist or a different drummer and said, 'Oh boy, I've got to hear this.' Nothing happened. It was always the same. Because it was a group. I devoted my life to that. I made some bad friends during the time – and busted up three marriages. That's okay, I wanted to do what I did. I'm sorry that I could not fully understand the needs of the women that were in my life.

"If I go in for something, I go the whole way. I kept going for marriage. But it has to be more than a one-way street. In these declining years of mine, I love to play and I still can play, thank God.

"I thought about my life, and I realized I was no hell to live with. But I don't think I was *that* bad. I've seen guys who were just terrible that women worshipped."

Oscar stayed on in Los Angeles after the El Camino concert. On

March 10, 11, 12, and 13 he played at Ray Brown's club, Loa's. The drummer was Bobby Durham. The bassist, of course, was Ray Brown. They were together again.

The Gerry Macdonald tapes remain a historical oddity. Gerry has stored safety copies in a vault. They are of a significance comparable to the Duke Ellington 1932 stereo recordings uncovered early in the 1980s.

Norman Granz filed litigation against MPS records, demanding the return of the masters of the recordings Hans Georg Brunner-Schwer made with Oscar. The MPS material has passed into the hands of Polygram, which also owns the Limelight and Verve catalogues, including all the albums Oscar made for that label. Some of the MPS albums are available, but not *The Way I Really Play*, which is still tied up in legal problems. Since this and some of the other albums he made for MPS, along with the Gerry Macdonald tapes, cannot currently be sold to the public, some of Oscar's finest work lies in limbo. Perhaps some day the legal problems will be resolved, and this remarkable material will all be made available again. Richard Seidel, who heads the jazz program at Polygram in New York, says that the Peterson albums in the Verve catalogue are so numerous that it is impossible to keep them all in the market-place. He said it is a joke within the company that if a project to issue *The Complete Oscar Peterson Verve Recordings* were undertaken and completed, it would take a truck to carry them, even in compact disc form.

In January 1987, at the age of sixty-seven, Norman Granz retired from the record business for the second time, announcing the sale of his Pablo label to Fantasy. When all the assets, including the tapes of an estimated eight hundred albums, many of them Oscar's, arrived at the Fantasy office in Berkeley, California, from Beverly Hills, there was hardly any publicity or historical documentation at all to accompany it.

Granz continued to reside in Switzerland, managing Oscar's career from there. Then he moved to his flat in London. He and his second wife, Grete, parted. His problem with glaucoma grew worse. On March 4, 1988, he underwent further surgery on his eyes, but his doctors extended little hope of saving his sight.

Herb and Patti Ellis, their children grown, bought a house on a lake in Arkansas, and live there. Herb still travels, playing jazz and playing golf.

Hans Georg Brunner-Schwer removed himself entirely from the record business and lives in semi-reclusion on his estate at Villingen. Baldhard G. Falk still works as a financial and business consultant in San Francisco. Eric Smith is retired and lives in Los Angeles. Lil Fraser Peterson's two brothers, George and Bill, retired from the railways respectively in 1984 and '85, and Lou Braithwaite in 1987.

Oliver Jones travels the world and records as an increasingly important jazz attraction in his own right. He is often compared to Oscar, but the styles are quite different. Whereas Oscar echoes Liszt and Chopin, Oliver evokes later Romantic piano composers such as Rachmaninoff, and the part the blues plays in Oscar's music is taken by gospel in Oliver's. The similarity lies largely in the articulation, the legacy not of Art Tatum but of their common teacher, Daisy Peterson Sweeney.

"Daisy and Paul de Marky," Oscar said. "She was already studying with him. When I hear pianists supposedly influenced, quote unquote, by me, their playing often seems watery to me. They haven't got the articulation. Paul de Marky was fanatic about that. Never mind listening to him, I used to love to watch the way his hands moved, as they prepared the next movement, the next chord."

Paul de Marky died in Montreal Convalescent Hospital on May 16, 1982, nine days short of his eighty-fifth birthday.

Four of Oscar's five children by his first marriage live in the Toronto area. Lyn lives in Nova Scotia. None of them became a professional musician, although each of them studied music. His daughters are married and have families. Norman works for the parks department of North York. Oscar Jr. has two jobs: he works for a picture-framing company and as his father's recording consultant and engineer.

Audrey Morris was stricken with cancer, underwent treatment, and experienced a complete remission. She continued to play piano and sing in the Chicago area. Her husband, Stuart Genovese, retired from teaching music. Sometimes Oscar would visit them in Chicago, sometimes they would spend part of the summer with him at his cottage in Haliburton, Ontario, where he would disappear for hours at a time, fishing on the lake.

He told them a story.

One autumn day he and Oscar Jr. were raking the leaves around the cottage. The road that passes by the house had been much improved in recent years. A motorist stopped and said, 'You're doing a good job.' He said he was looking for a gardener and asked them to come over and do his place.

Oscar said, "Yeah, as soon as we finish my place."

The man said, "What, do you live here?" Deeply embarrassed, he hurried away.

Incredibly, Oscar recounted the incident with amusement.

Audrey and Stuart told another story. They were visiting Oscar at the cottage towards the end of summer. On August 15, one of Oscar's friends dropped over for a visit.

"His name was Greg," Oscar said. "He used to run the general store. He and I were sort of buddies. He wanted to go down to the dock and have a drink. We all went down to the dock, Greg and Audrey and Stu and I. We were sitting there when a boat came around the point with about six teen-agers in it.

"Then I saw the prow of another boat, then a third. And then I realized they were coming toward my dock. I thought, 'What's going on?'"

"It was very ominous," Audrey said.

"A flotilla of rowboats," Stu said.

Oscar said, "And there were more and more of them. It could almost have been like the situation that day with Anwar Sadat, and I was really apprehensive. Then they raised all these signs that said *Happy Birthday, Oscar.* And they all started singing *Happy Birthday to You.* It turned from a moment of apprehension to one of embarrassment to one of love. All these kids singing. It was very moving. Greg said the kids had found out it was my birthday and they wanted to do it."

After a time of laughter and waving, the boats went away, leaving the lake as still and empty and serene as it had been before.

In 1987, Daisy Peterson Sweeney was awarded an honorary doctorate by Laurentian University in Sudbury. The last time I saw her, she was awaiting a pupil. A car pulled up in front of her house in Notre Dame de Grâce and a little girl in a snowsuit got out and ran towards her. I can still see her unconscious body language: arms slightly outheld, welcoming the child to a world of music.

May Peterson has never married.

"May's story is a poignant one," Oscar said. "I feel Daisy and I, and my brother Chuck if he were alive, owe May a great debt. She gave up part of her life to be with my mother when she was a shut-in. I moved Mum to Toronto because I wanted to be close to her. But when she felt the end coming, she wanted to go back to Montreal. So I moved her back to Montreal. During this, Daisy was teaching and studying, and I was travelling, and when Mum took ill, May stayed with her. May ended up being the one who lived with my mother. That's difficult. In such circumstances, you sometimes bear the brunt of the anger and ill feelings of someone who is in pain. It was very harsh for May, and she took my mother's passing very heavily, as we all did.

"When it was over, I talked May into working for me as a sort of personal secretary, to handle private mail and family matters and pay my bills and keep my schedule. She does it to this day. I wanted her to have some security. She comes to the house three days a week, and the rest of the week she teaches piano."

I have seen Oscar a number of times since the concert Roger Kellaway and I attended in Milan. But somehow the image of him after the concert sticks in my memory. We had to leave – Gigi Campi, who produced the concert, Roger Kellaway, Norman Granz's wife, Grete, and I. Oscar was signing autographs at a table at the entrance to a dressing room backstage. We were leaving him alone, surrounded by people who did not speak his language, whose language he did not speak. I remembered that time he drove me home through the Detroit River tunnel and we heard the bagpipe band and he told me the music was in B-flat.

"See you at home," I said, and he waved, and we left him there.

SOURCES

Magazine articles

Paul Zimke, "Hot Piano," *Maclean's*, 10 / 15 / 45

Harold Dingman, "Oscar Peterson," *Liberty*, 1 / 12 / 46

Jim Butler, "Canada's New Piano Sensation," *Metronome*, 1 / 47

McKenzie Porter, "Three Thousand Nights on Wheels," *Maclean's*, 3 / 15 / 49

Henry F. Whiston, "Watch Peterson, Say Canadians," *Down Beat*, 3 / 10 / 50

Mike Nevard, "He carries a torch for jazz and racial freedoms," *Melody Maker*, early 1950s

Don Freeman, "I Still Have a Long Way to Go, Says Oscar Peterson," *Down Beat* 1 / 11 / 52

"Granz Glad 'New Yorker' Panned His Astaire Album," *Down Beat*, 2 / 11 / 53

Bill Simon, "An Oscar for Peterson," *Saturday Review*, 4 / 28 / 53

Nat Hentoff, "Europe Jazz Lags Well Behind Ours: Peterson," *Down Beat*, 6 / 3 / 53

"How He Proposed, by Mrs. Oscar Peterson," *Tan*, 8 / 53

"Swing, with Harmonics," *Time*, 12 / 28 / 53

Oscar Peterson, "My Enjoyable Family Life," *Copper Romances*, 6 / 54

"Granz Duz All," *The Billboard*, 7 / 2 / 54

"Jazz: North to Newport," *Newsweek*, 8 / 2 / 54

Oscar Peterson, "The Jazz Scene Today," *Down Beat*, 9 / 8 / 54

Whitney Balliett, "Pandemonium Pays Off," *Saturday Review*, 9 / 25 / 54

George Simon, "Oscar!," *Metronome*, 10 / 14 / 54

John S. Wilson, "Granz Presents a Jazz Concert," *New York Times*, undated

283

Don Freeman, "Can Piano Be Mastered? No, Says Oscar Peterson,"
  Down Beat, 1 / 25 / 56
Max Jones, "I refuse to have any junkies in JATP," *Melody Maker*,
  5 / 23 / 56
Leonard Feather, "Norman Granz," *Esquire*, 1956
John Mehegan, "Jazz Pianists 1," *Down Beat*, 6 / 13 / 57
June Callwood, "The Oscar Petersons," *Maclean's*, 9 / 25 / 58
Leonard Feather, "Oscar Peterson, Gentleman Cat," *Nugget*, 196?
"Barred from Bar," *Toronto Telegram*, 2 / 1 / 60
John Tynan, "Take 5 (Norman Granz)," *Down Beat*, 3 / 3 / 60
"Granz Sells But Holds," *Down Beat*, 2 / 2 / 61
Kay Kritzwiser, "Oscar Peterson, Muscular Giant of the Piano,"
  Toronto *Globe Magazine*, 2 / 4 / 61
"Oscar Peterson's Jazz School," *Ebony*, 3 / 61
Max Jones, "Jazz giants still cling to Granz," *Melody Maker*, 3 / 11 / 61
Don DeMicheal, "Oscar Peterson on the Teaching of Jazz Piano,"
  Down Beat, 9 / 27 / 62
Clarke Wallace, "Jazz School with an Oscar," *Weekend*, 1 / 26 / 63
Patrick Scott, "Prisoner of the Assembly Line," Toronto *Globe and
  Mail*, 8 / 23 / 64
Jack Batten, "Oscar Peterson," *Maclean's*, 4 / 17 / 65
Leonard Feather, "Mr. Brown Goes to Hollywood," *New York Post*,
  11 / 14 / 65
"Art Buyer Claims He Took a Trimming," *New York Times*, 4 / 1 / 66
M.C. Ramonet, "Delicat Oscar," *Jazz Hot*, 5 / 66
Phil McKellar, "Oscar Peterson," *Performing Arts in Canada*, Spring
  1966
Leonard Feather, "The New Life of Ray Brown," *Down Beat*,
  4 / 9 / 67
"Being Black in Montreal," *Maclean's*, 12 / 68
P. Cresant, "Oscar Peterson," *Jazz Hot*, 9 / 69
"Norman Simmons Talks to Mark Gardner," *Jazz Monthly*, 10 / 70
Max Harrison, "Peterson in Private," *Times* of London, 11 / 5 / 70
François Postif, "Oscar Peterson," *Jazz Hot*, 4 / 73
Jack Batten, "Oscar Peterson," *Saturday Night*, August 1973
Len Lyons, "Oscar Peterson: Piano Worship," *Down Beat*, 12 / 18 / 75
Mike Hennessey, "An Interview with Oscar Peterson," *Gallery*, 7 / 76
Len Lyons, "Oscar Peterson," *Contemporary Keyboard*, 3 / 78
Marsha Boulton, "The Piano Man," *Maclean's*, 6 / 4 / 79

Marguerite de Sackville-West, "The Elusive Oscar," *Performing Arts in Canada*, Fall 1979

John Mcdonough, "Norman Granz," *Down Beat*, 10 / 79 and 11 / 79

Karl Dallas, "What's Going on, Oscar," *Melody Maker*, 11 / 15 / 80

Bob Doerschuk, *Contemporary Keyboard*, 12 / 80

Interview, "Talking with Oscar," *Jazz* (Sydney, Australia), 7 / 81

Frank Conroy, "Oscar Peterson," *Esquire*, 9 / 81

Paul Colbert, "Oscar Oscillates," *Melody Maker*, 10 / 24 / 81

Jacques Reda, "Oscar le grand," *Jazz Magazine*, 2 / 82

Mike Hennessey, "First Bass: An Interview with Ray Brown," *Jazz Journal*, 7 / 82

Richard Palmer, "Oscar Peterson: Genesis and Revelation," *Jazz Journal International*, three parts 7 / 81, 7 / 82, 7 / 83

Gene Lees, "The Trouble with Jazz Piano," *Down Beat*, 10 / 29 / 59

Gene Lees, "Oscar Peterson and a New School," *Down Beat*, 9 / 1 / 60

Gene Lees, "In Walked Ray (Brown)," *Down Beat*, 8 / 31 / 65

Gene Lees, "Oscar Peterson," *BMI* magazine, 4 / 66

Gene Lees, "Greatest Jazz Piano in History?" *High Fidelity*, 4 / 67

Gene Lees, "Oscar Peterson Playing," *Holiday*, 4 / 67

Gene Lees, "The Face behind the Performer," *High Fidelity*, 8 / 70

Gene Lees, "The Best Damn Jazz Piano in the Whole World," *Maclean's*, 7 / 75

Gene Lees, "All That Oscar," *Toronto Life*, 9 / 81

Gene Lees, "O.P. – Growing Up Canadian," *Jazzletter*, 9 / 81

Gene Lees, "An Afternoon with Herb Ellis," *Jazzletter*, 10 / 84

Gene Lees, "Boy with Drum," *Jazzletter*, 2 / 86

Books

Collier, James Lincoln. *The Reception of Jazz in America: A New View*. Brooklyn, N.Y.: Institute for Studies in American Music, Brooklyn College, 1988

Feather, Leonard; and Ira Gitler. *The Encyclopedia of Jazz in the Seventies*. New York: Horizon, 1976

Gridley, Mark C. *Jazz Styles: History and Analysis*. Englewood Cliffs, N.J.: Prentice Hall Inc., 1985

James, Burnett. *Essays on Jazz*. London: Sidgwick & Jackson, 1961

Lyons, Len. *The Great Jazz Pianists*. New York: Quill, 1983

Palmer, Richard. *Oscar Peterson*. Tunbridge Wells, England:
  Spellmount Ltd, 1984
Thomson, Colin A. *Blacks in Deep Snow: Black Pioneers in Canada*. J.M.
  Dent & Sons (Canada) Limited, 1979
Winks, Robin W. *The Blacks in Canada: A History*. Montreal: McGill-
  Queen's University Press; New Haven: Yale University Press, 1971

Radio and TV sound tracks

Sound track, CBC-TV, Oscar Peterson portrait, 2 / 83
Peter Clayton, BBC, Oscar Peterson radio interview
Gene Lees, CKFM, "Portrait of Oscar Peterson," radio interview,
  1973
André Previn, BBC-TV interview

Other

Hopper, Lou. *That Happy Road* (unpublished autobiography). National
  Archives of Canada
Israel, William Emerson. *The Montreal Negro Community* (unpublished
  master's thesis, McGill University, 1928)
Time magazine, private internal office memoranda, 1951 and 1953

INDEX